The Song of Africa

Isaac Benatar

Writers Club Press

San Jose New York Lincoln Shanghai

The Song of Africa

Published by Writers Club Press
an imprint of iUniverse.com, Inc.

For information address:
iUniverse.com, Inc.
620 North 48th Street
Suite 201
Lincoln, NE 68504-3467
www.iuniverse.com

ISBN: 0-595-09947-5

Printed in the United States of America

This book is dedicated to the memory of the two most wonderful
people in my life, my father and mother:
VICTOR AND RACHEL BENATAR
M.T.D.S.R.I.P.

Chapter One

Light rain was falling on the surface of majestic Lake Washington, as I sat alone on the angled slope of a grassy embankment close to the water's edge. My attention was fixed on the millions of little ripplets which seemed to cascade in waves across the surface of the inland lake. Ahead in the distance, through a haze of heavy mist, stood evergreen Mercer Island, and beyond I could see Seattle's skyline. It was a very special occasion that had brought me to this place, for today was the last day of 1999. Tomorrow, would see the dawn of a new century, and be a year away from the era of a new millennium. I considered myself as being fortunate to have made it to this point in time and wanted the solitude, to reflect on my experiences of the years that had gone past.

The combined effect was quite peaceful, and I was thoroughly enjoying the tranquillity of the scene when I glanced toward Marine Dive, a roadway curving around the southern part of the lake. An automobile slowly wended its way along the drive, passing a gleaming Rolls Royce limousine parked at the side of the road. A tall, handsome black chauffeur stood like a sentinel under cover of a nearby tree and patiently watched and waited. Glancing toward the grassy embankment, he saw me, smiled, and quickly looked away.

Curiously, the vision of the black chauffeur remained with me as my attention was refocused toward the ever-widening ripplets on the lake. His features began to alter and his smart uniform transformed in my mind's eye, to that of the face and the clothing of a warrior of Africa. My thoughts began to wander to another time, another continent, and I began to hum a tune that I had composed many years ago. The words and lyrics to the music were so special, that they existed only in my heart. I had named the melody, " The Song Of Africa!"

The lilt was soft with the beat of the African drums and the words told of the country of my birth.

As I hummed the tune, distant images began to reappear with profound clarity; events, all but forgotten, came thundering back into my mind; and through the magic of the moment, I was transported back to Africa. Visions of the wide open spaces of the African bushveld began to unravel from my memories. I pictured the scenes of beautiful and graceful herds of Antelope, Gazelle and Springbok performing their spontaneous running and leaping ballet of the African jungle. I saw the great elephant herds feeding peacefully off the high tree leaves, the sheer enormity of their size commanding distance and respect from all the creatures of the wild.

I recalled the sun settling over the western horizon, climaxed by the flight of the millions of Flamingoes and Cranes taking off from the lakes and rivers, clouding the evening skies, their pink and white ensemble contrasting against the red, orange and blue hues of the magnificent African sunset

I visualized the currents on the waters of the river I had known and enjoyed as a child growing up in Africa. and found myself, Ivan Bender, back on my parents farm near the banks of the Mazoe River, in a country then known as Southern Rhodesia, a British colonial territory in the center of Southern Africa.

It was my fifth birthday, the year was 1948, and something awesome that my parents referred to as World War Two had been over for three years. For me, a white child growing up on his parents' large tobacco and cattle farm in a predominately black nation, life was wonderful. I played in the tobacco fields, scampered about with the livestock, and chattered away with the local tribesfolk in their native tongue, Shona. All this had seemed to be a natural way of life in my upbringing. But, my memory had settled on this date because of a shocking encounter I had then, and was about to learn a lesson that day about untamed Africa: that despite the peace and tranquillity that seemed to reign in this beautiful, lush, semi-tropical land, nature also provided its crueler moments.

I was excited; my birthday present from my parents was a brand new fishing rod. I could hardly wait to take off to the banks of the nearby Mazoe River, some three hundred yards from the homestead. I called to Bimba, my Maltese puppy, and together we walked toward the river. Once comfortably perched on the banks of the river, I cast my line into the water and lay back to enjoy the warm African sunshine. Bimba played nearby, scampering in and out of the tall bushes, and neither of us saw the two slitted eyes keenly observing us from its camouflaged position in the clump of reeds behind us. Slowly, stealthily, a large crocodile circled to position itself between its intended victims and the river. As the crocodile drew closer, Bimba reacted, but too late. Huge jaws clamped down, the puppy yelped, and in the next instant it was swallowed whole.

I turned just in time to see the horrifying drama, and the crocodile, now only a few yards away, lunged toward me. Sheer instinct made me dive out of the way before the menacing jaws could clamp down, and drag me off into the river. Overcome by the terror, I ran screaming toward the homestead.

Rae and Vic Bender, my parents, alerted by the terrified yells, came running from the house, and I, in breathless gasps, told them what had occurred. Hastening back into the house, my father emerged a few seconds later with his rifle, and marched off in the direction of the huts where the farm employees and tribespeople lived. Some twenty minutes later, my father returned with a hunting party of thirty tribesmen, and I was told to direct the party to where I and Bimba had been. The search commenced for the crocodile, the keen eyesight of the Africans scoured the river, and before long the crocodile was discovered hiding behind a log on the river bank. My father carefully aimed his rifle and fired a single shot, hitting the reptile between the eyes. It turned belly-up and floated on the water's surface. After observing that the floating carcass made no further movement, the workers tied ropes around the reptile, dragged it out of the water, and brought it to the front of the homestead, where the trophy was left on display for all tribesfolk to come and view.

The death of the dreaded crocodile was cause for the locals to celebrate with a beer drink of Skokian, a concoction of fermented maize. Soon a bonfire was built in the center of the tribal village, and the inhabitants of the village, which consisted of about forty mud houses constructed in a circle with a large communal area in the center, came out to join in the festivities. The party started in the late afternoon and lasted well into the early hours of the next day, with the beating of drums and tribal dancing. I had been accepted as an "honorary tribesperson," and joined in much of the dancing, but to my chagrin, was not allowed to partake of the Skokian. The beating drums telegraphed the news to the surrounding areas, and tribesfolk and farmers from miles around made their way to the farm to join in the celebrations.

The vast size of each farm and the sparsity of human contact which resulted made an occasion such as this an excuse for the locals to get together, socialize, and recount how they were faring on their respective farms and in their villages. It was easy to sense the deep feelings of warmth and friendship that existed among the people who lived in this remote area. At midnight, I, with much protesting, was packed off to bed while the celebrating continued in full swing.

The next morning I was up early to again examine the cause of the previous day's frightening experience. Once outside, I picked up some pebbles and started to play a game to see how many pebbles I could hit the crocodile's head with. The first two pebbles thrown hit the motionless body, but the third pebble struck the reptile's eye—and it blinked! I stood frozen as I watched the creature rise to its feet, and walk off in the direction of the river. Frightened tribespeople who had been standing nearby gave the alarm, and within minutes, a search party was formed to look for the crocodile, but despite a lengthy search along the river and the embankments, it was never seen again.

After this incident, my parents decided to assign one of the new farm workers to be my constant companion and protector. The man's name was Motorcar, and I was filled with awe when I first saw the former Zulu, with his brawny muscles rippling throughout a 6 foot, 6 inch body. The man's muscles were clearly apparent, for he was dressed only in a loin-cloth which was actually made from a lion's skin. The same skin was used as his headdress. He had a warm smile and sparkling white teeth, which were accentuated by his jet black face and body. A friendship quickly developed between us, and I would sit and listen, enthralled by the stories my new friend would tell me about his Africa. Motorcar explained that although he was now a nomad, he was originally a member of the Ndbele Tribe which lived some three hundred miles to the west in the Bulawayo area of the country.

The story that captivated me the most, was when Motorcar explained that the Ndbele had originally been a part of the Zulu nation which lived in South Africa and how, under their powerful and fierce King Chaka, the Zulu nation had developed into a powerful warrior race, overcoming all other tribes and reigning paramount in South Africa. Chaka had developed a battle plan that divided his warriors into regiments known as Impis. The Impis, each led by a general, had been detailed to carry out conquests, to defeat neighboring tribes and thus enlarge the Zulu empire.

One of these Impi regiments had been led by Chaka's favorite general, Mizilikaze. In one of the forays, he failed to yield the treasures of the conquest to the King as was customary. This had displeased the Zulu chieftain, and instructions were sent through Chaka's messengers for Mizilikaze to return home with his regiment. Fearing Chaka's wrath and impending death for himself and his regiment of Impis, Mizilikaze disobeyed the instructions, and fled from the Zulu empire and South Africa.

Pursued by Chaka's regiments, he eventually reached the Limpopo River, and crossed the border into unclaimed African territory which was later to become Southern Rhodesia. Where Mizilikaze formed the new warrior nation of the Ndbele in Matabeleland. This small nation spent little time before establishing itself, conquering the neighboring Shona Tribe. The Shona had greatly outnumbered the Ndbele, but what the Ndbele lacked in numbers, they made up in fierceness and bravery to achieve military victory.

Motorcar was born thirty years earlier in Bulawayo, and his father, Chinoya, had been an Impi general in the new Ndbele nation. When Motorcar was a few months old, his father and mother, Umfani, become embroiled in a bitter land dispute with another Impi general, resulting in the two regiments battling each other. During the skirmish the opposing general and several warriors were killed. This incident incurred the wrath of the Matabele chief, who ordered the death of Chinoya, Umfani, and their infant son. Motorcar's parents were killed, but through the help of Chinoya's lieutenants, he was hidden and given to childless peasants living on the outskirts of the Ndbele tribal land. The loyal lieutenants had falsified his death, and Motorcar's life was spared.

At the precise time that he was being handed over by the lieutenants, the first motorcar his new parents had ever seen came chugging past. They were so impressed with the horse less wonder, that they promptly named their new baby, Motorcar. He grew up on the outskirts of the Ndbele nation, where as a young adult he learned of his true circumstances. A few years later he decided to make his way many miles East, to the Mazoe valley, where he found odd jobs on different farms before starting to work for the Bender family.

I would sit and listen for hours, engrossed with Motorcar's stories, then the two of us would take off into the bush to travel and explore the areas that surrounded the farm. We often followed the winding rivers, occasionally stopping upwind when wild animals were sighted, and we would hide in the bushes to watch lions, deer, and elephants drinking from the waterways. Nature, as wild and untamed as it was in this area, brought with it a breathtaking beauty that I thought surely existed all over the world.

Motorcar became my tutor in the ways of Africa and showed me how to make a bow and arrow, a slingshot, and how to pick up a firm straight branch and whittle it into an assagai, which was the African version of the spear. Toward evening when the sun began setting, and the African sky showed all its vivid reds, oranges, and purple hues, the two of us would set off toward Motorcar's hut in the village, and the warrior would continue to fill my mind and imagination with new and exciting stories of Africa,

The events of one fateful day would always remain indelibly in my memory. We had been picking mulberries and exploring the bushes in a hilly area containing many ancient caves. Motorcar had climbed on a rock for a better view of the mulberry pickings when he unwittingly stepped on the tail of a snake sunning itself on the rock. The snake was a vivid green, and in an instant it turned and lashed at Motorcar's bare foot, biting him on the ankle. Motorcar yelled, "Mamba," the name of the deadliest of all snakes in Africa, whose single bite was sufficient to kill any man—first causing a paralysis and, ultimately, a slow and agonizing death. The snake slithered away into the bushes, and Motorcar sat down on the rock, his shoulders drooped, his head hung low. I climbed up to the rock to join my protector, and my young quivering voice asked, "What's wrong, Motorcar? What's wrong?" Only Motorcar's eyes moved as he looked across at me, and whispered in his native tongue, "I am dying!"

It took much persuading from me to get Motorcar to leave his perch and head back toward the homestead where, hopefully, he would be able to receive attention for the wound. Very slowly, we made our way back to the homestead. Calling for my mother, I ran into the house, and in as few words as possible, explained what had happened on the rock. My mother sent a messenger out into the farmlands to summon my father, and together they examined the two puncture wounds where the snake's teeth had sunk into the ankle. From the description of the snake, it indeed appeared to be a green mamba which had bitten the Ndbele warrior.

A messenger was dispatched with an urgent message for the closest doctor, who was twenty miles away. It was now late afternoon, and an hour had passed since Motorcar had been bitten. The Ndbele expressed his belief that nothing could be done to save him, and advised my family that it was now time for him to return to his hut and prepare himself for the inevitable death that would come in the next few hours, after nightfall. Although my parents pleaded with him to stay at the homestead, nothing could change Motorcar's mind, and he walked slowly toward his home in the tribal village. I was upset and confused, and followed a short distance behind. Upon arrival in the village, Motorcar entered his hut, and commenced to package all his belongings into a small, neat pile.

When the sun began to set, Motorcar built a fire outside his hut, brought out an old soap box, and sat on it. Turning to me, he said, "I have one last favor to ask of you, my young friend." I solemnly nodded my head, and Motorcar continued, "I want you to bring me a paper bag to put over my head so that when the pain and agony strike me, no one will be able to see my face, and I will be able to die like a warrior, without shame." I quickly ran home, and returned in a few minutes with a large brown paper bag, and handed it to my friend. Motorcar looked around him for the last sights he felt he would ever see, placed the bag over his head, and sat motionless. My parents watched from a short distance away, feeling very helpless, but praying that the doctor would arrive in time. Local tribespeople formed a circle around Motorcar's hut, and some of the older women from the village began to chant and sing lullabies in order to soothe and bring peace to the dying man.

Many hours passed, and the vigil continued. None of the tribespeople left the area, my parents also remained, and I sat a few feet away from Motorcar, praying silently that my friend would not die. In the pitch darkness of the night, the flames from the fire created shadows and lights which reflected off the tribespeople's faces, and the whole scene had a grotesque aura, with everyone awaiting what they were convinced was the inevitable. One of the elders of the village approached Motorcar, who had sat silent and absolutely motionless all this time, and offered him some water and nourishment. From behind the paper bag, Motorcar refused to have anything.

Shortly after midnight, the messenger who had been dispatched hours before, came running breathlessly into the village to announce that his efforts to locate and bring the doctor had failed. The doctor had been called out on an emergency in Karoi, some fifty miles away, and the few telephone lines that had been installed were not working. There was no way of making contact with the doctor to come to Motorcar's assistance. Immediate and complete hopelessness set in among all those who were present, and the solemn vigil continued throughout the long night. As the sun began to rise the next morning, a tribal elder made his way to where Motorcar had been sitting motionless for many, many hours, and spoke out, "Are you still alive?"

Incredibly, there was a reply from behind the paper bag. "Yes, I am still alive."

My father moved closer to inspect the wounds, and noticed that instead of an infection, the holes made by the snake's teeth on Motorcar's ankle had dried up, and were covered with two small scabs. He turned to Motorcar and said, "I think, Motorcar, that you were bitten by a harmless grass snake and not by a deadly green mamba?"

After a few moments of silence, the reply from behind the paper bag was, "No, sir. I am dying."

The vigil continued throughout the entire day, and every now and then one of the tribespeople would check on the status of the "dying man" by asking if he was still alive. This would be answered by only a nod or grunt emanating from inside Motorcar's paper bag. When darkness came again, Motorcar appeared to be in no worse shape, and although advised again and again by the tribespeople and my father that there was no chance of him joining his ancestors at this time, Motorcar remained firmly convinced that this was still the case. The tribespeople began leaving for their homes. Tired and exhausted from the vigil, I too went to bed.

Early the following morning I returned to Motorcar's hut to find that he was still sitting in the same position, still very much alive, and with the paper bag still firmly over his head. After a few minutes, Motorcar spoke, "Young friend, are you still here?"

I replied, "Yes, Motorcar. I am here!."

"I am hungry, young friend. Will you bring me something to eat?" I raced off to find something for Motorcar to eat, returning a short time later and placing the food of corn and meat on Motorcar's lap. Motorcar removed the paper bag from his head to reveal a smiling and beaming face, and without any further ado, began ravenously eating the meal that had been set before him. A day later, the doctor was located, he came to the farm and examined the Ndbele, and determined that the bite had, indeed, been that of a harmless grass snake.

The nights in the quiet, remote homestead were lonely for me as a young boy. The immensity of the large farm, which was built in the lush African veldt, brought with it the disadvantage of remoteness from neighbors. The nearest farms and other children were distant miles apart. Our home was a large one, with eighteen rooms, six of which were bedrooms, and the remainder made up of dining areas, lounge rooms, enclosed study, patios, and servants' quarters. During the weekday nights I could look forward to a meal prepared by the household cook, Tomani, and afterwards in bed would listen to a crackling short-wave radio bringing in the latest news from the outside world.

Friday evenings were the best of all because the family friends from the surrounding farms would make their way by scotchcart or motor vehicle over the treacherous, pot-holed, sandy roads to our farmhouse for a Friday evening get-together. This was the night of the week when I was allowed to stay up later to hear the weekly serial, and then would listen with fascination to the events that my family and their friends would talk about.

Conversations ranged from what had happened during the preceding weeks on the various farms to who had been taken ill with a bout of the dreaded malaria fever to the occasional story of how a marauding lion or leopard had sneaked its way into the farm cattle pens and taken livestock. The conversation would often drift to memories of the settlers' original homelands. Like our family, most of the friends had emigrated just after World War One, from the Mediterranean island of Rhodes, just off the coast of Greece. I would sit perched on the sofa listening while my parents and their friends discussed their ancestral history. My parents spoke about their heritage, dating back to Spain, and how they were descendants of the Jewish community which had flourished in that country during the Middle Ages, producing some of Spain's greatest jurists, philosophers, poets, scholars, and merchants. They spoke also of how the Inquisition led to widespread suppression of the Jews in the area through the promulgation of laws confining them to ghettos, effectively excluding them from most trades and professions, and barring them from owning land. Eventually, they were prosecuted and banished from the country.

I would listen as my father, Vic, remembered how he had met and married my mother, Rae, and how he had decided, shortly after World War One, to move to Africa because his uncle had told him of the vast opportunities and land that were available for development.

The choice to go to Africa had been a difficult one because my father also had offers from relatives who earlier had left for America. After much deliberation, he decided to leave by boat for the African continent, and once he had set up a home, my mother, would follow at a later time.

On his arrival, my father was surprised and disillusioned at the primitive state of development at the port of Beira. The black inhabitants were half-naked, and the men were dressed in animal skins that were just sufficient to cover the genital area. My father would explain with a reminiscent smile, that his first reaction to what he saw, was that the decision to travel to Africa had been a mistake, and he eagerly inquired about the next boat returning to the island of Rhodes. Having traveled this far, however, he decided to make the journey into the interior to a country which had been newly named Rhodesia, or more accurately, Southern Rhodesia.

At the railroad station, with his few bags, he climbed aboard a dilapidated and dirty railway carriage of the Rhodesian Railways. Powered by a steam engine, the train took two days to make the three hundred and fifty mile journey from Beira to Salisbury, a small town of five thousand inhabitants, with three main streets, each very long and very wide. The buildings which lined the streets were very British colonial in style, as were the people walking along its streets. The men dressed in tailored suits and the ladies wore smartly styled dresses and carried parasols— all apparently oblivious of the warm tropical climate.

The town was composed of a few white merchants operating out of the colonial buildings and many blacks who traveled from the tribal areas to the "new city" to trade, shop, or look for work. There were a few cars and bicycles traveling the streets, but the transportation was mainly comprised of scotchcarts, which were an open, box-cart-type carriage pulled either by donkeys or horses. Vic's Uncle Morris had established a farm in Marandellas, a little town forty miles east of

Salisbury, and it took another day of traveling by scotchcart for Vic to end his journey.

Uncle Morris welcomed Vic, and gave him a minor partnership in the tobacco and cattle farm which he had started a few years earlier. By 1921 Vic had amassed a savings of five hundred pounds, and decided that it was time to send for Rae to join him and to begin their own farming business. Rae arrived six months later, but apart from the happiness of being rejoined with Vic, she was a tearful and very unhappy bride-to-be. She was dismayed at this different and primitive territory that she was to call her new home, but after much reassuring and persuasion by Vic, the two of them took off by scotchcart to look at the surrounding areas where they could buy land and build a home. Their search took them from Marandellas toward Salisbury and then farther north toward Concession and eventually to the Mazoe Valley.

The area they liked was hilly and lush with tropical, fertile soil. Leaving the scotchcart, they climbed to the top of the tallest hill, and looked down at the large, winding, clear river below that began far beyond where their eyes could see and continued flowing past them toward the horizon. The land was green, giving the feeling of peacefulness—and totally uninhabited. Rae and Vic proceeded to the government offices to inquire about the land, and there the elegantly dressed English land officer informed them that the land by the river was selling at six pence an acre. A sixteen-thousand-acre tract was selected at a cost of four hundred pounds, leaving them one hundred pounds to purchase tobacco seed, a few head of cattle, and bricks to build a home.

Through the years, with good land and good rains, the farm had flourished, expanding eventually to its twenty thousand-acre size. After three miscarriages, a son, Leon, and a daughter, Babbette, were born, and when Leon matured and traveled to the University of Cape Town, two thousand miles away, to study medicine, and Babbette was enrolled in boarding school in Salisbury, Vic and Rae decided to have another child. I was born in 1943, but the age difference between my elder brother and sister made me often feel like an only child because I rarely saw them except for the times they came home for the school holidays. I would sometimes pray for a little brother to play with, but that prayer was never answered.

Chapter Two

The events that occurred during the following year as I approached my sixth birthday were dramatic, and brought many changes. My father suffered a bad bout of black water fever, the most serious strain of malaria, brought about by a simple mosquito bite. For many days and weeks my mother and I watched as he suffered through the delirium, fever, and sweating. Eventually, my father recovered, but as usual with this type of infection, the virus would never leave his body, and he would be subject to yearly attacks of the fever, although in milder forms.

These health reasons and the fact that I was due to start school, prompted my parents to decide to move to the city. The move would give them the opportunity to have me live at home during my school years, and my older brother and sister would be closer to their friends when they came home from their schooling. The farm was advertised for sale, and after a few months a large overseas English corporation made a bid which was more than satisfactory for the purchase of the property. My parents began to plan our move to the city of Salisbury, but I was not enthusiastic about the move because I would have to say farewell to my friends in the tribal village. I approached my father, and asked if Motorcar could join us in our new home in Salisbury, and after some deliberation, my father agreed that Motorcar could come and work for us in the city. Motorcar, unfortunately, was not enthused about the idea of traveling into a built-up area, but with the naiveté of youth, I was persistent that my friend should come with us!

Sitting on the Mazoe River embankment, I, for the umpteenth time again brought up the question with Motorcar of coming to the city with the family. Motorcar turned to me and graciously responded, to my youthful doggedness; "Young friend, my way of life is here in the wild, free to roam in the open spaces—not restricted by the man-made jungles that have been built in the cities." Pointing to a bird flying through the air, Motorcar explained, "That is how I feel:, able to fly away, roam, and be free. In the city I would feel like I was locked in a cage. Thank you, my young friend, for wanting me to come with you."

As the day of the big move approached, preparations began in earnest for transporting our family's belongings to Salisbury. The tribespeople appeared saddened that our family was leaving them. As a farewell gesture on the last Sunday before we left, the tribespeople gave a beerdrink. With drums beating early in the morning and continuing until late that night, the leader of the village gave a short farewell speech in Shona. In response, my parents presented the tribesfolk with two scotchcarts and mules to pull them. The scotchcarts had been used regularly around the farm, and the farewell gesture was intended to help the villagers carry their vegetables and produce to market.

My father once more saw the sadness in my eyes, and understood the doubts that must have been going through my young mind about leaving the farm, and "particularly" leaving behind my trusted friend, Motorcar. He decided to try some persuading of his own. Calling Motorcar aside, my father offered him a new Raleigh bicycle if he came to Salisbury, and after one year of working with the family in the city, enough money to buy ten acres of farming land in the tribal trust areas. At that time, Motorcar could decide whether to continue working in the city or to return to the rural life. Motorcar gazed toward the gleaming, flowing waters of the Mazoe River and the trees bending slightly by the blowing breeze. He slowly turned to my father and said, "I know that young Ivan is my friend, and he needs me. I will try the city for one year!"

Two days later, the family was packed and ready for our move. The new Chevrolet which had been purchased from part of the proceeds of the sale of the farm and our older car were loaded to capacity. With a neighboring farmer driving one of the cars, we were ready to commence the journey to our new life. I placed the last of my bags in the Chevrolet and sadly turned for my last look at what had been the only world I knew. My father had not told me of the deal he had made with Motorcar, so I took a deep breath, and prepared myself for my farewell to Motorcar. Motorcar was standing nearby the homestead when I walked up to him, and began to say a few words before choking into tears.

Looking down at me, his big white teeth showing through his smile, Motorcar said, "Well, young friend, I wouldn't want you to go into the big city without having me to look after you, so I will be coming with you to Salisbury." I yelped with joy, threw my arms around Motorcar, and together we proceeded to the vehicles to commence the journey from the free, open spaces to an area that would be every bit as new and foreign to me as it would be to my friend.

Salisbury was an attractive, clean city—not a large city by any standards, but growing, and if the trend continued, it would certainly grow one day to be a major city on the African continent. My parents had built a house in Belvedere, a new suburb three miles from the city center. Although it was a large contemporary brick home on an acre-and-a-half of land. It felt confined in comparison to the wide open spaces to which I was accustomed. To add to my initial displeasure, I was enrolled in a nearby government school. The school, named after a famous Rhodesian hero, Routledge, was, in fact, a World War Two converted army barracks and prisoner of war camp that had until a couple of years earlier been in continued use by the military. The army had moved out to better barracks on the other side of the city, and the department of education had decided to turn the facility into a school.

In typical English fashion and tradition, discipline was rigidly strict. I displayed my dislike for the rigidity by announcing to my teacher during the mid-morning break on my first day that I no longer wished to attend the school, and promptly took off, running in the direction of my new home. Followed and chased by the teacher and several of the school employees, I made my way home, and was finally able to evade my pursuers, only to be met by my mother, who had already been telephoned by the school's principal. After a tongue lashing for my exploit, I reluctantly returned to school the next day. With time I began to adjust to the city life; in fact, I took a distinct pride in the growth of Salisbury. I watched the mushrooming of new buildings in the city's center, and was struck with awe at the first skyscraper, Rhode-Elect House, a ten-story building which took up an entire city block and was completed in 1953 when I had just turned ten. When I heard of the plans to build a fourteen-story building, my interest peaked, and I rode my bicycle to the erection site daily. On completion, I stood at the base of the building, Trafalgar Court, staring upward to the top of the structure in total amazement at its height and tried to imagine what it must be like to stand at the bottom, looking up, at the Empire State building, a structure I had read so much about in New York City that had a hundred and two floors.

Then came the boom, and the three countries of Nyasaland, Southern, and Northern Rhodesia formed a Federation, with Salisbury as its capital city. The vast economic potential of the combined three countries brought in worldwide investments, skyscrapers sprang up, and the population of Salisbury grew to a quarter of a million people. In sharp contrast to the rapid growth of the city, much of the area around Salisbury remained wild with the tall veldt grass marking the only border between the suburbs and undeveloped Africa. Amazingly, a short trek into the veldt would find raw nature, with tall acacia and baobab trees, and wild animals ranging from lion and leopard to the mild gazelle roaming free. Strayings into the suburbs by these animals inflicted fear and disruption in the daily lives of the Salisbury inhabitants.

I enjoyed venturing beyond the suburban limits into the untamed grasslands, and often, after the school day was over, I would take off alone deep into the veldt, exploring the bushes and climbing tall trees. Armed only with my air rifle for protection, I was oblivious to the potential dangers that could lurk nearby should I accidentally wander into the path of one of the larger carnivorous animals. Somehow, except for one incident, I was fortunate this did not happen. One day when I discovered an unusual set of prints along the bank of a stream, and believing my air gun would protect me from any eventuality which might arise, I stealthily followed the tracks along the waters' edge and through the bushes and rocks until I unexpectedly walked into a clearing and looked into the eyes of a half-grown male lion. We both were equally surprised at the encounter, and both stood frozen, staring at each other. After what seemed to be an eternity to me, but in reality was seconds, the lion turned and loped off into the camouflage and safety of the tall grasses. I, after taking in a few gulps of air, ran for the safety of my home.

Gasping, I arrived home, and ran into the back yard where I found Motorcar tending to the vegetable and fruit orchards. Motorcar turned to look at me with his usual beaming white smile, which immediately turned to concern on seeing the breathless boy. "What has happened, young friend?" I was about to rattle off the tale of my experience, but quickly changed my mind, realizing that if Motorcar and my parents were to know of my recent adventure and the potential danger of my travels into the bushveld, I would be forbidden from going into the bush alone in the future. Reluctantly, I decided that the adventure would have to remain a secret, and proceeded to pour out a lame story to Motorcar about chasing after a gazelle in the bush. Motorcar gave me a disbelieving, quizzical look, and returned to tending the vegetables.

The big occasion each year was the arrival in the city of the circus, and the event was preceded by a parade of clowns, artists, elephants, and caged lions down First Street, the main shopping road of Salisbury. The circus would then set up a large tent at the fairgrounds, less than a mile from my home. The first year that I saw the parade, a lioness went into heat, sending her scent out for miles around as a calling card in the wild for every lone and rogue lion to follow. Overnight, city life and wildlife merged, with some male lions following the irresistible scent to its source. Patrons at the first night show were greeted by the sight of three male lions clawing at the cage of the lioness and a frenzied circus staff attempting to scare them away without success. The show was canceled. The police arrived with dart rifles saturated with drugs, and after shooting the amorous males, they loaded the sleeping kings of the jungle into a van, and deposited them miles away from the city.

Reports of lions roaming the suburbs caused city life to come almost to a standstill, some schools were closed, and few citizens dared to venture outdoors for fear of being mauled by a lion. The city council decided they had endured enough and a delegation visited the circus, and told them to leave town. Without giving a single perform- ance, the circus folded its tents, and departed with the lioness, leaving behind a city in chaos, with adult lions roaming the area—all looking for the lioness.

True to his word, a year after moving to Salisbury, my father spoke to Motorcar about the promise of land. Motorcar informed my father that he wanted to continue working for the Bender family; however, he wished to take leave for six months because he had saved enough money to pay Lobola, the African tribal custom of buying a wife. The woman he had found was from Inyanga, a beautiful mountainous area one hundred and twenty miles east of the city. He planned to take her to her parents to negotiate the Lobola payment and to purchase farmland in the tribal trust land in that district. He would stay with her to sow their first crop of maize and then return to continue working for us. My father agreed with this arrangement and asked Motorcar to look for a temporary replacement for the time he would be away.

A few days later there was a light rapping at the front door, and I discovered a young black boy about the same age as myself standing on the stoop. "I look for work!" he announced. I looked at him; he was dressed in rags, wore no shoes, and was blind in one eye. I called to my father, who took one look at the boy, told him there was no job for him, and walked away leaving the two of us to stare at each other. The one eye stared sadly at me. "Very hungry," the boy said, rubbing his stomach.

"Wait here," I said, and went to the kitchen and returned with a glass of milk and bread. The boy gratefully accepted the food, and sat on the stoop to eat. "What is your name?" I inquired.

"Enok," came the reply. I watched him eat, and noted he was having difficulty swallowing the bread, and guessed that it must have been a while since he had last eaten.

"Where are you from, Enok?"

"I come from the country of Mozambique," the boy replied.

"Mozambique? That is far away! Why are you in this country, and how did you get here?" I asked.

Between forced swallows, Enok answered, "When I was a baby, my parents, who are very poor, blinded me in one eye so that they could take me to the docks in Beira to beg from the tourists in the harbor. I did that for five years, and sometimes when I didn't bring back enough money, they would beat me. Two weeks ago they said that they would cut my fingers off so that the tourists would have more pity on me and I would bring in more money—so I ran away. I slipped inside a Rhodesia Railways train that brought me to Salisbury. I have no family now, so I sleep in the bushes at night and look for work by day."

I would eventually learn as I matured and learned more about the world surrounding me that maiming young children to increase their "take" as beggars was not uncommon on the continent. But today the boy's story shocked me, and I became pensive. Then an idea came to me. "Stay here," I told Enok as I walked away to speak to my father. "Dad, please can we give Enok a job?"

"He's much too young, Ivan. What could he do?" my father asked.

"Dad, he has no family, no place to stay, and no money to buy food. If Motorcar could teach him to tend the vegetables and the orchard, then he and I could do Motorcar's work while he is away!"

With a knowing look, my father understood my desire to help the young waif. "Very well, Ivan, he can have a job, but this means that you have the responsibility of seeing that he does his work well!" He said, placing the charge of the waif's employment squarely on my shoulders.

Enok started work that day. I found some of my old clothes and gave them to Enok to wear, and he was taken to the servants' quarters, where he was shown his room and given his weekly ration of food. My father introduced Enok to Motorcar, "This is your new assistant. His job is to help both you and your replacement while you are away." Motorcar put the boy to work, and Enok proved to be a hard worker, and learned quickly. I sensed, however, that Motorcar saw something about Enok that he did not like.

A month later, Motorcar was ready to take his leave, and he brought his bride-to-be, Sheila, to meet my family. Shelia was a large, friendly black woman with a warm smile, and she quickly endeared herself to us, smiling and laughing as she talked. Motorcar was genuinely proud of her large size, saying that there was more of her to enjoy. He also introduced Tickey, a man almost as powerful-looking as Motorcar, who was to be the temporary worker during Motorcar's leave. Fond farewells were spoken, and Motorcar and Sheila left for the bus station and their journey.

Fate at this time began to weave its intricate web, setting events in motion for the future. Tickey lasted only three days before being arrested for nearly beating a man to death in a beerhall fight, so Enok was left to tend the garden on his own with my help. A few days later I answered the front door to find another young black boy, perhaps a year younger than myself, standing on the stoop. "I hear that you look for a gardener. I am a very good gardener," he said.

I sensed an air of genuineness about the young boy, and asked, "What's your name?"

"Amos," the boy replied.

"Why are you not home with your parents?" I inquired.

"I am an orphan. My mother was killed by a crocodile while washing clothes in the river by my tribal village. I do not know my father, so I come to the city to look for work."

I went to find my father, who wasn't too receptive about giving another waif a job. "Dad, he really is a nice boy, and we do need someone to work in the garden with Enok," I pleaded. My father eventually agreed to hire the young boy, but also let me know that I had reached my limit in accommodating stray waifs. Enok and Amos worked well together tending the orchards and vegetables, but the highlight of each day was after five in the afternoon, when I had done my homework, and the boys had finished their work in the garden. Then the backyard became a playing field, and we played soccer and cricket, and took turns shooting at targets with my air gun. During the weekends we would venture off into the bush to spot wild animals, and during the school holidays we would be allowed to camp out overnight. Sometimes in the middle of the night we could hear the growl of a large animal close to the camp or the laugh of a group of hyenas searching for scraps nearby.

A trust developed among the three of us that went far beyond friendship. On one of our overnight camping excursions into the bush, we sat around the campfire, and talked about what we would like to do in the future. I wanted to become a lawyer. My mother had given me the middle name of Boris, after the lawyer who had defended Dreyfus, the French Jewish officer who had been wrongly accused of being a traitor to France, and was sentenced to Devil's Island. The day Dreyfus was acquitted, Boris was gunned down and murdered on the steps of the court house. It was such a sensational incident during my mother's childhood that she had decided to name one of her children after the dedicated advocate. I was also intrigued with the idea of being a defender of those who needed my help.

Enok wanted to be a businessman and own mines. He had heard talk in his tribal village in Mozambique of discoveries of rubies which had been kept secret from the Portuguese prospectors, and one day he would go back to mine the fields. Amos wanted to become a policeman, because after his mother had been taken by the crocodile, a policeman from his village took him in and looked after him when he had no place to live—before he had traveled to Salisbury to look for work. Amos said jokingly to me, "You can defend the people that I arrest."

Quiet fell on our group while each thought of what the other had said about the direction we wished for our future. Then I vocalized my concern, "There is one problem, Enok. You want to be a businessman, but you can neither read, write, nor add. Amos, you want to become a policeman, but you need a Standard Five education certificate to show that you can read and write. What are you going to do?"

Our little group became very quiet, and after a few minutes, I came up with an idea. "I can teach you when I come home from school each day!" Enok and Amos's faces lit up in delight; the idea of learning to read, write, and add set them off jabbering in excitement. "Yes, I will teach you," I reiterated. When we arrived back at the house, I turned a portion of my bedroom into a "classroom," and each day after school I spent time with Enock and Amos, teaching them the basics of the three Rs.

My mother watched this development with amazement, and not only was she pleased, but she also seemed impressed with the arrangement. She saw that I, through my teaching, became a better student and more dedicated to my studies. The teaching eventually extended to chess, droughts, and an attempt at languages. My mother had taught me French, Spanish, Italian, and Portuguese, and I had picked up the country's regional tribal dialects of Shona, the language of the local tribespeople from daily contact with them, and Sindebele, the language of the Ndbele. I had also learned a spattering of Zulu from Motorcar, but my attempt at languages with Enok and Amos was not successful, so I concentrated on other, more fruitful lessons.

When Motorcar arrived back from his six-month leave, he received a warm welcome from my family. I was particularly happy to see my old friend back home. He was introduced to the new addition, Amos, and seemed to take warmly to the boy, though I could sense that Motorcar's wariness of Enok still existed. It was obvious that there was something Motorcar saw about the boy that made him distrust him, but he never spoke about it.

Motorcar was perplexed to see the daily event of the "classroom" and the lessons taking place each day, but he like everyone else, accepted the situation. The lessons continued for several years, and not only did Enok and Amos pass the Standard Five certificate examinations, but they went on a few years later to pass the Form Two senior high school diploma.

Chapter Three

Shortly after the family's' arrival in Salisbury, my father commenced his search for a new business, and after investigating many options with my mother, decided to open a bicycle shop. Conditions appeared to be prime for that type of enterprise because large numbers of tribal people were flowing into the urban area, attracted by the lure of new jobs opening in the expanding city. Because of the level of these incomes, the main form of transportation would be the bicycle. He leased a shop on the corner of Manica Road, which was the city's longest business street, and the second busiest concourse, and was also the main gateway to the eastern districts of the country. Three blocks from the railway station, the location was ideal because new arrivals looking to purchase transportation around the city could walk there.

My father worked hard developing the enterprise, which he named Royal Cycles. He hired mechanics to do repairs and provided what he believed to be the formula for a successful business: quality, good service, and fair prices. The business thrived, and the boom period of the Federation of Rhodesia and Nyasaland gave him the opportunity to import crates of bicycles directly from the source, and he soon began supplying other retailers.

About this time, my cousin Benny came to my father looking for work. He had just returned from the University of Cape Town, after failing in his second attempt at fourth-year medicine. I had a dislike for this relative, who was known for his meanness. He was a short, prematurely balding man of twenty-two, who, in the company of adults, wore a phony smile and gave the appearance of congeniality and kindness, when, in fact, he was the opposite. I was also aware that the feelings of dislike were mutual between my cousin and myself, so I was not overjoyed when my father announced that he hired Benny as a salesman in the business.

The business continued to expand, as did Benny's position in the company. Suddenly, Benny was the general manager. The Rhodesian iron and steel industry was growing in Que-Que, a town one hundred and twenty miles west of Salisbury (pronounced Kwe-Kwe by the tribespeople, after the sound of the frogs croaking in the streams surrounding the town). Benny approached my father with the idea of manufacturing bicycles at a new plant. The idea was a good one, and after many months of discussions and haggling, my father and Benny entered into negotiations with the Rhodesian Iron and Steel Board. A year later saw the birth of a small bicycle Industry.

Bicycle frames began being forged at the new plant, while other parts were imported from around the world—bicycle spokes from India, saddles from England, chains from Czechoslovakia, tires and tubes from South Africa—all making their way to the assembly plant at the new warehouse on Railway Avenue, Salisbury. Wealth and prestige flowed in with the growth of the business, but the one thing that remained unchanged was Benny. He went out of his way to be unpleasant to me, barring me from entering his office, and giving me a "friendly" punch on my shoulder every time we met. The punch was not friendly, but was intended to hurt! Benny also, never missed an opportunity to criticize or be demeaning to me.

I eventually spoke to my father about Benny. "Why does he behave like that, Dad?" I questioned. My father's forehead creased with concern and he said, "I have been meaning to have a talk with Benny for a while now, but I had hoped that he would change. Ivan, I think there are two reasons for his behavior towards you. First, he is jealous of you, and the second is more complicated. This business is really all that he has; he doesn't have any friends or much social life. I think he is afraid that one day you will come into the business and perhaps take away the one thing he does have—his power over this enterprise!" I thought carefully about my father's words, and said, "Dad, he is a fool if that is the way he thinks, we should be able to work together, as a family, to build and expand the business you started!"

My father replied, "You and I know that, Ivan. The problem is I don't think Benny wants to share anything with anyone!. He wants everything for himself, and that is what I am going to have to talk to him about!" My father soon afterwards spoke to Benny, emphasizing the need for a change in his attitude and the way he treated people. Benny, projecting his usual, studied smile, promised to make the effort to be more agreeable. For almost a month, Benny was actually pleasant to everyone, including me, but the change was temporary, and he soon reverted to his old ways.

While the business continued to grow and become established, I entered Prince Edward Senior High School, one of the more prestigious of the public schools in the country, with a reputation for strict discipline and high academic and sports achievements. It was 1955, and I was twelve years old. Here family wealth played little part, and everyone wore the same smart maroon uniform so there was no distinction between rich and poor. The dress code was strictly enforced under threat of a caning dealt out by prefects, teachers, or headmasters for any violations. At Prince Edward, each pupil's standing among his peers was determined by either academic or athletic merit.

Halfway through the first term, a new pupil with his arm in a sling was introduced into my class. His name was Robert and he sat in the seat next to me. At lunch break I talked with the new boy, asking where he was from and how he had received the injury to his arm. Robert explained that he was a recent arrival from Kenya, and his parents had owned a farm near Nairobi. I had heard about the problems that country to the north of Rhodesia was having with terrorists called the Mau-Mau, who were fighting for independence from Britain. The Mau-Mau were known for the atrocities they had committed against white farmers living on isolated farms, and I had also read that their initiation ritual was barbaric—new members were required to slaughter an animal, and drink the fresh blood mixed with milk.

Robert told me that his family had been attacked twice by Mau-Mau. The first time had been a couple of years ago, but on that occasion guard dogs had sounded a warning in the middle of the night, giving them time to call for help and to arm themselves to fend off the attack until help arrived early the next morning.

The second incident was far more serious. The Mau-Mau had come into the workers' camp, and under threat of death, made the employees feed the dogs poisoned food. Cutting the telephone and electrical wires, the attackers, numbering about thirty, surrounded the house that Robert, his mother, and father were in, and opened fire on the homestead. Bullets smashed through the windows, and whizzed over the heads of the three sleeping people, ripping holes into the inside walls of the house. After the first attack, the family had made a practice of going to sleep armed with rifles for protection, and with the second attack they dived out of their beds, and under cover of the walls by the windows, returned the fire. The situation seemed hopeless, so Robert's father instructed his family to make their way to the garage by the side of the house where the Land Rover was parked.

They would attempt to escape. Robert and his mother made a run for the vehicle while Robert's father stayed behind providing fire cover. As the engine started, two bullets struck his father, one in the stomach and the other in the arm. Throwing down his weapon, he, too, made a dash for the car, jumping into the back seat while the mother gunned the engine and raced out of the homestead, as the vehicle roared down the road, a bullet came through the window, hitting Robert in his left shoulder. Looking back they could see their homestead being set afire, with flames beginning to leap into the sky, and as they made their way to the nearest town, they were grateful just to have made it out alive. That had been nearly two months ago, and was the reason for Robert's arm being in a sling. While Robert and his father were recovering from their injuries, the family decided to move to the safety of Southern Rhodesia.

The classroom bell sounded, signaling the end of lunch break. As we headed back to class, I was disturbed, and pondered if such things could ever happen in my country. A few months later Harold Macmillan, the British Prime Minister, made his famous "Winds of Change" speech at the South African Parliament in Cape Town during a visit to that country. He predicted that powerful forces of change would sweep down across the African continent, and aided by the Soviet and Chinese fueling and feeding of dissension in Africa, the forces of change blowing in would be too strong to hold back. True to the prediction, the next few years saw the disintegration of the Federation of the Rhodesias and Nyasaland, with the emergence of nationalist leaders who would set the direction for the future. In Nyasaland, Dr. Hastings Banda, a London-educated physician led the insurrection; and in Northern Rhodesia, there were smaller riots led by Kenneth Kaunda. Southern Rhodesia was politically divided by leaders of two tribal groups, the Shona, headed by Reverend Sithole in the East; and the Ndebele, led by Joshua Nkomo, in the West.

The country to the north of the Rhodesias was the Belgian Congo, a territory administered by the Belgians as part of Metropolitan Belgium, with no central government. Katanga Province, which adjoined Northern Rhodesia, was the wealthiest area, and was rich in copper and mineral mines. There had been political rumblings in that territory, too, and the Belgians were preparing to give the country early independence. The problem was that the emerging political leaders had received no preparation in running a country, and there was division based on tribal lines between the leader of the Katanga province, Moise Tshombe, and the leader of the rest of the country, Patrice Lumumba.

It was 1959, and I, now sixteen and in my fourth year of high school, watched the developments with interest and much concern. Independence was granted to Belgian Congo and the name was changed to Zaire. Overnight, all hell broke loose as Moise Tshombe seceded the province of Katanga. Civil war erupted, with fighting between the troops, shooting and killing of the whites in the streets and homes, and rampant looting of the shopping districts. Shortly after hearing the news on the radio, I received a phone call from my high school French teacher who told me that several aircraft filled with refugees from Zaire were being flown in to Salisbury, and the first was due to arrive at five a.m. the next morning. They urgently needed people who could speak French to act as interpreters for the refugees, who would be ferried from the airport to the buildings at the showgrounds. Clearance had been given by the headmaster; would I assist? I agreed to help.

Early the next morning, I made my way through the darkness to the showgrounds to await the arrival of the first wave of refugees. Shortly after five a.m., the first buses arrived, and the plight of the refugees as they stepped out of the vehicles was heartbreaking to see. Most had been in bed asleep when the shooting had broken out in the middle of the night, so some had made the dash to the airport still wearing their night clothes, and others had barely enough time to throw on some clothes in their attempt to get away. What they stepped off the buses with was all they had left in the world.

The volunteers and helpers from the Rhodesian side did a wonderful job serving a warm breakfast, tending to the children, and patching injuries. I helped by interpreting, serving food, and assisting in calming people down. Over the next two hours, buses kept arriving, and they delivered more than eight hundred refugees. On one stop, I saw the most stunningly beautiful girl step from a bus. She appeared to be close to my age, had shoulder-length, blonde curly hair, green-blue eyes, and the figure of a Venus. She was wearing a blouse and shorts, but no shoes, so I surmised that in the frenzy of leaving, she hadn't time to finish dressing, and mentally nicknamed her Brigitte Bardot, after the French actress.

When I offered her a plate of food, she smiled at me as she accepted it, and during the rest of the day, I would glance at the girl, and each time I could see that she was also watching me. By the time evening came, I was exhausted, and I walked outside the showground building and past some bushes to a log where I sat down to rest. Lost in my own thoughts, I unexpectedly heard the rustle of feet walking on dried grass and looked up to see Brigitte walking in my direction. Approaching me, and speaking perfect French, she introduced herself and sat on the log beside me. Her name was Chantelle, she was from Elisabethville and had arrived on the refugee plane with her parents. They, like the others, had been asleep when the shooting started and had barely made it to the airport as the last planes were leaving. As we talked, the strain of her ordeal surfaced, and tears began streaming down her cheeks. I moved closer, intending to comfort her, and put my arm around her, meaning to hold her waist, but accidentally cupped her breast. A little embarrassed, I moved to try and take my hand away, but she captured it with her elbow, and pressed my hand firmly into her body. I sensed the excitement build inside me as I felt her firm breast and hardened nipple, under the pressure of her grip, then moved my hand away. I held her gently, and kissed her tenderly. The touch of her lips sent emotions through me that I had never before experienced! After the kiss we stood up, and Chantelle asked me to hold her once more—and from that moment everything else became irrelevant, and only the stars, the moonlit sky, and the two of us existed.

Slowly we made our way back to the building where the refugees were being sheltered. Chantelles' father approached us, and I was introduced to him. He was a handsome, blond haired, blue eyed man.

His hair was disheveled and he was wearing only a sports shirt, slacks and a pair of sandals. Obviously, he had snatched the nearest set of available clothing to wear, before they had make their escape. We walked together to where Chantelle's mother was quietly seated near a corner of the building. She too, was wearing ruffled, bare necessity clothing. On being introduced, I was immediately struck by the observation, that despite not having had the time to brush her hair or wear any make up, she radiated warmth and natural elegance. She greeted me with a beautiful smile. Chantelle's father informed us that the Belgian airline, Sabena, was sending a convoy of aircraft, which would arrive at midnight, to airlift them to Brussels. I felt a sadness swell inside me at the thought of Chantelle leaving so soon!

I traveled with Chantelle and her parents on the bus to the airport, and shortly after midnight a string of aircraft, in rapid succession, flew in and landed, took on passengers, and flew out again. I said farewell to Chantelle, and watched her aircraft take off. As the plane soared into the sky, I wondered if I would he ever see her again.

I stood by the departure window for many minutes after Chantelle's flight had disappeared from sight, thinking of the emptiness that now suddenly existed inside of me, without her.

My thoughts were interrupted by someone calling my name. "Ivan! Ivan!" It was my French teacher, Mr. Gallant, waving from the other side of the airport building, and signaling me to come over. "Ivan, they need help on the border because some of the refugees who were not able to be evacuated by aircraft or road convoy are trying to make it on their own by car to the border. We have an aircraft leaving in half-an-hour to take us to the border so we can help them. Will you come with us?"

I phoned my mother, and after telling her of the circumstances, she reluctantly agreed to let me go on the teacher's mission of mercy.

Our flight arrived in Ndola during the early hours of the morning, and the passengers were immediately bused to the border. On the flight, Mr. Gallant had briefly explained that we were flying in to assist the other volunteers who were providing help to the refugees as they crossed into Northern Rhodesia. I was totally unprepared for what I saw along the route to the border! The roads were littered with cars of all sizes and shapes, some were riddled with bullet holes, and others with bullet holes and blood. At the border there was a hive of activity in a makeshift camp, where the volunteers were giving temporary aid to the refugees before they moved on to the next available sanctuary. There was also a regiment of five hundred men from the Rhodesian African Rifles who had been sent in to secure the border. The regiment had a history of valor under the name, The King's African Rifles, and they had served with distinction in Burma during World War Two. The five hundred black soldiers and their two white officers were considered the elite troops of Africa.

Shooting could be heard from the other side of the border as the Zaire troops began to take control of the strip of land leading to the border from the Katanganese forces. On the Zaire side of the border there was a clear stretch of land running about half-a-mile before becoming obscured by trees. Suddenly the shooting sounded closer, and I looked in the direction of the shots to see a minibus racing out from the trees into the clearing toward us, chased by soldiers firing from an open Jeep. The soldiers continued peppering the side of the minibus with bullets until the vehicle made the crossing to our side of the border. At that point, the Jeep turned away, breaking the chase.

Fortunately the passengers, a husband, wife, and four small children, except for a few grazes, suffered no injuries. Very soon another small vehicle broke into the clearing with steam blowing from its engine and swerving dangerously because of several shot-out tires. The soldiers in the Jeep turned their attention to the car, and fired on it. When the vehicle came to a halt in the middle of the clearing, the Jeep skidded to a stop alongside it, and the troops jumped out. Racing to the car, they opened the passenger's side, and the body of a dead woman fell on to the road. On the other side the wounded driver, a man, opened his door and begged for his life before being riddled with bullets.

The whole scene hit me with such horror that I let out an involuntary yell at the top of my voice, "FOR GOD'S SAKE, STOP THE KILLING!" I screamed. My voice loudly carried across the open clearing to the jeep and its soldiers that had just murdered the couple The commander of the Rhodesian African Rifles, a captain, was standing nearby. I saw the soldier's face turn blood red, and anger spewed from his eyes. He called for a radio transmitter, phoned headquarters in Salisbury, and after explaining the situation, was patched through to the Cabinet Minister's office. He was put on hold while the minister telephoned the Belgian Ministry in Brussels, and the instructions came back that the captain was to speak to the Zaire commander for the region, and if that did not stop the killing, to take what steps he deemed necessary to do so. He was warned that Rhodesia did not want an "international incident," and if things went wrong, he would be held responsible. As the captain put down the transmitter, I heard him mutter, "Screw the job. There are lives to be saved!"

The captain sent a runner under a flag of truce to the commander on the other side, and a meeting was arranged half way into the clearing on the Zaire side. The captain and his aide walked over to the meeting point, and were joined by the Zaire commander and a group of his men. As they talked, I could see the discussions were becoming heated, suddenly the Zaire commander pulled out his revolver and waved the gun, threatening to shoot the Rhodesian captain. Almost in unison there was a loud clicking sound of five hundred rifle bolts arming bullets into their barrels. The Zaire commander turned to see five hundred Rhodesian African three-o-three rifles pointed directly at him and his men. Realizing that pulling the trigger of his revolver would be the last thing he ever did, the commander holstered his pistol, and marched off with his group. On his return to the Rhodesian side, the captain ordered his men to load onto the trucks, and they took off singing their regimental song, driving across the border into Zaire. I returned to my work tending the refugees. Five hours later the troops returned, once again singing their troop song. They had mopped up and cleared the area of Zairean soldiers without incurring a single injury!

Chapter Four

The next day I flew back to Salisbury, tired, shaken, and exhausted from the experience. I could not shrug off or forget the horrors I had seen, and I threw myself into schoolwork, my classes with Amos and Enok, and reading books to keep my mind occupied.

During the following months when I lay in bed at night, alone with my thoughts, I kept thinking about what had happened, and tried hard to understand why such things could happen. Eventually, I came to the conclusion that as civilized as man believed himself to be, he was really still in the dark ages of human development, despite the rapid technological advances that were being made. A section from a book I had recently read, *Gullivers Travels*, put a lot of what I was trying to understand in perspective: the King of Lilliput was preparing to go to war with the neighboring island kingdom, and was attempting to enlist the help of Gulliver. It turned out that his reason for wanting to go to war was because the king of the neighboring island had visited Lilliput, and during breakfast a dispute arose between the two kings regarding a custom by the one to cut a hard boiled egg in the center and the other to cut the egg at the top.

Absurd as that dispute sounded, I could compare that with real life events, where men went to war or killed over disputed boundary lines that are all imaginary, religious beliefs, or simply because of the pigmentation of another's skin—all in the heat of a brief moment of time, ultimately to be forgotten, or to be hidden in the pages of history books. As an illustration of this, I thought of America's once bitter enemy, Germany, who was now its friend, and the bitter Cold War between the Western and the Soviet ideals. Perhaps because of my youth, I was oversimplifying the situation, but it worked for me. To prove my own point, I mentally made three predictions and hoped that I would be able to see them happen during my lifetime.

The first was that the Soviet Union and the United States would become friends and perhaps even allies. The second was that man would eventually become color blind, judging each person on merit, rather than the pigmentation of his skin. The third was that man would learn to understand that religious beliefs are personal, and believing in a higher power in one's own way poses no threat to anyone. Then I would think of beautiful Chantelle and turn over and go to sleep with the image of us together in the moonlight.

With the countries to the north gaining independence, the situation in the Federation got worse. Army call-ups become the order of the day, with riots in the Northern Territories becoming more frequent and anyone over the age of eighteen who was not at school being con-scripted. There were riots in Salisbury, to a lesser extent and more con-trolled, but it was becoming obvious that the three territories would soon split. When the break-up of the Federation finally came, two of them, Nyasaland and Northern Rhodesia, were granted independence by Britain.

Nyasaland, under Banda, changed its name to Malawi. Rumors began to filter to Salisbury that Banda had achieved a "God complex," banning all opposition, jailing people for any criticism of him, and placing his British bowler hat on top of a pole in one of the main streets of Blantyre, the capital city, and requiring people to pay homage to it when they passed by.

Northern Rhodesia, under Kaunda, changed its name to Zambia. He, in true African "democratic" style, turned the country into a one-party state, banning all opposition parties, with the rationale that you could vote for whomever you liked, as long as it was for his party! He then embarked on an ambitious space program, and the training ground of the hand-picked astronauts was a high hill. Incredibly, at the top of the hill were barrels which the astronauts would climb into, and the barrels were then rolled off the hill, spinning down one hundred and fifty yards to simulate travel in Space, and voila, Kaunda had a space program! At the bottom of the hill he had very dizzy and battered astronauts. Kaunda was also awarded an honorary doctorate from a university in the United States which he had visited, and although he had received no high level education, he insisted that he now be referred to as Doctor Kenneth Kaunda.

Southern Rhodesia, now simply called Rhodesia, although self-governing since 1923, was denied independence by Britain until the precondition of majority rule was attained. The Rhodesians, a large number of whom were ex-British and veterans of World War Two, had watched the events take shape in the countries to their north, and decided that they did not like the break down of law and order or African-style Democracy. Digging in their heels, they became the boundary between the "Black North" and the "White South."

With the Federation now gone, a semblance of "normality" returned to Rhodesia. There were minor disturbances, but for the time being nothing of significance. I, like all other Rhodesian schoolboys fifteen or older, was required to attend military cadet training each Friday afternoon at the high school. From time to time, the powers that be would put on a show of force, so that the locals could observe the country's potential military might. The cadets, numbering a few thousand from all the high schools, assembled in full military uniform at the drill hall near the city center, and were marched through the main streets of Salisbury. It was a ludicrous sight to see. Here were young boys marching in full military attire, carrying antiquated rifles, some dating back to 1896—with no rifle bolts or firing pins.

When I turned seventeen, I was approaching my last year of high school. Academically, I had done reasonably well, and athletically I had excelled playing rugby and cricket for my school. On my own, I had taken up body building, turning one of the three garages at home into a gym with weights. Amos and Enok had long come to the conclusion that what was good for me was good for them, so they, too, took to training with the weights, and the three of us developed impressive, powerful physiques.

The bicycle business had grown to be a major Rhodesian industry. My father was now exporting cycles to the neighboring countries of Zambia, Zaire, Mozambique, and even South Africa before that country started its own plant at Springs, near Johannesburg. Now a rich man, Cousin Benny, in his own deceitful way, contrived to make as many people as possible believe that the business was his and that my father worked for him.

Motorcar was starting to grey a little around the temple, I knew my boyhood companion and protector was a true and trusted friend, who was content to work with his hands from morning to the time the sun set in the evenings. He was the person I loved to work with in the garden for an excuse to talk and especially listen to him tell one of his wonderful tales of Africa. It also fascinated me the way Motorcar could be totally focused on the task at hand and at the same time carry on conversation and his flow of stories.

Motorcar now worked for my family only nine months of the year. The other three months he would spend in Inyanga to be with Sheila, with whom he now had three children, all boys. There he would reap the crops on his ten-acre plot of land. According to African custom, the women and children tended to the family land, a remnant of the times when the men were busy fighting tribal wars and only returned for brief periods to help reap the crops. The men still left the tending of the land to the women and children, but instead of going off to fight a tribal war, they left to find work and earn money for their families.

Amos and Enok were preparing to write the Form Two Certificate examinations, a level that showed achievement of second-year-high-school competency. They had both written and passed the Standard Five junior high school tests three years earlier, and with my encouragement, continued the "classroom" studies to this next level. I realized that passing the exams would mean Amos and Enok would soon leave to find better positions in life, but this was what we had spoken about as we sat around the campfire in those early bushveldt years, and this was why both had studied so hard.

Examinations were spread over two days, with four, three-hour tests. The day of the first exam I accompanied Amos and Enok to the Salisbury Polytechnic, making sure they had their pen, pencils, and ruler before heading off for school myself. The next two days I behaved the same way a nervous expectant father did when awaiting news of the birth of a child. The second day I even arrived half-an-hour before the exam ended and proceeded to pace up and down the Polytechnic hallway, in nervous anticipation. When Amos and Enok finally emerged, I had asked, "Well?" The response was a fatalistic type of shrug from both young men, which had the effect of making me feel doubly apprehensive.

They were to be informed by mail of the results in approximately three weeks, so now began the waiting game. Three weeks later, to the day, two letters arrived in the afternoon post, and I went out to the garden, and handed each of them their mail. Amos opened his letter immediately, a worried frown betraying his anxiety, but it soon disappeared as he read the report. I heard a yell of joy; he had passed! Enok sat on the grass, staring at his envelope and announced that he wanted to sleep on it, and would open the letter the next morning. There was no way Amos and I were going to let Enok prolong the suspense, we put all kinds of pressure on him to open the letter—now! Slowly, Enok tore the letter open, and as the one eye read the results, a huge smile appeared on his face, and he began to dance and jump about with joy. He, too, had passed.

With the classroom now closed, I began to concentrate on the studies for my own exams. Rhodesia offered the Cambridge University overseas high school certificate, set by the University in England. Once the students had written the exams, they were sent back to England for marking and a waiting period for the results, which could take up to a couple of months. Rhodesia at that time did not have its own university, so most students were obliged to complete their higher education at universities in South Africa. The South African government subsidized a large portion of the education expenses of their colleges, but the large number of Rhodesians studying there had become a drain on their resources, so they proceeded to make entry more difficult by requiring Rhodesians to have a very high pass mark on their Cambridge Certificates before being allowed into their universities. I knew I had a tough task ahead of me.

I had become friendly with a student from the Girls High School, who was also in her final high school year. Her name was Shana Garrick, and from time to time we studied together. Her father, Stan Garrick, was a politician, not a successful one, but a politician, nonetheless, who had run for office in the Highland Suburb of Salisbury several times, and lost by wide margins on each occasion. He had subsequently formed his own party, the premise, which was thought to be very radical, was because it believed that Rhodesia should do what the Americans had done—declare its unilateral independence from Britain!

Shana's father was a self-made millionaire, having acquired his money from mining and real estate. He loved to talk politics and would take any opportunity to get up on a soapbox and vend his views. Each time I visited Shana, Stan Garrick would corner me for at least a forty-five minute session of fervent, impassioned political talk: "We should declare independence and go our own way! Forget what those armchair critics who are trying to dictate our future from a safe distance think we should do! We are the ones who will be affected! Do you think the world will come to our rescue once the slaughter begins? With independence, we will have control over our own destiny!"

I would politely listen, but deep down thought Garrick's ideas were crazy. "Do you think if we declared independence that Britain would let us go our own merry way without a fight, or possibly a war?" I asked on one occasion, with a hint of sarcasm.

Stan had replied, "To a large extent, yes! With a quarter-of-a million Rhodesians who were formerly British, and all the families, relatives, and friends we have in Britain, it would topple the British government to go to war with us. Besides, the British economy is doing poorly, so I don't believe they can afford a war. The worst that can happen is that they form an economic blockade against us, but sanctions have a very poor history of working, particularly with South Africa and Mozambique having a vital self-interest in our survival. The ocean gateways would remain open to us."

An election was due to be held shortly in the Highland constituency, and I followed the campaign with interest. When the results were published in the daily paper, *The Rhodesia Herald*, Garricks opponent won with 4,867 votes; invalid, spoiled papers amounted to 89; and Stan Garrick received 78 votes. It was the first time I ever heard of a candidate running in third place behind spoiled papers. Poor Shana, she was teased by her schoolmates and friends over the voting results, but remained staunchly loyal to her father. Little did anyone realize that those ideas would in a few years take firm root in Rhodesian politics and be implemented under the leadership of another man, Ian Smith!

The longest serving prime minister in the British Empire was the present Rhodesian Premier, Sir Godfrey Huggins. His thirty years of leadership, until the formation of the now-defunct Federation of Rhodesia and Nyasaland, had been a model of stability. Was there inequality between the races? Yes, there was; however, most societies tend to gravitate toward a system that works for them for that moment in time and history. Here were two societies living alongside each other: the black, steeped in their tribal customs and tradition, and the white, with their European culture and technology.

I believed there existed a large silent majority among the races who were content to live their lives in harmony, letting time take care of the evolutionary process of the merging of the two cultures. Who wants to fight or go to war with people one has grown up with? There was plenty of land and potential opportunity for all. For the moment it meant the whites lived in the urban areas or farmlands under European tradi- tional rules, and the blacks lived in rural areas under tribal rules and values; however, in a case of conflict over the systems in the urbanized areas, the European rules would prevail. When a native had enough of the European or commercial way of life, there was the option of heading back to the sanctuary of his tribal lands where a vast majority had their own plots of land.

A perfect system of society? No. Far from it, but the friendly smiles, well-fed people, and low crime rate must have been a reflection of something working. Unfortunately, there were the radicals on both sides, the ones who made the most noise and gave the impression of representing the majority view. With the whites there was the left, which felt that the blacks were getting a raw deal and should be pro- tected and nurtured like little children. On the right there were the bigots and racists who hated the blacks and would stoop to any level to undermine them.

There were honest black politicians who sought to improve the standard of life in their tribunal communities, and there were also corrupt, greedy politicians who seized on any opportunity to grab power and wealth for themselves. In time, these corrupt men became both the manipulators and the manipulated. As manipulators, they made promises they never intended to keep in order to gain the support of followers—promises of land, property, fancy homes, and cars to be handed out once those leaders gained control of the country. They were promises no society in its wildest dreams would be capable of providing to each of its citizens.

They became the manipulated because their greed made them easy prey to the outside ambitions of the Soviets and Chinese who fed that greed for their own political expansion purposes; in effect, turning those black politicians into puppets of their regimes. As the Chinese gained a stronghold among the Shona politicians, the Soviets targeted the Ndbele, and the same Communists who had mastered the art of causing dissension in the countries to the north now began to apply their tactics systematically in this region. Their propaganda was powerful and unrelenting, and the external effect was that the world now viewed Rhodesia as a racist colony.

Rhodesia, although a separate country from South Africa, was unfairly lumped together in the world's perspective as having that country's system of Apartheid. In actuality, Rhodesia had introduced a Qualified Franchise, which meant that irrespective of background, as long as one could show a level of education of at least two years of junior high school and was able to write one's name, that person could vote. Different from Universal Franchise, where everyone over a certain age has the vote, the Qualified System was introduced to make education the criterion, rather than race. The legislators were fearful that the introduction of a Universal Franchise would lead to the same break down of law and order that they had witnessed in countries to the north.

Politics, because of the troubling events taking shape in Africa, was a major topic in most Rhodesians' everyday thoughts and conversation. It was inescapable. even with the final school exams approaching, I found myself juggled my interests between my studies and the terrifying events occurring around the country. Amos was awaiting his eighteenth birthday so he could file his application to join the police force, while Enok was not quite sure which direction he wanted to take with employment that he hoped would start him on the journey to being a businessman.

There was now, one new very disturbing element that had begun to surface. It was difficult to not observe a change that had taken place in Enok from friendly and outgoing to sulking and introverted—almost withdrawn. In the hope of finding the cause of the shift in personality, I spoke to Amos, but Amos appeared reluctant to talk about Enok's situation, and merely shrugged his shoulders. Then, after reflecting a while, Amos told me, "I think Enok is going about with older men who are putting strange ideas in his head, and I also think he is doing dagga with them." Dagga was the African term for marijuana. I was very disturbed, and was going to have to find the right opportunity to talk to Enok, and try to help him through this problem.

I came home from school the following day and headed out to the garden to see Enok. As I approached the garage area, I heard Motorcar angrily yelling at Enok, "I don't want to hear you speaking about such things again!" Motorcar said, ending the conversation with an openhanded clip to the back of Enok's head that sent the boy reeling sideways. I quickened my pace to find the cause of the trouble, but at that moment, I heard my mother calling me from the house. Putting my curiosity on hold, I walked back to the house.

"Ivan, the consulate of Belgium phoned and left a message for you while you were at school," my mother explained. "Someone has written to you from Brussels, but didn't know your address, so she asked the consulate for help in locating you—I have the person's name written down—Chantelle Roget. Her letter is waiting for you at the consulate's office!"

"Chantelle!" I thought. She was the girl I had met while helping the refugees from Katanga! Barely had my mother finished speaking when I was already out the front door, heading for the consular office. For the moment, everything else was forgotten! At the consular office, the official handed me the letter, and I eagerly opened it. The letter was written in the most exquisite handwriting, and started, "Mon. Cher Ivan," and went on to say Chantelle hoped the letter would find its way into my hands with the help of the consulate. She was living in Brussels, and her father had found a job as an economist with a large Belgium company. She was now in her final high school year and was also successfully modeling for the covers of French and Belgian fashion magazines, but she planned to study at the Brussels University for a degree in photo-journalism. The letter ended with the words, "Please, Ivan, write to me whenever you have the time. Don't lose touch with me. I often think of our night together when I flew in as a refugee from Katanga and left my heart with you under the Rhodesian sky. Thank you for being there. Love, Chantelle."

That night I sat down and wrote to Chantelle, and from that day letters from the two of us flowed regularly. It would take about ten days for letters to get to Brussels and ten more days to receive a reply. The theme that grew out of that correspondence, was that we both wished one day to be together again and to share more than a brief moment with each other under the African sky.

Chapter Five

At the homestead the situation with Enok progressively worsened, as he seemed to develop a definite resentment toward me and my family, as well as for Motorcar and Amos. He had strange mood swings, ranging from quiet and introverted, to angry and belligerent. I decided the time had come to talk with Enok and perhaps find out what the cause of the problem was. Finding him one day working alone in the garden, I approached him and asked, "Enok, what's been the matter with you lately? I see that you have been getting upset a lot with all of us recently. Is there a problem?"

Enok glared at me, "You are the problem! You whites have stolen my country and my home!"

I stood in front of Enok, momentarily perplexed at the accusation and then replied, "Enok, if I remember correctly you came from Mozambique! As for stealing your home—what are you talking about?" My reply seemed to anger Enok even further.

"You whites came to this country, and stole our land and our homes. One day we comrades will throw you out, then we will become a strong communist country, and we will live in your fine houses and drive your fancy cars!" Enok continued to glare at me, and I felt anger surge from within my body. This was not the Enok I had befriended and grown up with. These were someone else's words that he was parroting, but further discussion with him seemed fruitless, since Enok was obviously in a determined mind set.

Turning to leave, I said, "Enok, if you believe that you are a fool! Nobody is going to give you wealth without working for it. The people telling you that are feeding you rubbish; their only purpose in doing it is to use you!"

"White bastard!" Enok retorted with a snarl.

I lost control and flew into Enok, my fist smashed into Enok's chest, and sent him reeling backwards. Quickly recovering, Enok lunged forward, and the two of us became entangled in a vicious fist fight raining blows on each other. We continued throwing punches until I caught Enok with a hard blow to the chin knocking him to the ground. Dazed, he stood up and prepared to take another swing at me. From his condition, I recognized that one more punch to his chin would probably knock him unconscious. At that moment, Motorcar and Amos arrived, stopping the fight and pulling the two of us apart. Motorcar ordered me to return to the house, while they helped the unsteady and dazed Enok back to his room.

I had won the physical contest, but it was an empty victory, and when I returned to the house I was emotionally shattered over the fight with Enok. That night I ate dinner with my parents, but remained silent about the fight with Enok. The situation with Enok never improved, and two months later, after receiving his pay, Enok packed his bags and simply disappeared, leaving without giving notice or saying goodbye. Shortly after learning that Enok had left, I went to the garden to speak with Motorcar. To my surprise, both Motorcar and Amos were happy with the departure of Enok. "It is a good thing that Enok has left; he would have caused much trouble. The people he is with are Satan nyoka, Devil Snakes!" Motorcar stated in a solemn voice.

I thought a few seconds, and then asked, "Remember a couple of months ago, Motorcar, when you had an argument with Enok, and it ended with you clipping Enok on the back of his head? What happened?"

Motorcar replied, "Enok's people wanted to organize an attack in the middle of the night on the homes of white people, while the whites were asleep. They wanted to kill many whites and cause fear among those that survived the attack. His people could not get enough support to carry out their plan, so there never was any threat of that happening, but I was angry with Enok for suggesting that to me and for being a supporter of such a terrible act. That is why I struck him!"

Amos, who was standing nearby, nodded his head in agreement. "It is better that Enok has gone and taken his bad ideas with him, but trouble walks in his shadow, so I don't think we have seen the last of him. Now it will depend on how large a shadow he is able to cast in the years to come."

Gradually, Enok's departure drifted into memory, life continued, and I became engrossed in my daily studies since the time to sit the Cambridge exams was now only a few weeks away. Life in Salisbury was fairly stable with the exception of minor political demonstrations, which appeared to occur with more frequency and was carried out by the same few people. The disturbances must have been greatly exaggerated by the overseas media, because there were constant inquiries from friends and relatives of the family in the United States and Europe regarding our well-being in the light of the "riots" and "killings" that they were reading about in the American and European press.

Even Chantelle called from Brussels, afraid that we may be going through the same situation that she and her family had found themselves in Katanga. I reassured Chantelle that life was calm in Rhodesia and there was little substance to the reports she was reading. I could not hold back telling Chantelle how happy I was to hear her voice, and we talked a little while, the conversation ending with the two of us using those precious words; "I love you!".

Then came a letter from my Uncle Jack, my father's younger brother who lived in Hermosa Beach, California. He, too, had read the exaggerated reports that were being printed in the press and wanted to know if the family was safe. He was particularly concerned about my future safety in a land which was indeed headed for political instability. He and his wife had not been able to conceive children and they asked if I would be interested in their sponsoring me into the United States with the possibility of studying at the University of Southern California. They had been successful in business, buying property on Sunset Boulevard and building a small shopping center where they leased out shops. Jack stated that they had a large beach front house and that he and his wife would love to have a child who was a member of the family stay in their home. They felt it would make their lives more complete, even if for a temporary time while I completed my studies.

This was a wonderful opportunity for me, although I had already applied and been tentatively accepted for admittance to the BA, LL.B. law course at the University of Cape Town in South Africa, the college where most of my friends were going to study. I had always dreamed of traveling one day to America and Europe and this would afford me the possibility of combining travel with my studies. My parents placed a phone call to Uncle Jack in the United States to accept his offer, and Uncle Jack promised to start the sponsorship process immediately. During the conversation, I learned that I would have a window of time to wait before I could start my studies at U.S.C., since the academic year in America started in September and ended in May, which was different from the Rhodesian, Southern Hemisphere academic year of March to October or November. It was now early October, 1961, and if all went well, I would enroll for the following September intake of students.

I took the Cambridge examinations at the end of October. The day I finished writing the last paper I set about applying for immigrant status with the United States consulate. Surprisingly, the process was relatively easy because the consulate had already received documentation from Uncle Jack and Rhodesia was one of the few countries in the world that rarely used up its allocated immigration quota to the United States. It was a matter of a few weeks before I completed the requisite medical tests, police reports, and had the final immigration interview with the consular official. The interview ended with the petition for immigration to America being approved.

With ten months to wait before my departure for the United States, my father offered me a job as salesman in the bicycle company. I jumped at the chance to learn the family business, and indicated my enthusiasm to start work immediately. Although relieved to know that my intended departure for America would soon remove me as a threat in the business, Cousin Benny had a difficult time hiding his jealousy when he observed the pride with which his uncle introduced his son to the other employees. Benny vowed to make my stay in the business as unpleasant and difficult as he could manage.

I spent the next six weeks traveling with the other salesmen, meeting the customers, and learning the trade. I enjoyed the contact with the clients, who ranged from buyers for the large department stores to small farm shop owners living in the remotest outlying districts. After my initial training, I was given the outskirts of Salisbury as my territorial sales area, and was allocated a sturdy Peugeot van loaded up with spare bicycle parts, which allowed me to make immediate delivery of small orders. I also carried sales books to write new orders to be delivered by truck a day or two later. I enjoyed developing a good rapport with the customers, and was fortunate enough to bring in good sales.

Three months into my job with Royal Cycles, the situation in Salisbury's black townships worsened, with larger and more frequent politically motivated riots occurring. The government declared a state of emergency, with the intention of stabilizing the situation. The proclamation resulted in all the salespeople in the bicycle company, with two exceptions, receiving army call-up papers. The two exceptions were an elderly salesman, Dan, who was in his sixties and considered too old to be called up, and myself, with a temporary exemption until I completed my university studies.

With the shortage of staff, Benny seized on the opportunity to make life more difficult. He assigned the elderly salesman, Dan, to cover the sales area in Salisbury and its suburbs, while assigning the rest of the country, an area usually covered by several salesmen, to me. Sitting in his office, Cousin Benny couldn't resist snickering at what he had just accomplished. The task he had given me was impossible and required me to be on the road for lengthy periods at a time. He fully expected me to try to beg my way out of such an arduous task or ask my father's help to be assigned a smaller sales territory. Either way, Benny would have the psychological advantage of making me back down.

On learning of the assignment, my father called for a meeting with Benny, himself and me, to sort out the situation. Benny entered the office with his usual phony smile, and sat down, I also, sat down on the chair opposite him. Both of us faced over to behind the executive desk where my father was seated, he seemed to be deep in thought, while observing us. My father started the meeting. "Benny, the territory you are asking Ivan to cover is ridiculous; he is just a boy. I don't care if we service all the usual sales areas while our salesmen are on call-up. We will resume those calls when the men get back. It's just too much territory to expect one person to cover!"

Benny was silently gloating, and started to say, "Well, if it's too much…."

I calmly interrupted him. "Its okay, Dad. I can do it! I can cover the sales area; besides, it's important to maintain continuity with the customers while the regular salespeople are away on army duties." I knew what Benny was doing, and I had accepted the challenge! Looking straight at Benny, I said, "If you let me have a list of the customers, I'll leave first thing in the morning!"

I fully intended to turn the impossible task into an exploratory adventure. My goal was to maintain as many sales as possible, and at the same time, see some of this wonderful country that I had not yet seen. Leaving early the following morning, I headed east, stopping at the small farm stores before coming to Marandellas, a small town of five thousand people, forty-five miles from Salisbury. Continuing eastward, I watched the roadside scenery start to change from tall, brownish grass to more heavy, green grassland embedded with baobab trees. Those trees appeared awesome, only thirty to forty feet tall, bearing a coconut-type fruit, but some of the tree trunks were at least thirty feet in diameter.

By nightfall, I had made it to the Inyanga Mountains, a lush, green valley resort area speckled with a few hotels. On reaching the highest point, I could see beautiful green rolling hills, streams filled with rainbow trout, crystal-clear lakes, and high above each lake were resort hotels overlooking the splendor. I drove down a side road that would take me to the village where Motorcar's family lived. Sheila, Motorcar's wife greeted me with enthusiasm. She had grown plumper over the years, but was still as happy and pleasant as I had remembered her. I met Motorcar's three sons for the first time and gave them gifts of candy. Sheila and I sat around the village fire drinking Sheila's home-brewed beer, and talked for a couple of hours before I left for a good night's rest at the nearest hotel.

Early the next morning, I was on the road again, still heading east toward the city of Umtali, which was nestled in a valley only twenty miles from the Mozambique border, the Portuguese East African country. Umtali always reminded me of a movie I had seen about Brigadoon, the mythical Scottish village set in a valley that only appeared to mortals through the mist once every one hundred years. Similarly, after a lengthy, steep road climb, the city would suddenly come into view hundreds of feet below, as low clouds trapped in the valley appeared to float over the city below the roadway. This image, I felt, gave the town a mystic aura.

I spent two days in Umtali seeing customers and taking orders from merchants in this hamlet with a population of twenty thousand. My business completed, I set off again in a southerly direction on a journey of another two hundred miles that would take me to Fort Victoria, toward the South African border. The roadway now consisted of strip and dirt roads. Sixty miles from Umtali, I came to Hot Springs, a health spa in the middle of nowhere that consisted of a roadside store and a resort where the patrons were put up in one of several rondavels, a type of circular bungalow with an African tribal-style, thatched roof. In the middle of the resort was a well from which the boiling mineral waters bubbled up to the surface. These waters were drained from the well by a pipe to a large concrete swimming pool. The steam from the hot water sent off fumes that permeated the air with a powerful smell of sulphur that was almost overwhelming. Finishing my sales with the store owner, I was invited to a break and a swim in the pool. Despite the smell, the waters felt exhilarating, and I enjoyed the pool for a couple of hours.

Realizing that I had spent more time in Hot Springs than intended, I quickly dressed and continued my travels. I still had many miles to cover that day, but thirty miles down the road I encountered a herd of elephants sauntering across the strip road. I stopped the van two hundred yards away to give them a wide berth. A huge bull elephant with gigantic tusks was in the lead, followed by four cow elephants guarding two baby elephants. I knew that this type of animal was intelligent and usually quite peaceful unless provoked or felt threatened, in which case it could turn into the most powerful killer in Africa. I watched as the elephants crossed to one side of the road with the exception of one cow, who remained on the other side grazing in the grass. It was common knowledge that one never drove between a bull and his cow since this was instinctively taken as a threat to separate the two, and the bull would invariably charge the interloper.

I waited, but twenty minutes later there was no movement by the cow elephant to cross the road. Dusk was approaching, and I still had many miles to travel, so I edged the car forward, and the cow turned and moved toward the road. I stopped, and the cow stopped; I moved the van forward, and the cow moved closer to the road; I stopped, and the cow stopped. The movements had now gained the attention of the bull elephant who stood staring at the van. I waited another twenty minutes—still no movement from the cow! Uneasy and unsure, I edged the car forward, the cow edged closer to the road, and the bull flapped his ears as a warning. I stopped the car; and was becoming impatient with the cow's teasing.

After a few more minutes, I decided to chance it, putting my foot down on the fuel pedal and speeding through the gap between the elephants. The bull trumpeted, raised his trunk, and brought it hammering down, barely missing the van as I drove past. Looking back, I could see the huge bull charging after me, and in front I saw to my horror that the road did a dog-leg curve to the right, and the elephant was now taking a shortcut, thundering through the tall grass to cut me off. In my panic, I thought of a muddled version of a Pythagorean theorem on triangles: I was traveling from point A to point B to get to point C, but the God-damned elephant was charging from point A directly to point C to ram the van.

I pressed my foot harder to the floor, accelerating the vehicle to the maximum, spewing dirt into the air. The bull loomed menacingly closer, lowered his head with tusks extended and went into the ramming posture. I braced myself for the possible impact as the elephant drew closer and lunged itself at the vehicle. Miraculously, he missed hitting the van, although only by a few feet. Then the elephant regrouped, turned, and started to charge again, but I was now on a straight stretch of road, and putting more and more distance between the vehicle and my adversary. The animal kept charging, and maintained the chase for what seemed a lifetime, but as he fell farther and farther behind the van, he finally stopped. Shaking his head in anger, his trunk waving from side to side, the elephant bellowed trumpeted insults at my fast-disappearing vehicle.

I didn't even think of slowing down for the next twenty miles. My heart was pounding and my head ached from the stress, but I kept driving until late into the night, eventually reaching a small roadside hotel on the outskirts of Fort Victoria. After checking into the hotel, I lay across the bed and fell instantly into an exhausted asleep. The following morning I was up early and felt much rested from the nightmarish experience of the previous day. It was Friday, I had only a day-and-a half to complete sales in this area, since all stores closed at noon on Saturday for the weekend.

Fort Victoria wasn't quite big enough to make city status, but it was a small, friendly municipality of fifteen thousand people with a few business streets that serviced the large farming community surrounding the town. The social entertainment consisted of the local cinema and a very active repertory group and theater that regularly performed plays, but for the tourist there was one of mankind's few unresolved archaeological mysteries, the Zimbabwe Ruins, just twenty miles from the town. After finishing my last call at noon Saturday, I took a drive to the famed ruins.

The Zimbabwe Ruins were known to be at least three thousand years old. One of the theories of its origin, because of the unique fortress-city structure and Chevron designs (something not seen in any other archaeological find known to man) was that it was built by space aliens. The other, and perhaps more acceptable explanation, was that it was built by Arab traders, but that did not explain why they would build a city so far inland, hundreds of miles from the sea, and so far from any other known civilization of that time.

Arriving at the site, I saw a structure that took up several hundred yards in area. The wall surrounding the city was fifty feet high, constructed of large granite blocks, and etched around the entire top was a zig-zag Chevron design. The inner city was built in the form of a maze, also with granite blocks, with several seventy-foot-high domed buildings, but with no perceivable entrances. Along the maze were enclaves for statues, and though the statues were different sizes, they were all of the same object—the Zimbabwe bird, which was carved out of soapstone, a soft type of marble stone. This bird of unknown origins had become the adopted symbol of Rhodesia.

It was early evening by the time I finished exploring the mysterious ruins, and began the drive back to Fort Victoria. Taking advantage of the fact that I was now eighteen and able to drink, I stopped by the repertory theater for a beer before planning the next portion of the sales trip. I would head for Bulawayo, three hundred miles due north, and make several stops along the way at farm stores. Since the trip would probably take about three days, I would leave the next afternoon, which would be Sunday.

Leaving a farm store at dusk two days later, I passed a pan—a natural watering hole of the wild—a few hundred feet from the road. I stopped the van to take in the sight; this was truly Africa at its best. There was a spectacular orange sunset, and the water hole was attracting animals of all sizes, shapes, and colors to quench their thirst. At the farthest end of the pan a small herd of elephants was playing, rolling in the mud and spraying water through their trunks, and nearby zebra, long-horned gazelle, and a few warthogs. Monkeys scampered down from the trees to create some mischief before being chased back up the trees by the other animals, and at the other end of the pan, three tall giraffes were spreading their front legs to allow their long necks to bend down to reach for a drink of the water. I closed my eyes for a moment, and I heard the sounds of Africa: birds singing and chirping in the tall grasses and trees around the pan, an occasional roar of a lion in the distance, the resonating pitch of the laugh of a hyena, joined by the different chords of perhaps dozens of other not-visible mammals of the wild blending together into a perfect symphonic harmony of nature. Watching the panorama unfold in front, I reluctantly started up the van's engine, and wondered how different the sights and sounds of the American vista would be.

Chapter Six

A day-and-a-half later, I arrived at the Matopos, a hilly, rocky region just outside of Bulawayo. Here at Worlds View, Cecil John Rhodes was buried. A diamond magnate; founder of the De Beers Diamond Organization; Prime Minister of the Cape Colony in South Africa; and benefactor of the most prestigious education grant in the world, the Rhodes scholarship. He was the man who dreamed of expanding the British Empire, building a railroad system across Africa from Cape Town to Cairo, and settling the country that now bore his name. Standing by the grave, I wondered how it was possible for a young man suffering from ill health, who arrived in Africa at the age of twenty-one, could achieve so much by the time of his death at the age of forty-nine. In twenty-eight years he had accomplished most of his goals, and had become one of the world's richest men. Looking at the panorama from the site of the grave, I could understand why Rhodes had chosen this exquisite place as his final resting place. The view was exhilarating, the hills were not quite high enough to be mountains, but from this, the highest point, I could see miles of undulating, lush green valleys and rocky hills capped with natural-balancing rocks.

Legend had it that king Lobengula, chief of the Ndbele people who resided in this area, was also buried somewhere in the Matopos. It is believed that many of his tribespeople had worked in the diamond and gold mines in Kimberley and Johannesburg, and brought back many illicit diamonds and gold, which were handed over as tribute to Lobengula. The king had lived in approximately the same time period as Rhodes, but when he died, he and all his treasures were secretly carried by his generals to one of the myriad of caves that were hidden in the Matopos hills. There, Lobengula was buried, sitting in a regal position on chests filled with diamonds and gold, an assagai in one hand and a shield in the other. Treasures that would have rivaled King Solomon's mines were then sealed by the generals with a large rock, but the site has never been disclosed to the outside world.

During his lifetime, Lobengula was notorious for his strong and ruthless reign, sentencing hundreds of thousands of his followers to death. It was because of Lobengula's merciless rule that the nearby city was given its name, Bulawayo, literally translated from Ndbele as The Place of Slaughter. Bulawayo, Rhodesia's second largest city, with a population of a quarter-of-a-million people, was to be my next stop.

Arriving in the city I saw the widest streets on earth, which originally were built for ox wagons to travel on, and made wide enough for the wagons to easily do a U-turn. With the advent of motor vehicles, the roads were simply paved over with macadamized tar, and became eight lane highways—four lanes in each direction—and still leaving enough room for two rows of cars to park in the center aisle of the road, splitting the thoroughfare in half. Bulawayo was the industrial center of the country, headquarters of the Rhodesia Railways, and hub of the distribution of goods both inside and outside the country. I made my way to the Selborne Hotel, a colonial-style building opposite the large modern City Hall building, and after a fast shower, set off on calls to stores in the city.

The city was definitely growing, with a fair amount of construction in progress, and a large number of new buildings, a few with fourteen-and-fifteen stories. A certain amount of business rivalry existed between this city and Salisbury, and during one of my stops at a store, the owner jocularly referred to me as the boy from "Bamba Zonke," which translates to grab everything. It was a reference to the fact that Salisbury had earned a reputation for taking the plum situations in the country—capital of Rhodesia, capital of the previous Federation, and now the financial center, plus anything else Salisbury could lay its hands on. This caused much resentment among other localities in the nation, particularly Bulawayo, which believed there should be more sharing with the rest of the country.

Three days later when I finished my calls, I had several sales books filled with orders which I packaged and mailed to Salisbury before setting off on the next leg of my journey; the Victoria Falls, three hundred miles to the west.

Passing through some of the wildest and least developed parts of the country, the road alternated from natural dirt to two parallel, three-foot-wide tar strip roads to the luxury of a nine-foot-wide, fully tarred road. In some areas, just staying on the road became an adventure. The farm stores became fewer and farther apart as I approached one of the world's largest game reserves, the Wankie Game Park, a hundred and fifty miles out from Bulawayo.

The game park was unfenced, and the animals could wander in and out of the sanctuary at their leisure. It was an area abounding with virtually every species of African animals, who during their travel to and from the park needed to walk across the road at random points. Aware of the danger of collision with animals, and remembering my recent experience with the bull elephant, I slowed the vehicle to a crawl, and looked ahead to see a pride of lions emerging from the bushes and crossing the road ahead. I came to a full stop, and the royalty of the jungle proceeded with their crossing, barely acknowledging the van's presence. Farther down the road a large group of monkeys came into sight, some scampering across the route, while others were jumping from trees on one side of the road to trees on the other side. Again I stopped, but this time my presence received their full attention. Apparently in a mischievous mood, they clambered over the van, bouncing off the roof of the vehicle, pressing their faces against the windshield, and making faces.

With dusk closing in, I made my way to the Bumi Hills Safari Lodge for a meal and to rest for the night. Erected on the outskirts of the game park, the lodge was a large two-story structure built on the slope of a hill, from what appeared to be granite bricks. Most of the building was enclosed with large windows, and from the convenience of the dinning room gave a clear view of the outside scenery. The dinning room led to a large outside patio, built on stilts—a safe height from animals wandering about below. In front of the patio was a cleared open space resembling a well-maintained fairway on a golf course which led up to a natural water pan at the edge of the clearing. This was surrounded by heavy bushes and trees from which animals of the wild would emerge to drink from the water. At night the entire clearing and pan were illuminated by huge floodlights, giving a spectacular view of any creature that wandered into the limelight.

Night had fallen, and the lodge was full of European and American tourists mingling in the dinning room and on the patio. Suddenly there were "Oh's" and "Ah's," as four elephants wandered into the clearing to drink from the pan. I walked out onto the patio to join the tourists and catch the sight, but as impressive as it looked, found the setting a little too commercial to be enthused. I knew that just a few miles away, Wankie Game Park offered more spectacular sights in a natural environment, without the benefit of the lodge's contrivances. After a few minutes, I left to retire for the night.

Bright and early the next morning, I was up and ready to continue the odyssey. A few miles down the road, which at this point was gravel, I slowed to a stop. A huge lone elephant stood straddled across the road barring passage, his trunk was up in the trees pulling down leaves and shoving them into his mouth like an enormous feeding machine. The elephant stopped feeding for a moment, and faced my vehicle, flapping his ears. Thinking I was too close to the animal, I backed up the van a short distance, before realizing by doing so, I had shown weakness to the elephant by backing off. The bull did a mock charge, but I stood my ground. A second mock charge followed, and again I stood my ground, and the elephant, realizing he was not going to scare the intruder away, took off into the bushes. Beads of perspiration flowed down my forehead, and I continued along my journey, thinking that I would be perfectly happy if the only elephants I would see from now on were the small, tame ones in a circus.

Later that afternoon, I passed a road sign indicating that the village of Victoria Falls was now ten miles ahead. Continuing along the road, I could, in the distance, hear the sound of constant thunder, and the noise became louder as I approached its point of origin. In the distance, I could see huge clouds of mist rising from the ground upwards towards the sky, and realized I was nearing one of the seven natural wonders on Earth, "Mosi-A-Tunae." Translated, it means the waters that thunder, the name given to the falls by the local tribespeople before its discovery by the missionary and explorer from Scotland, David Livingstone. Livingstone had re-named the falls in honor of the reigning Queen Victoria of Britain.

Before going to the Falls, I took a small detour to see a very large baobab tree, whose diameter must have been thirty-five feet. In front of the tree was a carved rock bearing a metal plaque with the inscription that beneath this tree was buried the heart of David Livingstone. His body had been sent back to England for interment in Westminster Abbey, alongside former kings, queens, and other men and women who had achieved greatness in the British Empire. I momentarily pictured the historic meeting that took place here between the American newspaper reporter, Henry Morton Stanley, who had long been searching the dark continent for David Livingstone. Finally finding him, he greeted him with the now famous words, "Dr. Livingstone, I presume?"

I returned to the van, and drove to the Victoria Falls Village, which was situated a half mile from the thundering waterfall.

At the Village, I checked in at the Victoria Falls Hotel, an old and very large two-story, Colonial-style structure built at the turn of the century by the Rhodesian Railways for tourists. I was excited at the prospect of seeing the wonder of the falls, and after freshening up, made my way downstairs to the front of the building, which I saw contained a verandah, tables, and seats, with a patio bar at one end. In front of the verandah on a grassy area, a tribal Marimba band was beating out African music. I stopped and listened to the music for a few minutes before walking through the village streets which consisted of rows of old shops, some of which I would be visiting the next day to sell bicycles and spare parts. Hundreds of tribespeople were selling their hand-made artifacts, which ranged from wooden masks and carved soapstone statues to pure, knitted linens. Their selling technique was aggressive, and they approached anyone who resembled a tourist, and began to bargain. I walked the half mile to the falls, and as I got closer, the roaring sound of water became almost deafening. Suddenly, the thick growth of trees and grass along the road cleared, and in front of me stood the majestic Victoria Falls—an awesome sight one mile long, with two billion gallons of water from the enormous Zambesi River cascading over it every minute to the gorge four hundred feet below. To preserve the natural beauty, nothing man-made had been erected in the entire area—no fences, no observation platforms, and no protective barriers, which also made the region very dangerous.

I had read of tourists, who on occasion had ventured too close to the falls, slipping and falling to their deaths. I approached the brink of the falls very cautiously; it was an incredible view! Although one long continuous waterfall, different sections of the falls had been given descriptive names. The closest portion was the Devils Cataract, where water wended its way around the side of the river bank before doing a sharp turn and roaring downwards. I could see fish thrashing about in the waters, whose flow was too strong for them to fight, before they were pulled over the thundering breach to the gorge below. Amazingly, they all seemed to survive the fall, because I could not see any fish floating on the water below.

The next section was the Main Falls, where the largest bulk of the river flowed over the Falls, creating massive clouds of vapor before flowing down the ravine. The last portion was the Rainbow Falls, where the light from the sun struck the rising mist, creating a perpetual rainbow at the end of the falls.

A couple hundred yards up river, behind the waterfalls, was a small fifty-foot island, and three large crocodiles had climbed onto the small piece of land, and were basking in the sun. On one side of the embankment, a herd of zebra were drinking at the water's edge. The falls had been created by a large fracture of the earth millions of years ago, and I walked the full length of the cataract facing the falls, passing through the Rain Forest, a section of heavy, dense growth that was always saturated from the spray of the rapids. I eventually reached the point where the gorge became a river again, and on the other side was Zambia.

A large bridge connected the two countries, once the centers of busy traffic carrying commerce between the previously united territories. It now stood empty of travelers, and armed Zambian soldiers stood guard behind sandbags, their officers watching every movement on the Rhodesian side through binoculars. On the other side, the Rhodesians were less confrontational, with only two border guards and a solitary customs officer standing at the entrance to the bridge. The friends had become enemies, and I thought once again of "Gulliver's Travels" and the two kings' needless argument.

When I returned to the village after dark, the marimba band was still playing in front of the hotel, and the verandah had filled with a mixture of tourists and locals for the cocktail hour. I sat down, ordered a beer, enjoyed the music and estimated that I had a hundred and fifty miles left to travel to Kariba, the last leg of the sales trip. By that time, I would have covered two thirds of the country before heading back to

Salisbury, and the remaining third, the northern districts, was closer to Salisbury, and I would do that on a separate trip.

Driving to Kariba, I traveled through the new, developing area of the country, and I knew there would be an even larger number of wild animals crossing the slippery gravel roadways than I had yet encountered. It wasn't long before I saw a herd of hundreds of antelope come bounding out of the tall grass, cross my path, and disappear into the tall grass on the other side. Farther down, a twenty-foot-long Python snake, its stomach bulging from a recent kill, was laboriously slithering across a portion of the road. The next stop was for a family of eight cheetah, silently ambling along the side of the road.

On many occasions I passed vultures sitting on the tree tops by the roadside. Born scavengers, they continuously stretched their long necks, scouring the vicinity for remnants of a kill to peck on. I could not help cringing at the sight of the ugly birds. Finally arriving at the township in Kariba, which was situated on the Zambian border, I saw there was considerable construction taking place in this new community. A few years earlier, an Italian company had completed building the world's largest hydro-electric plant on the river which separated the two countries. It became the world's largest dam, successfully harnessing the mighty waters of the huge Zambesi River, but the damming of the river caused extensive flooding of the valleys in front of the Kariba dam, and in turn created the world's largest man-made lake.

The idea for the dam was born during the years of the Federation, with the intention of providing electricity for a large portion of Central Africa. With the Federation now gone, the dam was owned jointly by Zambia and Rhodesia, and there was a heavy white line in the center of the large dam indicating the split of ownership. The multi-lane highway built at the top of the dam in anticipation of the heavy traffic expected to move between the two countries stood empty. Like the scene at Victoria Falls, on the Zambian side there was heavy sandbagging, armed soldiers, and constant monitoring through binoculars. Again, the

Rhodesians were more casual, with a few guards and policemen at the border post.

Shops had been opening at a rapid pace around the area to accommodate the growing population of the township, and a fair amount of my time was spent opening new accounts. Mr. Germanis, one of the store owners, told me of a power boat that he had recently purchased, and when I expressed interest in fishing, Mr. Germanis invited me to join him on an evening fishing cruise he had planned for that night. I eagerly accepted the offer. We would be angling for tiger fish, a sharply-toothed fish, which ranged in weight from between two to ten pounds, and, although small, the fish always put up a tremendous fight, and made good sport fishing.

We had to navigate around a large blanket of Kariba weed that was growing like wildfire, and spreading over the surface of the lake. The weed's origin was unknown, but the flooding of the valleys had altered the environment, and this lily-like growth with intermingling vines was spreading at the rate of up to a hundred feet a day. The plant had become an uncontrollable menace, creating havoc with boats on the lake, and clogging the intakes of water turning the hydro-electric generators at the dam.

Mr. Germanis maneuvered the boat toward an island near the center of the lake and stopped. Less than a hundred feet away, diving in and out from under the surface of the lake, and spouting water through their nostrils were twenty to thirty hippopotamuses. Germanis handed me a fishing rod and tackle, and casually remarked, "By the way, keep an eye on that white center line on the dam, because if we stray too close to the Zambian side, they are likely to take pot shots at us!" Beginning to feel nervous over the risks involved in this fishing trip, I also, began to ponder the possibilities that the hippos playing nearby could get territorial, come under their boat, flip it over, and crush us—or once the boat's engine was started again, the propellers could easily get snagged on the weeds, leaving us to drift inadvertently toward the Zambian shore. I silently prayed that we could simply fish without something going terribly wrong.

It was almost dark before I caught my first bite, and from the fight the fish was putting up, it would be a nice size. As I struggled to reel it in, I saw out of the corner of my eye the outline of two hippos grappling nearby, possibly involved in a mating ritual. The animals, intent on their activity, were moving dangerously close, and suddenly there was a loud crashing sound to the side of the boat. The force of the impact caused the craft to rock violently, and I grabbed for the side rails to prevent being thrown overboard. As the boat finally stabilized itself, Germanis shouted, "Damn Hippos weren't looking where they were going, and crashed into us! Are you all right?"

Acknowledging Germanis's question with a frightened "Yes!" I noticed that the tiger tooth was still on my line, and attempted to focus my apprehension and energy to reeling in the furiously fighting fish. It was after midnight when the boat with our catch of seven fish edged its way back to the Kariba shoreline. I stepped safely on to solid land once again, and looking up at the clear sky, whispered a grateful, "Thank you!"

Returning to my hotel room, I switched on the radio, and the Rhodesian Broadcasting Corporation had, as usual, shut down at midnight, so I tuned in to the world service of the BBC. It was reporting that the Rhodesian Government had proclaimed a step-down of the army conscription, which meant that the salespeople would soon be returning to their jobs. I let out a sigh of relief to know that once I got back to Salisbury, I could return to my smaller regular sales territory.

I was awake at sunrise, elated with the feeling that after being away for a few weeks I would soon start the journey home. I planned a route across the country which would shorten the distance to less than two hundred miles, and set off on my homeward journey.

Arriving back in Salisbury, I was greeted with a hug and kiss from my mother and a friendly, warm handshake from my father. I started to speak with excitement about my harrowing experiences on the trip, but my mother interrupted to tell me the news that the Cambridge examination results had arrived, and I had passed with good marks. I was overjoyed, this finally meant that my trip to America would become a reality.

Allowing me to enjoy the good news, my mother waited a few hours before conveying the other news; that Amos had been accepted by the police force, and would begin his training in a couple of weeks. As good as the news was about Amos, I couldn't help feeling a sadness that my friend would be leaving. I went out to the garden, and Motorcar was first to greet me with his big smile and to inquire about the trip. I told him about the visit I had made to Sheila and about meeting his three sons. I warmly congratulated Amos on his acceptance into the police force; Amos, too, was saddened by his impending departure. "I will miss not working here. Thank you, Ivan, for helping me. We will always be friends!" He said simply.

I smiled and replied, "Amos, I will miss you also. No matter what the future holds for us, I hope that we will always be friends, and stay in touch."

I returned to work at Royal Cycles the following day, and Cousin Benny acknowledged neither my return to the business nor the high sales that I had achieved during the sales trip. My father, on the other hand, openly showed his pride, slapping me on the back in front the other employees, while commenting, "Job well done, Ivan!" The praise appeared to make Benny more resentful, and he skulked away to his office.

During the next few months, I spent much of my spare time reading as much literature about America and Europe that I could get my hands on. I planned to fly to London for a week to visit my brother and sister, and I had also arranged with Chantelle to fly to Brussels to spend a week with her, sightseeing together. From Brussels I would fly back to London for the flight to New York, and finally to Los Angeles—to my new life!

Chapter Seven

As the much anticipated day of departure drew closer, I had kept busy with work and preparations for the trip. I had tactfully resisted invitations from my sister Babette, and brother Leon, both now married, to stay with them in London. It had been a number of years since I had seen my brother and sister, and I felt it would be more "comfortable" to stay at the Overseas Visitors Club, an inexpensive lodging place in London, intended primarily for young tourists like myself who were visiting from Commonwealth countries. Staying at the club, I would also have the independence to come and go as I pleased.

Amos had started his police training course, and would often visit my home during his occasional day off from classes. Amos looked very smart in his pressed uniform, causing Motorcar to tease him, saying that Amos was not going to have any time to fulfill his future police duties, since he would be too busy fighting off all the women who would be chasing him because of his outfit.

Television had recently been introduced into the country, but the viewing hours were very limited. The black and white screens came to life at six in the evenings, and went off the air at ten. Social life was changing; instead of family conversations at night, everyone was now seated silently in front of the screen, making the most of the viewing time. On his occasional visits, Amos would stay to watch the evening programs, but Motorcar was at first horrified by the magic that kept people imprisoned inside the TV cabinet. He also believed that the actors on the screen could see him, and he would try to engage well known personalities such as Jack Benny in conversation. It was one of the rare times that Motorcar became annoyed with me, because I would double over with laughter at the attempted conversations.

I tried to make up for my disrespect in laughing, by explaining the essentials of how a TV set was like a radio receiver with a picture. This eventually seemed to placate Motorcar, and he would often come to watch the evening programs with the family, preferring to sit on the carpet with me. The American western, "Bonanza," and the British spy series, "The Saint," soon became our favorite shows.

Politically, there was no progress. The detention of the Shona and Ndbele politicians, Sithole and Nkomo, aggravated the internal situation. The Rhodesian government was unsuccessful in negotiating with the British government, and the talks with the black political leaders were fruitless. The main point of dispute appeared to be that the government wanted a gradual evolution to majority rule, while the black politicians wanted it immediately! A collision course between the two ideals appeared to be inevitable, and the political uncertainty that resulted was causing international investments and development of the country to come to a standstill.

Since the departure of the long-time Prime Minister, Godfrey Huggins, three others, Garfield Todd, Sir Edgar Whitehead, and presently Winston Field, had taken the premiership, but none was able to find a satisfactory solution to the country's problems. Each lasted a relatively short period of their intended terms. I watched and followed with interest the careers of two politicians, Ian Smith and Clifford Dupont, who were regarded as the rising stars in the political arena.

Ian Smith was a Rhodesian-born farmer, who had served with honor in the British Royal Air Force against the Germans in World War Two. He had been shot down in a dog fight with a German fighter, receiving injuries which ended his days as a fighter pilot. Dupont was a business entrepreneur, rumored to be a member of the wealthy French and American business families, and his financial power had gained him considerable influence.

The night before I was to fly to London, the family sat down for a dinner together. My mother gave me a long embarrassing hug, and my father went into a protective mode, giving me advice on situations that would require caution during my travels. Friends called to wish me a good journey, and Amos came by to say good-bye. Motorcar had made a bracelet for me which was woven from elephant hair collected during his travels. Presenting it, Motorcar blessed me with the traditional Zulu and Ndbele farewell, "Hamba Gashi—go in peace!"

The next morning, carrying two heavy suitcases, I made my way through the airport customs to the departure lounge. Outside on the airstrip I could see the Caledonian Airways DC 6 propeller aircraft that had been chartered by the Overseas Visitor's Club to fly our group of passengers to London. Once aboard the aircraft, I was pleasantly surprised to find that I had been seated next to a very attractive girl of about twenty-one, who was making her first trip overseas. Nadine Caldwell had long, light brown hair that fell to below her shoulders; bright, sparkling brown eyes; a peaches and cream complexion; and an air of total naiveté.

As Salisbury disappeared into the distance behind us, Nadine and I talked to pass the time, and she mentioned that this was actually her first trip anywhere. As I mentioned the places I was looking forward to seeing—Trafalgar Square, Piccadilly Circus, Buckingham Palace, Big Ben, Westminster Abbey, and the Tower of London—I realized the girl had no idea of what I was talking about. She had never heard of those landmarks! Puzzled, I asked her what places she intended to visit.

"I really don't know. I know nothing of the places in England." Even more puzzled now, I asked why she was going to London?

"Well, all my friends had saved up and gone on holidays there, so I thought I would do the same." I was amazed that she was making a major trip like this, with no idea of what she was going to do upon arrival.

Twelve hours later as the plane started its descent towards Kano in Nigeria for a refueling stop, the pilot announced, "Ladies and gentlemen, we will be landing shortly in Kano for a two-hour refueling stop, but we have just been informed that there has been an attempted coup d'état in Lagos, with some fighting in the streets of Kano and near the airport where we will be landing. Because of the refueling hazard and intense heat on the ground, passengers will be required to disembark until the refueling is completed. Please make your way to the departure lounge, and stay there! Do not, under any circumstances, cross over the barrier that has been placed in the lounge leading to the duty-free shops! Anyone doing so, in breach of the security situation they are facing at the moment, will be arrested and detained! Thank you."

As the plane descended, I saw that the houses below were made up of a large assortment of mud-constructed dwellings, which from the air looked like mud igloos. Intermittent puffs of smoke could be seen rising around the perimeter of the airport, and I wondered if that was as a result of gunfire. Nadine, myself and the other passengers nervously made our way to the departure lounge as instructed. As other aircraft landed, those passengers, were also crowded into the lounge, soon filling it to maximum capacity. The combination of a large number of bodies and the equatorial noon day heat was making the temperature unbearable.

Returning after one of the many trips I made to the cafeteria to buy sodas to quench our thirst, I could not find Nadine. Searching for her, I saw that she had wandered to the other side of the security barrier, and was looking into the windows of the closed duty-free shops. Two soldiers approached her and angrily began to yell at Nadine. Taking a firm hold of her by the arm the soldiers began to lead her away, I hurtled over the barrier. Approaching Nadine, I slowed to a walk, put on a casual smile for the soldiers, and said, "Nadine, that's not the way to the ladies room—I knew you would get lost!" I took her arm from the soldier, and walked back toward the barrier.

Momentarily taken off guard, the soldiers stood motionless. Then one of them raised his rifle, and shouted, "Stop!"

I countered with a yell. "Run Nadine!" We dived back over the barrier into the crowded lounge. The soldiers had obviously taken the trespass seriously, and followed into the lounge searching for us. Mixing with the other passengers, I asked one of the women if I could borrow the beret she was wearing. I quickly slipped the beret over Nadine's head, bunching her flowing hair under the hat, and pulled her to the carpeted floor with the other passengers who had been unable to find seats. Noticing that Nadine had barely any make-up on, I asked if she had brought any with her. She nodded, pointing to her handbag.

"Put it on—heavily!" I told her. Taking an eye liner pencil from her, I proceeded to paint a mustache on my face, blackened one of my front teeth to look like it was missing, ruffled my hair and put on sunglasses. The soldiers, still searching for us, approached within a few feet and stopped, their eyes scouring around the room. I held my breath. After a few seconds they moved on to continue their search in another part of the lounge.

The speakers in the lounge announced that our plane had completed refueling and requested passengers to embark on the aircraft. Walking in the middle of a group of people heading back to the plane, Nadine clutched my arm tightly until we were safely on board. I gratefully returned the borrowed beret to its owner, and sank into my seat with relief, shaking my head over Nadine's stupidity.

Nine hours later the aircraft passed over the English Channel and started a gradual descent towards Gatwick, the newly built airport just outside London. I was filled with excitement; finally, I would be arriving in a world I had only read of and dared to imagine—civilization, architecture, history, entertainment and a sophisticated society. My brother Leon had written to me, arranging to meet at the terminal in downtown London. Once the plane landed and I had passed through immigration, I made my way to one of the many double-decked buses outside the airport that would take us the forty miles to London. Nadine, it turned out, was also staying at the O.V.C. Club, so climbing aboard to the top level of the bus we traveled to the city together. As the bus wended its way into the city, I was fascinated by the spectacle of row houses after row houses that lined the streets into London.

Parting with Nadine at the terminal, I began to search for Leon through the mass of people arriving and departing the concourse. "I say old fellow, is that you, Ivan?" came a voice from my side. Turning, I saw a man wearing a bowler hat, a black pin-striped suit with a red polka dot tie, carrying an umbrella, and looking very British! This…is my brother? I wondered, staring at the man for a moment. "Jolly glad you could come for a visit, old chap!" Leon continued, taking my hand and shaking it.

"Glad to be here and to see you again!" I responded. And began to feel like a hick, as I was dressed casually in a white sports shirt and black slacks. Making our way out of the terminal and onto the street, Leon hailed a cab. It was still early morning, and the pavements were filled with pedestrians.

"Harley Street, Driver!" Leon told the cabby. I knew that my brother had moved to Harley Street, the inner circle of Britain's top physicians. As I listened to my brother speak, I began to wonder if part of the cost of being admitted to that elite medical circle was to learn to talk as though you had marbles in your mouth. We drove to the Harley Street residence, where I was introduced to Leon's wife, Ellen, a petite, attractive, and pleasant woman. By coincidence, she was also from Africa, had been born in Zaire of French parents, and was a trained nurse. They met while working at the same hospital, and after a lengthy courtship, they married.

Ellen fussed over me, and made me feel welcome. I started to feel less like a hick over my simple clothing. Leon announced, "Babbette sends her apologies. She had to go to rehearsal for a show she is doing tonight at Covent Gardens—Swan Lake. We will see her this evening, as she has sent tickets for us all to go to the performance." Continuing, Leon explained that he had appointments at the clinic to attend to, and suggested I check into the O.V.C. Club and that we should meet again that evening at seven to go to the theater. I was happy with the arrangement since it gave me a few hours to start the sightseeing I was so eager to do.

The O.V.C. Club was situated in Earls Court, and I traveled on the London underground rail system, the Tube, to get there. The Club was made up of several five-storied buildings, each named after a Commonwealth Country, I was given lodgings In "Australia House." The building was historic, so were the facilities. My room had barely enough space for the bed and a sink, I struggled to find a place to put my suitcases away. The room also contained meters for gas heating and electricity, which if not continuously fed shillings, at what I thought was an alarming rate, would cut off the facilities at the most inappropriate times. Down the hallway were the communal toilets and Bathrooms, which serviced all the rooms on that floor. I made up my mind to ignore the discomfort, as I had the independence to come and go as I pleased.

Catching the tube, I traveled to the center of London, I got off at Piccadilly circus, a roundabout with the statue of Eros in the center and surrounded by very large neon advertising boards, that even in daylight made a spectacular sight. Behind some of the facade of neon signs, were bombed out buildings, a reminder of the German V-2 missiles that had been unleashed on the city during the Second world War. It was now 1962, and the war had been over for seventeen years, I was surprised that nothing yet had been done to rebuild on these scarred, bombed out sites.

I walked the City continuing with my sightseeing, enjoying seeing for the first time, Trafalgar Square, Big Ben, The Houses of Parliament and Buckingham Palace, before returning to meet with Leon and Ellen to go to the theater. Babbette had a lead role in "Swan Lake" and was very good. We all went backstage after the show. Babbette came over to me and hugging me she said "Ivan Dah-ling!" It appeared that she too had acquired the taste of talking with marbles in her mouth! I was introduced to her husband, Gregg a tall thin man who also danced with the ballet company. We all went out for dinner in Soho at a posh French restaurant, where I attempted to talk as though I had marbles in my mouth, it was a poor attempt and just did not work with me.

Over the week that followed, I spent the days being simply a tourist, visiting the famous landmarks of London and taking day trips to the English Countryside. The nights were nearly always spent with my brother and sister, who spent a lot of their time hobnobbing with the elite of London society.

After a couple of days I saw Nadine in the lobby of the Club, I asked her how she was enjoying her vacation. "Wonderful!" She replied, and then proceeded to tell me how she had met a man the day before, who had told her that he was going to make a movie star out of her. "Nadine, I hope this man didn't pick you up from one of the tourist sites you were visiting?" I asked. "Why. Yes!" She responded, apparently amazed at my clairvoyance. "Nadine, you need to be very careful, you dress and look like a tourist, some men will take advantage of tourists, perhaps this one wants to try to get into your pants!" I gently told her. "Oh, He doesn't want to get into my pants, he just wants me to pose nude for photographs he is going to send to his director." She said, with total conviction. Looking at the doorway to the lobby, she said "I have to go now, Tom is waiting for me!" As she walked away, I called out "Be careful, Nadine!" She waved back at me with a smile, as she left through the lobby doors.

The next evening, I returned from my sightseeing to see Nadine on the pavement loading her suitcases with the help of a tall podgy man, who must have been twice her age, into a battered, little yellow Morris Minor car. On seeing me, she ran over, gave me a kiss on the cheek, and said "Goodbye Ivan, I am moving in with Tom, he is going to help me get into the movies." With that she got into the car, which spluttered into life with a couple of exhaust backfires, and took off into the evening sunset. I never saw her again!

At the end of the week in England, I had traveled and done as much sightseeing as time had allowed. London and surrounding areas had lived up to what I had hoped to see and experience.

Though, one fact was striking, although England had the history, population and wealth that Rhodesia did not have, here the wealth was in the hands of a very small percentage of the population. There was a very large amount of poverty apparent wherever I went, living conditions were dismal and people seemed to have a hard time trying to make ends meet—even though their income was higher than the Rhodesians. By contrast the quality of life in Rhodesia was vastly superior. Even the poorest of the blacks had the tribal trust land reserved for them, where they could return to their tribal villages and their tract of land. I came to the conclusion that "Wealth" and "Poverty" were subjective, to be defined by the circumstances in which one lived, combined with the quality of life one was able to enjoy. In that sense the "Wealth" of life in Rhodesia outclassed England.

Saying farewell to my brother and sister, with repeated thanks for their hospitality, I left on the bus to the airport to catch my flight to Brussels. This was a part of the journey I was looking forward to—seeing Chantelle again.

The flight was a relatively short one, arriving in Belgium a couple of hours after departing London. As the aircraft taxied on the landing strip towards the terminal building it was early evening, I felt my pulse rate go up, I was starting to feel nervous. Once the plane had docked, I walked into the arrival lounge, and then I saw her!

Chantelle was smiling, her green blue eyes sparkled, her blond hair still shoulder length was neatly coiffured around the sides of her neck. Her elegant woolen dress which stopped at her knees could not hide her curvaceous body and legs.—She had matured into a beautiful woman.

I, awed by her beauty, became even more nervous. Chantelle waved at me, calling out "Ivan!" Then she rushed into my arms, we embraced and tenderly kissed. I felt as though my legs were going to buckle. Collecting my luggage, we talked as we walked out of the airport, Chantelle was so relaxed in her conversation and manner that she made me feel at ease and my nervousness began to dissolve.

Reaching her car, I was quietly impressed to see that it was a black 1956 Ford Thunderbird sports coupe. We set off and Chantelle detoured through the city to show me some of the sights, we passed by the Atomium, a huge replica of neutrons around an atom, that had been the showpiece of the Worlds Fair held in Brussels a few years earlier, then on to the Royal Palace which basked in an array of floodlights, we stopped to look at the famous little statue of Mannequin Piss, built by the side of the Palace.

We drove to what appeared to be a fashionable area of the city and parked in the lot of a new high rise building, I recognized the name "Cimeiz" as the address where my letters to Chantelle had been addressed. We took the elevator and went up to the twentieth floor, entering into a luxurious apartment, furnished with contemporary furniture. On the walls were several enlarged glass framed photographs from famous European fashion magazines featuring Chantelle on their covers. Chantelle offered to get me a drink. When she returned, I was standing admiring the photographs on the wall. "Your parents have a beautiful apartment!" I complimented. Chantelle moved in close behind, putting her arms around me. "Ivan...this is my apartment, my modeling is bringing in a ample income. It has been good enough to pay for this apartment, car...and prepare me for my future career, my studies in photo-journalism at the University of Brussels." I turned and took her into my arms, just the touch of her made me feel good. Looking into her sparkling eyes I said, "I admire that, Chantelle, not only are you doing well now, but also preparing for where you want to go in the future!" She cocked her head, "You mean I'm not just a dumb

Blond?" She teased with a laugh. "If you are, I would pray to have some of that dumbness and do as well as you!" I countered, teasing her back.

Then I kissed her, I could feel my instincts taking over, Chantelle responded with her body softening into the embrace. We kissed, hugged and talked a little while longer, then I found the courage to take Chantelle's hand and lead her to the bedroom. We kissed on the bed and undressed each other slowly, savoring each part of the other's body. Chantelle's breasts were so firm she didn't need to wear a bra. Her skin felt soft like pure silk, feeling her sent electric impulses through my body. We caressed and tenderly explored every part of the other's torso, each touch seemed to bring with it a new and exciting sensation.

I stopped for a moment, and told her softly, "Chantelle, I have never made love Before!" Embarrassed at my own inexperience. Chantelle giggled nervously, "I haven't either, I am still a virgin!" Squeezing me tightly she whispered, "We will learn together!" We continued with our journey of exploration. I went inside of her and Chantelle let out a brief moan of painful ecstasy as I ruptured her virginity. We made love, kissed, talked, hugged and made love again through the night. It was the best sleepless night I had ever experienced.

In the early hours of the morning we were still both awake, and Chantelle lay snuggled into my side. We talked about our likes, dislikes, dreams and fantasies. Then I asked her, "Why me, Chantelle? You could have the pick of any man you want!" Her green blue eyes looked at me, and she answered "Remember the day we flew in from katanga—I watched you giving of your self to the refugees, you were so focused on helping the needy and making the people feel comfortable without thinking of yourself. Then, as I watched I saw you handle situations with gentleness and caring, there was a great strength of character about you. You became more and more handsome in my eyes. At the end of the day, I could see how tired and exhausted you were, yet you never asked for anything, instead you went outside the building to collect your thoughts. That's when I followed, to see if there was something I could do for you. I was very vulnerable then, and you could have taken advantage, instead you comforted me. When we kissed that sealed my feelings for you!" She said, giving me a kiss and continued, "I have often thought 'If I could draw a picture of the man I would love—what would he look like?' The drawing always comes back with a portrait of you!" We snuggled a little while, then as the sun rose, fell asleep for a couple of hours in each others arms.

When we awakened I went to shower, Chantelle after a few minutes joined me and we lovingly washed each other, playing and laughing under the water. The sex had been wonderful, though I found that just being together with Chantelle, holding her, laughing, talking and the sharing of our emotions, was equally pleasurable. I also, took delight from the lack of inhibitions that existed between us.

Once dressed, Chantelle took me out do more sightseeing, we viewed different landmarks, during which we talked, teased and laughed even more—it seemed that we could not run out of subjects to chatter about.

During the week of my visit, we dressed up to go to plays and visited night spots. Chantelle, in her different gowns and outfits always looked a picture of elegance and style. The days were spent equally comfortably dressed in jeans and scruffy tee shirts, seeing the countryside. We went for dinner one evening at the home of Chantelle's parents, they were a genuine, warm and pleasantly elegant couple. They had recovered well from the time of having to leave all their belongings back in the old Katanga province of Zaire. From them, it was apparent where Chantelle's honesty and charm had been inherited.

The last day of my visit to Brussels, Chantelle took me for a drive along the Belgian country side. As we drove, I spoke of my concern that with my studies in America, it may be some time before we saw each other again. Chantelle replied, "That thought has also been on my mind." Her eyes began to cloud, and she drove to a nearby rest area and stopped the car. Continuing, she said, "It seems that we both have a few years and some miles to travel before we will be able to settle down. My dream is to spend my life with you, mon cheri. My impulse is that if you were to ask me to marry you this moment, I would accept and go anywhere with you, whether it be America or Rhodesia. Common sense is, as we both know, you have a career to study for, and I have mine to continue and study for here in Brussels. So we will have to be together in spirit, no amount of miles between us, can separate my feelings for you, my heart will always be with you until you return with it and we are together again." "I love you, Chantelle." I said and determinedly added, "I make you this promise, even though we don't know when, that we will be together—and I will ask you to marry me when the time is right for both of us!" Chantelle smiled in response, "I love you too, and I accept!" We gently sealed our promises with a kiss.

We drove further into the country side and reached a clear running stream flowing by the roadway, we stopped and walked a short distance from the car, finding a small clearing surrounded by tall grass and reeds near the water, we sat down and enjoyed the scenery. I put my arms around Chantelle and kissed her. "Make love to me." Chantelle whispered softly in my ear. I did, we embraced and made love with a passion beyond what I believed could exist. Afterwards, totally spent I rolled over on the grass to rest, Chantelle cuddled into me and lifted my head to lay on to her silken thighs, stroking my hair as we talked.

We returned to Chantelle's apartment, reluctantly picked up my suitcases and drove out to the airport. As my flight was called, tears started to stream down the sides of Chantelle's cheeks, we embraced and she said "Au revoir, mon cheri!" Looking into her green blue eyes and wiping the tears from her cheeks, I told her, "There is no need to cry my love. This is just the beginning for us!" kissing her, I walked to the entrance to board the flight. I turned for one more look at her, She called out "Just the beginning, cheri!" I nodded and waved, before entering the passageway leading to the aircraft. I waited until I was seated aboard the plane to let out my emotions, and a tear streamed down the side of my face. As we taxied to the runway, I looked back and whispered "My visit with you Chantelle, was like drinking the nectar from Paradise!" Then the plane took off into the evening sky.

The flight to London was a short trip, arriving at Heathrow in time to catch the Connecting TWA 707 jet to New York. Seven hours later, it was still late evening, as my jet completed the crossing of the Atlantic into the different time zone of New York City.

One of the most exhilarating sights a nineteen year old from Africa can hope to see, is the New York skyline at night for the first time. I had hailed a Yellow cab from the TWA terminal at Idlewild airport and seated by the back seat window looked up in awe, as we passed the succession of tall buildings leading into Manhattan. Most of the offices in the buildings had their lights left on, and the lighted windows added to a dazzling display of the illuminated skyscraper city. I had a reservation at "The Victoria Hotel." The taxi dropped me off in front the hotel and I noticed it was situated across the road from the famous "Winter Garden Theater," that carried live stage shows. A crowd of people were exiting from a performance, as I started to walk up the steps to the hotel entrance. Suddenly there was the sound of gunfire, people scattered in all directions, I dropped to a crouch on the steps behind my luggage. Within a few seconds, several police cars came screeching to a halt at the scene, lights flashing, sirens wailing, two of the cars mounted the pavement, before coming to a stop. Police officers ran out of their vehicles with guns drawn and the area was soon cordoned off. I turned to a couple standing near the steps, "What is happening?" I asked. "There has been a gangland hit, this is the way the 'Families' solve their problems!" The man answered. "Oh shit, you mean this doesn't just happen on T.V.?" I exclaimed loudly, causing some of the bystanders to turn and stare at me. I entered the hotel, the receptionist appeared to be either unruffled or did not care as to what was going on outside the hotel. "Please fill in this form with your name and address," she said. I filled in the address; "Glamorgan Ave…, Belvedere, Salisbury. Rhodesia." The receptionist read it, "Sir, I am not familiar with the suburb of 'Rhodesia',

which part of New York is that in?" She asked. I couldn't believe I was
standing in an international hotel with the receptionist asking me
which suburb of New York, Rhodesia was in! " It is a Queens Colony!"
I responded. "Thank you, sir." She replied, and wrote in the words
"Queens, N.Y." on the address card. Giving up on the address, I told her
I wanted a room which had a view, for two days. "Yes sir, a room with a
view for two days, you are booked in to room 1902, on the nineteenth
floor." She said, handing me the keys. I went up the elevator, and opening the door to the room, I saw it was very comfortable looking, with a
king size bed, a T.V. set and its own bathroom, very different to the
room I had in London. I switched the T.V. set on, C.B.S. was running a
commentary on the current Cuban missile crises. From the quotes of
President Kennedy's speech, a showdown with the Soviets seemed
imminent, unless one of the two powers was prepared to back down. I
began to wonder about the timing of my coming to America. "I may
have arrived in the 'safety' of the United States just in time to be nuked
out of existence!" I thought cynically, to myself. I showered and afterwards was eager to see the view of New York, I went to the window and
pulled open the curtains. There was a great view…of the brick wall of
an even taller building built alongside the hotel. It was just after midnight, the hotel brochure had advertised that it was a few blocks from
Times Square, so I decided to take a stroll.

Reaching the downstairs pavement, I could see that this truly was a
city that didn't sleep, people were walking everywhere. I too began to
walk in the direction of the neon-lit up area which seemed to be about
five blocks away. After entering the third block I saw an elderly couple
at the end of the block, approached by a tall man waving something that
looked like a knife. The elderly man reached into his pocket and handed
something over, and the couple proceeded along their way. The tall man
approached another couple waving his knife, the same thing happened,
they handed over what appeared to be money, and were allowed to walk
on. The tall man went up to a man walking on his own, again the same

thing happened. I could see that the people were being mugged. Anywhere else in the world, the victims would have raised a hue and cry, police would have rushed to the scene, the man arrested and dragged off to jail. Here the tall man's activities seemed to be accepted to the extent that he had created a production line of people he was mugging. Two blocks further down, I could see a policeman sitting astride his sturdy horse, guarding Times Square, apparently unaware of what was happening a couple of blocks from him. The tall man started to walk in my direction, I walked across the street to the pavement on the other side, to avoid him. The tall man followed, he crossed the street, approaching me, he said, "Gimme your money!" "Screw you!" I told him. "What?" said the tall man, obviously not used to rejection. He began to wave his knife, I violently kicked him in the crotch, and walked away, leaving the tall man writhing on the pavement in agony.

I started to seriously think about cutting my visit to New York short, if I encountered any more mugging incidents. Reaching Times square, the place was a hive of activity, people were everywhere, shops were open selling everything from electronics to souvenirs. The huge neon billboards flashing around the square brightly lit up the constant motion of life. I entered a shop to buy postcards to send home, they also sold foreign magazines. Sitting on the shelf was an issue of "Elle" magazine from Paris, featuring Chantelle on its cover. I picked it up and before paying for it, started to browse through the other ladies fashion books on the stand to see if she appeared in any of them as well. My actions must have been misinterpreted, as a man standing nearby, wearing bell bottoms and very definitely gay walked up to me and said with a heavy lisp, "Hey sugar, would you like to have some fun tonight?" I laughed inwardly at the mistaken approach and replied with a straight face, "No thanks, I think I have already had all the fun I can Handle for tonight!" Continuing to browse, I started to feel the effects of the long flight and exhaustion taking over. I returned to the hotel, keeping a careful watch along the way for the tall man with the knife, I made it back to my room without further incident. The next morning I was up bright and early to explore more of the city. By day, New York was a completely different sight with most of the blazing neon lights turned off, the image became accentuated with tall bland concrete skyscrapers surrounding a cacophony of cars fighting to make headway on the streets below. The pavements were filled to capacity with pedestrians walking in every direction, trying to get through the heavily congested traffic intersections to their destinations. I walked along the crowded streets until my feet ached, stopping to browse through Macy's, the world's largest department store, glimpsing through the variety of merchandise being sold there, it took me two hours to walk the ten floors of the shop. I walked across the street to the base of the Empire State Building, to fulfill a boyhood dream. Looking up the one hundred and two stories of the building, I remembered standing at the base of the newly completed fourteen storied "Trafalgar Court" building in Salisbury in awe, wondering what it must be like to stand at the base of this building looking up—now I knew. With so many other tall buildings around the Empire State Building, the height of the skyscraper lost some of its impact!

I did what most tourists do, entered the building and went up the three tiers of elevators to the observation floor on the one hundred and second level. Listening to the conversations on the way up, they all seemed to revolve around one topic; the crisis with the Soviets and their placing missiles in Castro's Cuba. Somehow, the prospect of a nuclear war seemed so unreal, "Surely mankind isn't so stupid as to blow ourselves out of existence?" I thought to myself.

At the observation level there was a spectacular view of New York City's other Skyscrapers. The traffic and people below looked like ants scurrying around giant anthills. Out in the harbour the Statue of Liberty made an impressive sight at the shipping entrance to America, with her offer of freedom and liberty for all. Suddenly I felt spent, I began looking beyond the statue over the ocean to Chantelle, and become very aware of just how much I missed her.

The following day I traveled to Idlewild airport, for my flight to Los Angeles. The seven hour flight seemed to take forever. I tried to prepare myself for what lay ahead. Apart from my father's side of uncle Jack and his wife Emily, my mother had her family of six brothers and sisters living in the west Coast of America. My mother had not seen any of her sibling brothers or sisters seen since leaving the Island of Rhodes over forty years previously. Although, they had always kept in close contact through letters. There was a brother Maurice, and sister in Los Angeles. The sister Rena, had married a dentist and they had two daughters, both of them had won beauty pageants and landed small roles in movies. The remaining family, a brother and three sisters lived in Seattle, mostly with families of grown up children, who were much older than me, cousins that I looked forward to meeting at some time during my stay in America. Similarly it was closer to fifty years since my father had seen Jack, who sailed for America at the age of thirteen. Although Jack and wife Emily had written regularly to us in Rhodesia, unlike the other relatives they had never sent photographs of themselves, except once, thirty years previously when they had sent a photo of themselves as a young, slender and handsome couple. So I had no idea what they looked like today. The stewardess on the flight had taken a fancy to me, and spent a lot of time flirting and fussing over my comfort. The seat next to me was vacant and she sat next to me during her free moments from work. As the plane descended into Los Angeles, she slipped me a card with her phone number and hand written in the words, "Call me!"

At the airport, The full compliment of all the families of Aunt Rena, Uncle Maurice and Uncle Jack were waiting to meet me. I was also introduced to the cousins Elaine and Jody, who had won the beauty pageants and they were almost as poised and attractive as Chantelle. Jack pulled me aside to introduce his wife Emily, She waddled up to me, and I knew instantly why no photographs had been sent, the lady was extremely overwieght! She was munching at a large chocolate bar as she put her arms around me to give a welcome kiss.

As time went by, I adjusted to my new surroundings and explored the city, learning more about the vast spread out metropolis of Los Angeles. I tried to stop myself from making comparisons, but being in a new country, it just seemed natural to observe the differences between what I had been used to, what I was now seeing and what I had expected to find. Surprisingly, although much larger and substantially more populated than Salisbury, the way of life was not all that different. The hi-tech existence I had expected to see was more a myth than reality. The telephone system was substantially more efficient, there were three major T.V. networks, a lot more cars and an advanced highway system. Everybody seemed to be involved in giving out or collecting Green stamps with every purchase from gasoline to food. On the other hand, except for a few mansions in Beverly Hills, the houses in Salisbury were bigger, built on larger plots of land and more individually designed.

The main contrast was that the Rhodesians had a more relaxed way of life, with clean breathable air. The misconceptions of the life in Africa amongst Americans was remarkable, I was asked several times by people I was introduced to, if I lived in a tree house in Rhodesia, if I had kept a lion as pet, why I spoke English, how come I was white and did white people really live there? The university was a good place to meet new friends, though I felt the standard of education in Rhodesia was higher, some of the topics in the courses being taught, I had already covered while in my last year at high school.

Getting to and from the university on buses had become very time consuming, so I decided to invest some of the two thousand dollars I had brought with me, in a car. I found a red and white 1956 Corvette in good condition, the seller wanted seven hundred and fifty dollars for it and after "Heavy negotiations," settled for five hundred in cash. I felt on top of the world with the purchase of my "New" car.

Together with my new friends from campus, I joined in the Friday night Los Angeles ritual of cruising bumper to bumper down Hollywood Boulevard, watching the pavement sideshow. What a show it was too, the once grand, but now run down street had a constant parade of people that wanted to be noticed walking along its pavements. There were the weirdo's dressed in the strangest outfits, gays and lesbians holding hands, aspiring starlets made up of beautiful women and handsome men looking for that glimpse of recognition. Also, part of the attraction was the conversations and exchange of phone numbers with the girls driving in the car stuck alongside us, in the never ending traffic jam down the Boulevard.

Afterwards I would go with my companions to either "Pandora's Box" a night spot on the Sunset strip to listen to a band, or "P.J's" bar to catch a performance by the famous Trini Lopez. The fact that my friends and I were not quite twenty one years old yet, did not seem to merit much attention. Uncle Jack was a pleasant and good man, astute in business, and reminded me of my own father. Aunt Emily on the other hand never did anything without an ulterior motive, and that was to eat, she was totally obsessed with feeding herself. Conversations held with her were made between her mouthfuls. They had an office in their shopping center on sunset boulevard, near Schwab's drugstore where many famous movie personalities hung out at the coffee and soda fountain there. Often when visiting my aunt and uncle's office, I took the opportunity to stop in at the drugstore for a soda and watch the passing parade of celebrities, sometimes becoming involved in conversations with them. I met Max Baer Jr. from the new hit series "The Beverly Hillbillies" and was surprised to learn from him that he was the son of the of the former world heavyweight boxing champion, Max Baer. Coincidentally, I also met "Sgt. Doberman" from "The Phil Silvers Show" who bore a striking resemblance to my aunt, he was a regular customer who would sit down with the other actors and comics, and spurt spontaneous jokes with them for hours. I was often invited to sit at the cubicle with them and spent many hours just listening to the never-ending comic genius that flowed between these people. My cousins, Elaine and Jody, had each won beauty pageants. Elaine the eldest at twenty nine had a few years earlier won the "Miss California" title, and Jody, a year older than me, was a current "Miss California" beauty finalist. They lived together with their parents in a large Beverly Hills Home on Rodeo Drive, with all the wealth and social trappings of life in that exclusive area. As beautiful as they both were physically, their characters were equally ugly. Spoilt, self centered, arrogant and vindictive to the extreme. Through their outward attractive appearance, they got away with bad behavior that most people would not even think of attempting. On one occasion I had been invited to join my cousins, their parents and about twenty guests for a dinner at an exclusive Beverly Hills restaurant. During the course of dinner, Elaine became angry, as she felt her new boyfriend was not paying enough attention to her. She picked up a large bowl of spaghetti and meatballs from the table, took aim and threw the contents into the boyfriend's face—this gained the man's attention very quickly! Surprisingly, this did not end the relationship and the poor man dated her for another three months of unending punishment before Elaine tired of him and moved on to some other man waiting in the wings for his turn at being abused.

Jody was not quite so physical in her way of getting attention, she merely splurged out venom most of the time she opened her mouth. Amazingly, she looked like butter wouldn't melt in her mouth and even appeared lady like when her lips opened. But what came out, ripped at you like a Piranha biting straight into the Jugular vein. I of course not being a potential suitor, and not interested in Jody in any way other than as a relative, did not put up with the poison emanating from Jody's venting. And I usually, handed back to her as good as she dealt out. The two of us learned to keep a cautious distance from each other.

Both Elaine and Jody were involved through a movie agent in appearing in commercials and often received calls to do small parts in

Hollywood films. They had become friendly with Michael Landon of "Bonanza" fame and his soon to be bride Lyn Moe. During my visits to my cousins home, I would often meet Michael and Lyn there, and in time also became friendly with them. Michael invited me to the Paramount Studios set where scenes for the Western series were filmed.

A few days later I arrived on the set to find Michael Landon already in costume, preparing to film a new episode. Michael had just made a purchase, a brand new Corvette Sting Ray sports car, metallic silver in color. Michael proudly showed me his new toy and we compared my '56 Corvette with the latest designs on Michael's new car. After a few minutes we were joined by Lorne Greene who played the father in the T.V. series and Dan Blocker who played "Hoss" in the show. I was introduced to the two men and was impressed by their height and size. I estimated Michael's height to be at least five feet ten, and these two men must have been eight to ten inches taller than him—no wonder "Little Joe" looked so small on the T.V. screen in comparison to these two "Giants". After admiring Michael's car for a few minutes we all walked to the stage sets to start that day's filming for the series.

The main fixed set was a replica of the living room of the "Ponderosa" home, which consisted of half a living room, complete with dinning table, staircase and the walls had fitted mountings of cattle heads and horns. The other permanent set was a jail cell. For this episode a stage had been built depicting the inside portion of a cabin, complete with windows. On the other side of the windows, a live horse had been placed to give the appearance that it was an open space with the steed grazing outside. I was fascinated by the illusions of filmmaking which looked so real on the screen.

During a break in filming, Michael handed me a copy of that days "L.A. Times", which carried a front page article about Rhodesia, stating that there had been rioting in the main street of Salisbury. "Looks like the Natives are getting restless! What do you think is going to happen in your Country?" Michael asked. "I don't know Mike, I just wish they

could sit down and work this out without the interference of the
Soviets and Chinese." I Replied. Lorne Greene was standing nearby and
overhearing the conversation, commented "We are having our own
problems with the Soviets and the Cuban missiles, looks like the
Russians are trying to push us too far this time!" To which I responded
with a concerned, " I hope it doesn't end up with someone being stupid
enough to press the button that starts a nuclear war, because then it
wont matter about the politics here, Rhodesia or anywhere else. We will
be too busy trying to survive the nuclear fallout!" The conversation at
that moment was interrupted by a call to do the next scene. I continued
to watch, fascinated by the workings of filmaking.

At the end of the day I gathered the courage to approach Michael
Landon and ask; " Mike, I have never acted in front of a camera before,
do you think it would be possible for me to try and get some work as an
extra?" To my total surprise Michael's response was very receptive "Sure
Ivan I'll get it set up for you!" In the next few weeks, with Michael's' help
I joined the actors union and obtained my actors card, with the bonus
of being hired as an extra in two of the episodes of "Bonanza."

Encouraged by these events I found myself an agent and started
doing part time work as an extra in several movies in-between classes at
the university. The pay was good, at the scheduled ninety five dollars a
day union rate. More than the money, I enjoyed the fun of being in the
make believe world of the movie industry. Sneaking a camera on to the
sets I was working on, I took photographs of myself with the stars,
which were regularily sent back home with my letters to my parents and
to Chantelle in Brussels. To my surprise and delight, I found myself
being increasingly called in for casting calls and landing a few tiny
speaking parts in major movies.

A director friend of Michael Landon phoned me to say that he had
been talking with Mike about a new T.V series he intended to produce
and direct for N.B.C. in the next season. It was to be a "Spy" series and
the script called for a regular minor role actor with an "English" accent.

Michael had recommended me for the part. The Director wanted to know if I would come in for a screen test. My instinct was to yell out "Yes please! Please!", but with difficulty, held back my excitement to a polite "Yes, thank you, when would you like me to come in to audition?" The director set up the interview for two days ahead at his studio on Sunset boulevard. The screen test and interview went smoothly, and a week later the casting director called to tell me that I had been selected for the role in the series, which was at that time still unnamed, but tentatively called "The Agents". I was beside myself with joy! I couldn't believe that this was really happening, " I am going to be on a regular T.V. series!" I shouted out aloud. There was no one at home to hear me, but I wanted to hear the words anyway, to bring in the impact of what had happened. I switched on the T.V. set to watch what the "Other actors" looked like on the small screen, as if I were seeing it for the first time, and became involved watching a soap opera.

After a few minutes, the show was interrupted, the announcer appeared on the screen to say that President Kennedy was due to address the Nation that day on the ongoing Cuban missile situation. I, like many other people in America that day held my breath, fearing the worst—had the situation gone beyond the point of no return, were we about to get into a nuclear war with the Soviets?

Later that day Kennedy spoke to the nation, the developments were not good, he spelled out graphically with maps and pictures, the dangers that were being put into place by the Soviets installing missiles in Cuba and how easily they could be launched to hit the main cities and cut off the lifeline of the United States. His address ended with the announcement of a naval blockade of Soviet ships into Cuba.

The ball was now in Kruschev's court, would he blink, or was this to be the beginning of a disaster, with nuclear weapons being unleashed, where no one could predict the consequences either in devastation or the effect on future mankind. After listening to Kennedy's address, I walked outside my uncle's house in Hermosa Beach, I wanted to think, and the best way I did that was to stroll along the road watching the passing events. Somehow, this usually had the effect of helping to clear my mind and to see things more in perspective, as I walked I passed by a supermarket. Long lines were starting to build outside the store and the people who had already been inside were coming out loaded with all sorts of canned food. Kennedy's speech was bringing about a minor panic and some citizens were taking the precaution of buying food to hoard in the event of a war. I continued to walk, further down I came to another food store, the identical situation was developing there, with lines building up and customers coming out with whatever was available in canned food. I stood and watched for a while.

The scene unfolding in front of me seemed very unreal, I felt more like a spectator than a participant of the events happening around me. Then I realized how much I missed the wide open spaces of the African bushveldt, my parents and home, the genuiness and warmth of Motorcar and Amos's friendship. I tried to rationalize my feelings and questioned the surge of "homesickness" I was going through, wondering if I too was suffering emotions of anxiety over the developing threatened conflict, wanting to be with the ones I was closest to at a time like this. With a sigh, I continued walking, I didn't have an answer to the confusion I was experiencing. But, one thing I was going to do, was place a long distance call to my parents in Salisbury, at least speaking to them and hearing their news would help soften some of the homesickness I was encountering. After a few days, Kruschev "blinked" and ordered the Soviet Navy sailing towards Cuba with missile parts to stop and hold their position, eventually ordering them to turn around and sail back to Russia. The crisis with Cuba was temporarily over. While many Americans breathed a sigh of relief, a new threat loomed on the horizon, in a place very few knew or had heard much about, a country called Vietnam.

The former French colony of Indo-China, had recently been granted independence from France and changed it's name to Vietnam. The communists were gaining a foothold in that country and the West was determined to stop them from advancing and swallowing up other nations in Asia. Many analysts warned that involvement in that country could lead to a major conflict similar to what had occurred in Korea. In T.V. interviews, the politicians said that they would never let that type of conflict happen again, but, that pressure had to put on the communists to stop them from enveloping other countries, as far away as they may be. I drew a parallel with what was going on in Rhodesia, did anyone realize or more pertinently, care that the same was happening there in my home country. The Marxists had systematically strolled down the African continent, focusing on one country at a time. feeding and fueling whatever dissension they could. The communists were devious enough to let the local populations do their fighting for them in the name of "liberation" and "freedom" and once the fighting was over, switching their focus and moving on to the next country, leaving behind a Marxist government and a population enslaved by a system worse and poorer than before.

What was not common knowledge, despite the publicity given to the Russians and their aspirations of domination, was that the Chinese were subtly and cleverly matching the Soviets step for step not only in Asia, but in Africa too.

I placed my call to Salisbury. It felt so good to talk to my mother and catch up on the events happening at home. Though, some of the news was disturbing, my father was suffering from his annual recurrence of the Black water fever, the illness that had been a major factor in our selling the farm in the Mazoe Valley and the move to Salisbury. The fever this year had been particularly severe and the doctors had admitted him that morning to the General Hospital as a precaution and for treatment. My mother said she would pass on the news of my success in landing a part in the T.V. series to my dad, and knew that he would be as happy as she was to hear the news. They looked forward to seeing the series when it eventually came to the little screens in Rhodesia.

I put down the telephone and felt cause for concern, each year I had seen my father suffer through a recurrence of the Black Water fever and each time after recovering, he had seemed that little bit weaker. My father had never in the past needed to be hospitalized, and I hoped that this was just an unusual circumstance.

The next few weeks were busy for me, the script arrived for the pilot of the T.V. series, meetings were held to define the character that I was to portray, rehearsals and filming schedules at Paramount studios were being arranged, this combined with University studies, left me time to do little else. Fortunately my aunt and uncle were very supportive during this time, proud that their nephew was to become a "T.V. Star", did all they could to help.

Elaine and Jody on the other hand were dumbfounded that their upstart cousin from Africa had been able to capture a role in a T.V. series, which was something they had been unable to do. They superficially complimented me, however their resentment was more than perceptible, with snide comments and predictions that the series would never get off the ground. I realized that they were envious and calmly let their comments slide, which had the effect of upsetting my cousins even more. A week before filming was due to start, my mother telephoned, "Ivan, your father's condition has not improved, in his weakened condition the doctors are concerned about his heart, they are doing everything possible for him, but the next few weeks will be crucial, he may not survive this seizure. I have phoned Babbette and Leon, they have both decided to come to Salisbury to be with him, it is up to you whether you also wish to come back home." In my mind this was not a matter of choice, the decision was plain, I would leave for Rhodesia to be with my family, as soon as I could. Within a week, the Corvette was sold. The film company was more than understanding and launched a search for a new replacement for my role in the series. Uncle Jack did everything possible to convince me to stay and not throw away the potential for a wonderful future and career, but my mind was made up.

I was going to be with my father, whatever the cost. With the proceeds of the sale of my car I bought the air ticket to return home.

Seven days after receiving my mother's phone call, I was on a plane flying home to Rhodesia. At Salisbury airport, my mother, together with Leon and Babbette who had arrived a couple of days earlier, were there to meet me. It felt wonderful to be back home with them, and to smell the fresh, clean air of Africa again.

We drove straight from the airport to the hospital. My father was delighted with our reunion and clearly it lifted his spirits to have his family all together with him. For me it was heartbreaking to see my father's condition. He had been a well built man six feet tall and a strong one hundred and eighty five pounds. Now he was thin and drawn, barely weighing one hundred and twenty pounds. His mind was as alert, strong and sensitive as ever, I knew it would take more than an illness to affect that. He maintained his sense of humor to lighten the seriousness of his condition and health. I thought to myself, how much I respected my father more than any other man I had ever met.

After visiting hours, we returned home. I had been away for eighteen months and it was pleasing to see that nothing had changed. Motorcar was there to greet us, I threw my arms around my old friend, "Motorcar, I have so much to tell you about America!" and showing Motorcar my left wrist, I said "See, I never took off the bracelet of elephant hair you gave me—it brought me luck all the time I was there!"

Motorcar showed me his usual beaming smile and said " It is good to have you home again young friend, I hope your father recovers from his illness soon."

For the following three weeks the vigil continued with my father, his condition slowly deteriorated, the family was with him day and night. On one occasion, I was alone talking to my father when he said "I am glad to have this opportunity to speak with you alone, Ivan. If anything should happen to me, I am concerned about Benny's handling of the business. He doesn't care who he steps on to get what he wants! I have willed everything to your mother, but be cautious in your dealings with Benny, and be sure to see that your mother is protected from his self-ishness." "I promise Dad!" I replied, "But there is no need to talk about that, you will get better soon!". I added hopefully.

Two days later, my father suffered a heart attack and with the family around him, passed away in the early hours of the morning. As the family tearfully walked away from the hospital, I put my arm around my mother's shoulder holding her in her time of need. I looked up at the sky, and saw across the clear African night, a shooting star blazing its way through the heavens.

Chapter Eight

My father had earned a lot of respect among the community, both with friends and business associates alike. Messages of condolences and compassion flowed in to our family. Many of the friends visited our home to offer their sympathy in person. Benny, also made his appearance at the house with the other well wishers. To my astonishment, his first comment to my mother as he walked into the house was a dramatic, "What is going to happen to the business, now that Uncle Vic is gone!" I glared at him, the man's selfishness and total insensitivity was hard to believe. Fortunately, Benny's words seemed to bounce off her, as though they were sounds without meaning. My mother was too preoccupied with the devastating family loss, to give any thought to the material or business aspects of life.

Emotionally, it was difficult for me to cope with the fact of losing my father, and life seemed to be at its darkest. Then I remembered what my father had taught by his own example; strength of character, kindness and sensitivity to others. Perhaps that was the finest legacy my father could have left me and I prayed that I too, had inherited a fraction of those qualities. Right now my mother needed all the support and strength I could give, and it was important that I focus on being there for her. Hopefully, that would also help me to get through this difficult time of sorrow.

Leon and Babbete stayed in Salisbury another three weeks before returning to the demands of their busy schedules in London.

I too, gave a lot of thought to returning to my studies and possible film career in Los Angeles. But, that would have left my mother without any of her children, in a country that was heading towards an unstable future. Finally, I decided that I would stay in Rhodesia with her. Perhaps, I thought, that was what destiny had planned for me all along, to live in the country of my birth.

I discussed my feelings about remaining in Salisbury, with my mother. Although she made no attempt to influence my decision one way or the other, I could see the sense of relief in her eyes at the thought of my remaining with her. That was all that I needed to confirm my intention to stay. "I will meet with Benny tomorrow, Mom, to discuss coming to work in the business!" I said at the end of the conversation.

The next morning, a meeting was arranged. The meeting consisted of my mother, who as the sole beneficiary of the estate, was now the Chief Executive Officer of Royal Cycles, Benny the corporation's President, and myself as the prospective employee.

I explained to Benny my decision to stay in the country and expressed my desire to work in the family business. The Phony smile appeared and spread across Benny's hardhearted face. "Ivan I would be glad to have you come on board in the company, however, like all new employees, you will have to start at the bottom. I am prepared to offer you a position as a clerk at minimum wage, then in a few years, perhaps, you could work your way up to being a salesman in the organization."

Benny's response took me by surprise, "Wait a second Benny, this is my fathers business in which I have already worked as a salesman, If I interpret your offer correctly—what you are suggesting would mean in effect, that it would take years before I would be in a position to handle any of the executive intricacy of this organization,…. or is that what you really want? To make sure that I am kept from learning too much about the organization and the decision making, which ensures your keeping control of this business? If that is your fear, then it is groundless—rest assured that my intention is purely to work together as a family, I don't wish to threaten your position!" I replied.

The phony smile never left Benny's face. "Take it or leave it, that is my offer!" he responded. I looked at my mother, she said nothing, and looked down to avoid my questioning glance.

There was something seriously wrong here and I needed to speak to my mother to find out exactly what was happening. "Benny, I would like to think about the offer, I will get back to you, as soon as possible." I said, ending the meeting.

Alone with my mother later in the day, I questioned her silence, why hadn't she stood up for me? Tears flooded into her eyes. "I am sorry, Ivan, but I had no choice. Just before you came in Benny and I had a meeting with the accountants. They told us that the death duties payable in your father's estate, came to over five hundred thousand pounds. All our money is tied up in the business and the only way we can pay it is by taking a loan from the bank. To complicate matters, Your father and Benny were the only ones that had control and knew the complications involved with the operations of the business. With your father gone, Benny is the only one who knows that now. He is like the Lion that has realized the full potential of his strength, he threatened to resign and walk out if he is not left in charge to run the business as he sees fit. My fear is, if I force the issue about the level of your position in the firm, he might leave. There isn't anyone with enough knowledge to continue running the company. We would be forced to sell off the business to pay the death duties and debts—and be left with nothing!"

I reeled back at what my mother was saying. Benny was taking advantage of the situation to the hilt, serving his own selfish ends. The question was, what to do about it?

There was no point in forcing the issue with Benny, if I did that, Benny might just walk from the business, leaving my mother and the company in chaos. If I accepted the position as clerk, I knew Benny would make life intolerable, as well as ensuring I was kept from advancing to any decision making post in the company, that way Benny could maintain his strength and hold over the organization.

I thought of the alternatives, one was to find a job with another company, or, even more appealingly, start my own business.

"Mom, I am going to tell Benny that I am not accepting the job offer, if I did, he would try to gain control over me too, this way I can keep a watch over him freely, from a distance!" I told my mother. "What will you do?" She asked. "I am not sure at the moment. There are a few options I would like to look into, One of them is to start my own company!" "Doing What?" She queried, "Frankly, I don't know yet." I answered candidly, "But I am going to look around to find where there is a need for trade and open my own shop."

"You are so much like your father, Ivan. I wish you every success!" My mother said, wiping the tears from her eyes.

I considered my status. My position wasn't exactly a strong one, I was barely twenty years old, I had a little over three hundred pounds left over from my trip to America—and very little commercial experience! Granted, not much to start a business career with, but I believed I did have guts and determination. Thinking about the type of shop to open, I knew about bicycles and that industry the best of all, perhaps that was the way to go! I would start looking around for a suitable retail location the next day.

My search took me to the "Avenues" a newly completed shopping center, two miles from the heart of the city. It was in the hub of a highly populated high rise apartment dwelling district, a good area comprised mostly of middle class inhabitants. At a conservative estimate, I thought there were about 30,000 people living within walking distance to the shops.

There were twenty shops, yet only five had been leased, namely, a Supermarket, hair salon, bakery and two restaurants. The other shops lay empty. The political situation was deteriorating to the extent that very few people were prepared to take the risk of opening up new ventures in the light of the uncertainty. I thought that I could use that fact to negotiate a lower rental for the premises. Also with so many apartment dwellers, they were sure to need household appliances, tools, light bulbs and electrical parts. Why not supply that too? That was it—I would open a bicycle and hardware store!

The owner of the shopping center, a Mister Johnson, was handling the leasing of the shops personally, from a suite of one the hotels he owned in the town center. I went to see him. "Yes, son, what can I do for you?" Mister Johnson asked. "I am interested in renting one of your shops in the Avenues." I replied. Johnson eyed me cynically. "The rent is one hundred and twenty-five pounds a month, can you pay that?" Johnson asked. "No sir, I can't, I am prepared to make you an offer though, I would like three months free rent to help me get started, then one year at sixty pounds a month, after which I will take a five year option on a lease at the full rate you are asking at one hundred and twenty five pounds a month!" I responded.

"You're crazy! Why would I lease ideal premises at such a ridiculous rate." Johnson spluttered out at me. "Because it would be in your best interests to have more shops leased and receive some income coming from them, rather than none! Also, the more space you rent and the busier the center becomes, the better an attraction it is for others to lease space from you, or, would you rather have them sitting empty with no rent coming in at all!" I stated. Johnson reclined back into his heavy leather seat and looked at me, "Tell you what, I will accept a hundred pounds a month in rent!" I stood up from my seat, and said "I am sorry, but the offer I made you is the only agreement that I am prepared to enter into!" I turned and started walking towards the door to leave. "Come back here, young man!" Johnson called out to me, I turned around to face Mr. Johnson. "You really do have balls young fellow, taking on a crusty old businessman like me! Hardware and bicycles…Huh; that would be an attraction to get people shopping at my new center—I like that! Very well, we have a deal, on the terms you have offered. When do you wish to take possession?" I gratefully responded, "One month from today…and Mister Johnson, thank you!"

As I left the hotel, I thought, "Well, step one is complete, I have the location. Now to arrange for a loan and goods to put into the shop. I returned home and went to the garden to tell Motorcar the news. Motorcar listened intently as I told him what I was about to do, then he asked, "Young friend, you taught Enock and Amos to read and write, do you think you could also teach me to sell?" A little confused by the question, I answered, "Yes I think I can, but why are you asking me that?" Motorcar beamed his smile "Because I would like to work for you selling goods in the shop!" He replied. I put on a mock caustic expression, "Huh, you certainly do have balls to ask a crusty old business man like me a question like that!" Then with a laugh, I said, "Yes, of course, it would perfect to have you working in the shop, though, I can only afford to pay you the same wages as you are getting now plus a commission on sales, but, as business improves I will increase your salary! If that is acceptable, I will arrange with my mother for you to continue living in your quarters here, and you can come in with me to work each morning. Do you want to think about it, Motorcar?" "I have thought about it young friend, and I wish to work for you!" Motorcar replied. "Done!" I Said , extending my hand in agreement.

That evening I told my mother the news of finding the store and its location. "Ivan," she said sadly, "Benny doesn't want you to open the shop!" "Oh, why not?" I questioned. "Benny says that if you open a bicycle shop, our customers will associate you with "Royal Cycles" and it will look like we have gone into competition with them on the retail trade. He said that it will be bad for our business." My mother informed me. "Mom, don't you see that is just an excuse, to stop me from doing anything that may be successful, frankly, he does not have the right to try and stop me!" I continued, "I had intended to go to 'Royal Cycles' tomorrow to open an account for the new shop…do you think Benny will create a problem for me to do so?" I asked. "I don't know, but I will do what I can for you. I am so sick of Benny's hard attitude towards you!" My mother replied.

The next morning I went in to the accounts department of "Royal Cycles." I initially spoke to Ian, the company's accountant. "I am sorry Ivan, but Benny has given instructions that if you were to come in, we were to refer the matter to him!" Ian said in an apologetic voice. " That's fine Ian, let him know that I am here!" I said with a raised feeling of dejection. Benny kept me waiting for nearly an hour before making an appearance. "Ivan this company can not be associated with you in any way. The retailers that we deal with will believe that we have opened a retail shop that is going to compete with them. So we can't have you on our books." Benny said. "Listen Benny, accept the fact I am going to open my shop. All that I am asking for is the same credit terms extended to "Royal's" other customers, nothing more, and no favors." I replied. Benny Glared at me "You would be a bad credit risk, you are only twenty years old, what the hell does a little pip-squeak like you, know about business anyway?" Benny said challengingly. I tried to remain calm, "Probably a whole lot more than you did at my age, when my father was good enough to give you a job in this business!" Benny nearly choked with anger. Ian, who was seated behind Benny broke into a fit of coughing that sounded a lot like laughter. Benny turned to give Ian a threatening look and the 'coughing' stopped. Turning back to me, Benny said "Anyway, your mother has spoken to me about this, the best I can do is sell on a cash only basis, so that there will be no record of us dealing with you!"

I held back the urge to smash the phony smile off the little man's face, instead I said, "That's fine Benny, I will get my supplies elsewhere! Your foolish hunger for power and greed has stopped us from working together as a family…unfortunately for you, one day you will regret what you are doing!" With that comment, I turned and left the premises.

I realized that I was in a predicament, I needed goods to stock up the shop. The problem was I did not have the cash to lay out, so I needed goods on credit to give me the breathing space and momentum in time, to turn sales over, then I could apply the profit to build a cash basis, to pay for expenses—and eventually own the stock in the shop.

I went to the see the manager of the bank that my family had used for several years. The manager was polite, but he too, took on an apologetic tone, "Ivan, we received a call from Benny this morning; he said that if you were to approach us for a loan, that he was notifying us that you had no connection with the family business and that as far as he is concerned, not to rely on the good name of the family to assist you in obtaining a loan!" " Does that mean that the bank won't help me with a loan?" I asked. "Well there is one way we would be prepared to give you a line of credit, and that is if you can find a financially sound guarantor who will sign for the responsibility of the debt, we would lend you a thousand pounds." The manager replied.

I left the bank feeling dismal, Benny had gone to extraordinary lengths to try and shut every door in my path to opening the business. One factor though that Benny had underestimated, was that the barriers were making me more determined to open the shop and succeed. I milled several concepts around in my mind, on how to get around those obstacles.

Then a strange thought came to me. I had always gotten on well with Benny's father, uncle Joe. Joe was my mother's younger brother and the only other close relative we had in Rhodesia. He wasn't rich, but had owned his own clothing store for over thirty years and was certainly financially sound enough to sign as a guarantor with the bank. The irony of going to Benny's father to help me get around Benny's adversity, at first seemed a bizarre notion, but the more I thought about it, the more the idea made sense. Besides, if my uncle wouldn't help, I would be no worse off than I was now!

I phoned my uncle and a meeting was arranged at his clothing store for later that day. When I did arrive at the premises I was warmly greeted by Benny's father. Suddenly, I felt a surge of nerves and began to feel serious doubts concerning the wisdom of what I was doing. Holding back on my nervousness, I explained the recent developments, and my reasons for coming to seek his help as a guarantor for the bank loan. Joe listened without interruption until I had finished. Then he said, "Your mother has also been keeping me informed of what Benny has been doing. I am sorry that he has brought this hardship on her and the way he is treating you. Regrettably, since he became a 'Big shot' in the bicycle industry, I hardly ever see him—and he certainly wouldn't listen to any advice that I would try to give him!"

Joe put his hand to his forehead in thought, after a few moments he looked at me and said, "I would be happy to sign as guarantor, I think that is the least I can do to help in the circumstances—However, there is one condition attached; Benny must never Know that I have done this for you!" I gratefully acknowledged my uncle's offer to help and we ended our meeting with my emphasizing on my promise never to reveal my uncle's assistance, to Benny.

As I left my uncle's store, I felt a twinge of sadness for Benny, even his own father disagreed with his methods. Surely, I thought, Benny must have been aware that his pursuit of power at the cost of others, was alienating him from his family and relatives—people who could have been his strongest supporters and source of strength. As far as friends the man had none, except for a few who hung on to his coat tails in the hope of reaping some financial benefit being thrown their way from the business.

I shook the thoughts from my mind of softening up towards Benny. The reality was, that Benny had chosen to be an adversary and I in my business dealings had to treat him as such.

The next step for me was to secure a source of supply of Bicycles.

Mr. Buchanan of "African Cycles," was a distributor of bicycles and
had been a friend of my father for many years. I went to see him. Mr.
Buchanan appeared puzzled by my request to buy from him. "I will be
happy to supply to you, and also extend terms of ninety days for payment; but Ivan why are you buying from my company, when you could
get what you need from the source that supplies to me, your family
business?" He asked. "Mr. Buchanan, thank you for the terms, as far as
not buying from my family's business—I would prefer not to discuss
that!" I answered. Buchanan nodded his head knowingly, "It's Benny,
isn't it?" I made no attempt to respond.

Next, I opened an account with a hardware and electrical supplier. I
made arrangements to build a shop counter and for simple fixtures and
fittings to display the shops products. Finally, partitioned off a section
at the back of the store for bicycle repairs and hired a mechanic by the
name of Solomon, to do the repairs.

During the next few weeks Motorcar and I worked day and night,
putting together the fixtures and fittings, receiving the products ordered
and organizing displays. The political life had taken a secondary place in
my mind with the intensity and activity of getting the shop into order
and preparing for it's opening. However, a conflict was brewing
between the internal factions and Britain. Politics was playing a major
role in almost every aspect of daily life, to the detriment of social life,
business, and the security of the future course of the country.

Winston Field had resigned as Prime Minister of Rhodesia and two
men, Clifford Dupont and Ian Smith had vied for the position of the
Premiership, with the Rhodesian born Ian Smith edging out his opponent for the leadership of the country. Dupont took on the position of
deputy premier.

A charismatic man, Ian Smith, soon won the admiration of the white
population in the country by voicing and standing up for his beliefs.
One of which was that if Britain continued to pressure for majority rule
before granting independence, Rhodesia would do what the Americans

had done; declare unilateral independence from Britain. I thought about that notion and how only a few years earlier when Stan Garrick had espoused that idea, he had been ridiculed by the mere handful of votes he had received at the polling booth, now the tide was changing dramatically in favor of that once "absurd" direction. The unilateral declaration of independence or "U.D.I." as it was commonly being referred to, was on everyone's lips.

World opinion had turned adversely against Rhodesia, the press reporters that had flowed into the country all seemed to be competing for who could file the more "sensational" story about the country back to their press rooms overseas. One over zealous photographer had gone to the extent of taking a picture of Cecil Square, a park in the center of Salisbury, where a number of blacks would go to lie down and relax during their lunch hour. The photograph appeared in the overseas press with a caption to the effect that the men relaxing in the park were in fact dead bodies and victims of a mass shooting after rioting had broken out in the capital city.

Reports such as these were doing incalculable damage to any hopes the country may have had of sorting out the political differences. Many Rhodesians came to believe that their backs were up against a wall and their only hope for survival was to stand their ground. Ian Smith, the former fighter pilot and native born Rhodesian, seemed to be the strong leader needed to guide the struggle for survival.

The black political factions were also consolidating their positions, the Soviets were backing Joshua Nkomo in the west, and the Chinese were supporting the reverend Ndabaningi Sithole in the East, Unfortunately, the moderates had no great powers to back them and were losing ground fast to the power players.

Business life had drawn to a standstill as Rhodesia was now considered a bad risk for international investors and there was little incentive for the locals to spend, to build houses, or, plan for an uncertain future. I too, was being told by some of my friends that I had chosen a very bad time to open my shop with so much uncertainty about the future and that I had little chance of success. I merely shrugged off the negative comments. People needed to buy products whether times were good or bad. I just hoped that I had selected the right products to sell. Motorcar and I worked on. It was the last Friday in October and the store which I had named "Ivan's Cycles and Hardware," was due to open the following Monday, the first day of November, 1964.

After putting the last finishing touches to the store, Motorcar and I sat down in the middle of the shop on the cold vinyl floor, exhausted, looking around at our handiwork. I turned to Motorcar and for the first time voiced my concern; "Do you think anyone will buy from us, Motorcar?" Motorcar merely returned my gaze with his own questioning look. The absurdity of my "unanswerable" remark hit both of us at the same time and we broke into fits of laughter. "Well, young friend, if no one buys from us at least we have built a good looking shop! Now let us rest this weekend and be fresh for Monday when we open!" Motorcar replied, putting his hand on my shoulder in a comforting fashion. "Good idea, have a good weekend Motorcar!" I answered, and we commenced to lock up the store. Once outside, Motorcar briskly climbed on his bicycle and waved a goodnight, saying that he was going to spend the weekend visiting friends. I waved back at him as he rode off into the darkness.

As I walked towards my auto, I caught sight of a Jaguar sports car at the far end of the nearly empty parking lot and paused. A cold shudder suddenly ran down my back. Benny was sitting in it, watching me.

That evening when I arrived home, Chantelle phoned from Brussels to wish me success with the new shop. The two of us were thousands of miles apart and had really spent little time together, yet we had become so much a part of each others lives. The conversation ended with my having to soothe Chantelle's fears about what was happening in the political sphere of Rhodesia.

Sitting down for dinner with my mother, she also wished me success in the new venture. However, she too, was nervous about the circumstances and expressed her concern for my prospects of doing well in the light of the developments in the country. I was more than aware of the risks involved, but it was now too late to turn back. So, I calmly responded, "Mom don't worry about me, all I can do is my best, if the business doesn't work I will make sure no one will be hurt, I will find a job and pay off everyone that I owe!"

Sunday night I barely slept, thinking about the opening of the shop. Monday morning arrived, Motorcar and I set off to open the shop. Arriving at the parking lot, I was surprised to see a large crowd of people with bicycles milling around outside my store. I could hardly believe my eyes, "What is going on here Motorcar?" I asked.

"Well young friend," Motorcar replied, "I could see that you were worried whether anyone would buy from us, so I spent the weekend in the African township around the beerhalls telling everyone that you were opening a bicycle shop, that you are a good man who will treat them fairly, and that they should support you. So, I suppose they listened to what I had to say!"

"Thank you, Motorcar!" I said, with my eyes clouding, "Let's go and look after our customers!"

Motorcar and I made our way through the crowd and opened the doors for business. To my delight the customers streamed into the store, and it was nearly midday before there was enough of a lull to take a breather. The poor mechanic was so overwhelmed by the number of bicycles left for repairs, that he had to stack them on the floor all the way up to the ceiling to maintain some space to work in.

After lunch time, Amos visited the shop with a group of his police friends. They too, brought their bicycles in for repairs and to buy spare parts. The evening brought a different type of customer, the apartment dwellers returning home from work, they stopped in to look around and purchase hardware and electrical needs.

As time passed, the prospects for the store to succeed began to look good. Motorcar, the mechanic Solomon, and myself, worked long and hard hours, keeping pace with the small but growing business. After a few weeks, I also found it necessary to hire a second mechanic to help out with the mounting repair jobs. At the end of the first month I made out a commission payment from the profits to Motorcar that was equal to nearly four times his usual salary.

When I handed the money to Motorcar, Motorcar looked at me in a puzzled way. "What is this for?" He asked. "That is the commission I promised for the sales you have made!" I replied. "What is a commission?" Motorcar queried. "That is a percentage of profit from the sale of the goods!" I said, attempting to explain. "Percentage? Profit?" Motorcar repeated, looking down at the money placed in his hand. Then he beamed his big smile "I think I like this percentage, profit business!" He walked away gratefully shaking his head, murmuring to himself "Percentage?…Profit?"

Benny had banned the salespeople of Royal Cycles from making sales calls on my business. However, during the months that followed, many of them stopped in anyway, to make personal visits and offer their assistance. On one occasion, while Benny was away on business in Europe, a salesperson arrived with a truckload of bicycles, delivered with a note from my mother Rae, saying they were a gift from her to help in my business.

The intuition I had about opening my own business was proving to be the right one, but that was one of the few things going right around me. Benny was tightening his grip on the family business, I could only watch, and wait for the right time to take on Benny. I wanted to be financially strong to handle the battle. Politically, the confrontation between Rhodesia and the rest of the world was building up to the country's detriment. Britain as the colonial power, lead the way as the main adversary.

Ian Smith and the British Prime Minister, Harold Wilson held several rounds of negotiations. They had come close on many occasions to reaching an agreement on several issues, but stumbled on the main point of majority rule. Citing the chaos and corruption that had ensued in the newly independent countries to the North, the Rhodesians were standing firm in their conviction that the country was not yet ready for majority rule. They submitted alternatives to get around the stumbling block; such as an "A" and "B" voting rolls. The "A" roll votes would be for the whites voting for their members of parliament and the "B" roll for the blacks electing their members, which would ensure a form of parity in electing members to the legislative body. Britain held steadfast to the notion of majority rule, before granting full independence.

Rhodesians felt frustrated, believing that a system that may have worked well in developed countries in Europe and America, had little chance of success when imposed and applied to a developing nation in Africa. Here the rules were different and the level of sophistication amongst the majority of tribespeople was a little above primitive. The breakdown of the systems in the countries to the North of Rhodesia after gaining majority rule, was living proof of those fears.

Ian Smith and the Rhodesian Government threatened to go the "U.D.I" way, and declare unilateral independence, if Britain insisted on the majority rule pre-condition before the grant of sovereignty. The era of the moderates was fading, the time emerging was for which corner one chose to be in between the two pugilists, one side conservative, the other liberal. It seemed that if you were a white Rhodesian there was very little choice left…it had to be U.D.I.!

While the political tug of war raged, Rhodesians tried to make the most of living conditions under a stressful environment, attempting to maintain a semblance of social life. I joined a Jewish youth club, called "The Zionist Youth Organization." The club was comprised of some of the most decent young people, one could imagine. All in their late teens or in their early twenties, they were a fun loving bunch of young people who got together once a week for a social at differing venues, sometimes at one of the members' houses who had been brave enough to host about a hundred guests, sometimes at rented venues where guest speakers from all walks of life were invited to give talks.

The name of the organization was probably a misnomer, although most of the members were Jewish, it was more of a social club involved in socializing and charity work. We had set ourselves the goals of organizing functions such as dances and rock band competitions. The proceeds from which would go to charities, towards building our own youth center and for socials.

I enjoyed the organized activities and found it to be a pleasant break away from my daily business life. I progressed from being a member, to the groups' committee, and at the next annual election that year, was voted in as chairman of the society.

Youth groups were very popular in Salisbury, there were twenty-six such clubs, mostly representing religious or ethnic backgrounds. There was a lot of interaction and competition between the different youth societies. I and the leaders of the other various groups believed that irrespective of our backgrounds, we were all Rhodesians and as such, a lot of camaraderie and friendship flowed amongst these young people in inter-club sports, socials and dances.

The big event each year was the "Youth Mayor's Ball." A major youth function and dance. Where all the societies each nominated four representatives to run for election as the Youth Mayor and Mayoress of the city of Salisbury. The Youth Mayor's post was coupled with the position of Chairman of the Youth Council, which co-ordinated activities between the youth societies and was also, the representative of the youth of the city.

I was nominated as one of my clubs representatives, along with three of my friends from the society. It was October 1965 and the Ball and election were to be held the following January.

As proud as I was at being Chairman of the club and being selected to run for the position of Youth Mayor, I maintained my prime focus on the cycle and hardware business, which was growing steadily. Also, in October, Mr. Johnson the owner of the shopping center, approached me to inform that he had recently completed building a new shopping center a few miles away in the suburb of Borrowdale. He asked if I would be interested in opening a second shop in the new center on the same favorable terms as the present lease agreement. "I think you've got balls, young man. I'd be happy to rent you space—we'd be helping each other, you know!" Mr. Johnson told me.

I thought about the offer and after a few days agreed to lease the new space, setting a target date of opening the store in December, to be in time for the Christmas sales. I offered the position of manager at the new shop to Motorcar, which he politely refused, saying that he was happy with what he was doing, with earning his salary plus "percentage...profit!"

Ian Smith had recently returned to the country after a last ditch attempt to solve the political problems. A meeting with the British Prime Minister, Harold Wilson, had concluded with both men holding stubbornly to their viewpoints. It was clear that the differences were irreconcilable. Wilson had also threatened that Britain might use force or sanctions, if Rhodesia decided to go it alone and declared unilateral independence. Rhodesians waited with baited breath as to what was going to happen next.

November 11th, 1965, Rhodesians were informed by the local newspaper and radio station, to listen to a special address to the nation to be given that morning by the Prime Minister, Ian Smith. An announcement was also made that there was to be a hook up of the speech on the South African Broadcasting Corporations network, to South Africa's listeners. I nervously, tuned in to the radio at my shop and listened to Smith's speech...The Unilateral Declaration of Independence was being made!

After the speech I turned off the radio and feared for the worst! Would there be civil war? Was rioting going to break out? I thought about my mother at Royal Cycles. If there were going to be problems, I wanted to be close by to protect her. Leaving my store in Motorcar's care, I got into my car and drove towards Royal Cycles. Along the way, what I saw, was the opposite of what I had expected; The street traffic was as usual, pedestrians of all races were calmly walking along the pavements, the city center appeared quiet with fewer shoppers, but everything else seemed normal...no rioting or problems of any kind.

I heaved a sigh of relief when I finally arrived at the parking lot at Royal Cycles, everything I had seen along the way, had been peaceful. Entering in to the business I passed Benny, we barely acknowledged each other with a simple nod. I went to my mother's office, and found her seated behind her desk, looking out the window and deep in thought. I went to her and gave her a hug. "Hello Mom," perching myself on the desk, I asked "What do you think of the news?" "I am scared!" She said and continued, "Like everything else, it is the fear of the unknown. If the world leaves us alone, we have a good chance of solving the political problems amongst ourselves, but I don't think we are going to be allowed the peace to do that! Politicians, sitting in the safety of their armchairs overseas are going to try and dictate what we should be doing, and that is going to cause a lot of turmoil in Rhodesia!"

"How do you think the political situation is going to affect business?" I asked. "It has been affecting our business for quite some time already!" she replied, "With the introduction of exchange control regulations and import quotas, we haven't had the foreign currency to buy parts for the bicycles, and the quota imposed by the government has limited us to purchasing seventy-five percent of what we bought last year. There is already talk that with U.D.I, the situation will become even worse, particularly if the sanctions that have been threatened by Britain and the rest of the world are imposed!" She said.

"It seems that I have picked a really bad time to open my second store." I said, feeling a small sense of forebodence, "Britain has threatened the first part of the sanctions will be the imposition of an oil embargo—if that does happen, people will be looking for alternative means of transport, namely bicycles!" I added. My mother looked at me and replied; "Yes, that could be a boost to business, but because of the currency restrictions and government quota, we won't be able to supply the demand, so what do we do?" "There's not much you can do on the import side, Mom, but I know what I am going to do at the retail end! I am going to buy every bicycle I can lay my hands on, to be prepared for that event!" I said, thinking that I could turn the bad situation into an advantage. "Aren't you taking a very big risk, by doing that?" My mother cautioned. "Yes, I suppose I am, but to use that old cliché, no risk, no reward!" I answered.

"Ivan, perhaps I can help you reduce some of the risk." my mother said thinking out aloud. "Benny does not need to know what you are doing. Buy as many bicycles as you can from your usual distributors and what you don't sell I will buy back from you. With the shortage in supply of bicycles, Royal will always be able to re-sell them even if it means taking a small loss!" "But mom, that means you are taking all the risk?" I questioned. "Yes, but the risk is minimal, and that is what I would like to do to help. Now, go and buy your bicycles!" She replied.

I left Royal Cycles feeling good. My mother was finally going to stand up to Benny by helping me in my business.

Driving back, I looked around me and saw the way Salisbury had grown over the years. "So much has changed!" I thought. Even the times when a marauding lion or other wild animal would venture into the city, was now a part of history. There were probably a few wild animals left within twenty miles of Salisbury, but most of them had been relegated to life in the large game reserves or parks as a necessity for their survival. Rhodesia was rapidly moving into the twentieth century, politically, socially, and environmentally.

Returning to my store, I was greeted by Motorcar. "How is your Mother?" He asked. "She is well!" I replied. "Young friend, what is this 'U.D.I.' that so many people are talking about?" Motorcar asked. I shrugged my shoulders at the immensity of the question, and attempted to uncloud the politics by explaining the events leading to and the meaning of the declaration of independence. When I finished my explanation, Motorcar shook his head in puzzlement, "We have a good life in this country, does this 'politics' mean that we are going to have trouble now?" He asked. I shook my head not knowing the answer and said, "I really don't know Motorcar, for everyone's sake, I hope not!"

The next few weeks proved to be very hectic for me, with the opening of the new shop in Borrowdale. There were problems in finding a suitable manager and completing the store shelving in time. Though, the grand opening did happen as scheduled, on the first day of December, 1965. I had been so involved with the new shop, that despite Motorcar's reluctance to be a manager, he was virtually left on his own with the help of an assistant to run the business in the Avenues.

I had bought every bicycle I could from the distributors which amounted to three hundred and fifty cycles, and rented a small warehouse to store them in.

The political events were also moving rapidly. Britain led the world in imposing sanctions. An embargo on oil exports to Rhodesia caused a minor panic among many Rhodesians who feared that they would be unable to buy gasoline for their cars. I had a run on both stores for bicycles. Customers who drove to my stores in Jaguars, Mercedes and other fancy cars, bought bicycles, to ensure that if petrol ran out they would have some form of transportation.

Within weeks I sold out of bicycles and all my distributors fearing a shortage in supply, rationed the sale of cycles to their customers. I decided to attend the police auctions, held once a month at the Market Square, where unclaimed bicycles from closed cases, were auctioned off. I bought my first lot, which consisted of a hundred bicycles in various stages of disrepair, carted them to my shops where the mechanics repaired them and then made a handsome profit on the sale of the used bicycles.

As January 1966 rolled in, it was obvious the chances that I had taken with the purchase of so many cycles had been successful...However, Rhodesians were beginning to adjust to life under sanctions. Petrol rationing cards and coupons were introduced which reduced the heavy demand for bicycles. Business settled in both my shops to sales of goods I was able to obtain and sell on a rationed basis.

The youth mayoral elections were now only a matter of a couple of weeks away. I knew that there was going to be stiff competition from the representatives of the other youth organizations. I had a theme in which I strongly believed: "Unity in youth; Planning ahead for a generation of co-operation and understanding!"

It was a simple theme—take out the politics and set instead common goals for the youth organizations, such as raising funds for a youth center or charity events; where young people from different societies and walks of life could work together without the barriers of politics or race. I based my thoughts on the premise that working together would help create a knowledge and understanding of the different cultures, overcoming the myths and fears of the unknown!

I believed that as the future generation took its place in Rhodesian society, the friendships developed during the days of our youth by the future leaders, would encourage a co-existence overriding differences of color, religion, and culture. I was hopeful that if selected as a finalist I would have the opportunity to present my thoughts at the ball. This was a small contribution to what I believed was the formula for a Rhodesia of the future to succeed. I also realized that my ideas put me in the same court as moderates, but it was what I believed, and I was going to speak out on my thoughts.

The days leading up to the election were hectic with many preparations and friendly competition amongst the contenders for the youth mayoral post. The delegates, voted by their youth society to represent them, had to endure an interview with an impartial selection panel comprised of six members of respected elders of the community. The panel was made up from diverse members of society and included the Dean of Law at the newly established University of Rhodesia, a well known Rhodesian broadcaster and the current Miss Rhodesia. Their job was to scrutinize each candidate on the basis of academic record, achievements, personality and ability to represent the youth in the city. They would chose Eight finalists, four men and four women, who would be asked to deliver a speech at the ball, on which the final decision for the selection of Youth Mayor and Youth Mayoress and the two deputies would be made.

The night of the ball arrived. The venue was a large ballroom at the Rhodes Community Center. The hall soon filled with members of the different youth organizations and the elite of Salisbury's society. The candidates running for election milled about nervously with the guests, attempting to look cool and relaxed. Then the process began, each candidate was interviewed by the panel in the privacy of a separate room of the facility. At midnight, the chairman of the panel announced the finalists. My name was amongst them and the announcement was followed by a loud round of applause.

I was pleasantly shocked to hear my name and made my way onto the stage to make the speech. I illustrated my theme of unity, by holding up a crystal glass goblet, and said; "As a whole this crystal glass serves a useful purpose. It can hold water to give us life for the future, but if I were to drop and shatter it, the broken pieces would become useless and serve no function. So would we too, if divided like those broken slivers of crystal!"

I ended my speech and returned to my table to listen to the speeches given by the remaining finalists. They were impressive! Each of the speeches presented by the selected participants had been well prepared, and were delivered to the audience with enthusiasm and skill. When the speeches were over the panel quietly retired to their room to make the final decision.

I sat at my table in quiet conversation with my friends. There was no point in worrying over something that was now in the hands of the panel, I concluded that worrying would not improve my chances of being elected, so I concentrated on enjoying what was left of the evening.

The panel returned and announced their selections; the deputy Youth Mayoress was from the Hellenic Youth Club, Helas Theopoulis. The deputy Youth Mayor was from the Harari township, the largest of the youth groups, and the first ever black elected, George Tambala. His selection brought a loud round of applause from the crowd. The Youth Mayoress was Anna Caulders, from the Sarum Youth Club. The announcement brought in even larger applause.

Finally, the announcement of Youth Mayor. "The new Youth Mayor is….Ivan Bender!" I was overwhelmed at hearing my name! I got up from from my seat and went to the stage to accept the Mayoral gown and sash of office, in doing so, I walked through a standing ovation of people at the ball.

The four of us newly elected youngsters stood in a huddled group accepting the congratulations of our peers and being photographed for the newspapers. The new black deputy, humbly extended his hand to me, "Congratulations…sir!" He said. I took his hand, "Congratulations to you too, George!. By the way, my name is Ivan, not 'Sir'…and I wasn't *just* making a speech about working together—I meant what I said!" George smiled and nodded in acknowledgment.

Chapter Nine

My social life was elevated to a new plain with the election as Youth Mayor. I attended formal functions, gave speeches on behalf of the youth of the city and spent a lot of time in organizing youth activities. Anna and I met on a regular basis with the City Council elders and the Mayor of Salisbury.

We were also invited to meet with the Prime Minister, Ian Smith, for morning tea on one occasion. The Prime Minister was a cordial man but very direct in his speech, who came to the point quickly and wasted few words. I found it very difficult to asses his feelings on the topics as we talked. While Smith's voice showed enthusiasm from time to time, his gaze remained with the same constant bland expression as he spoke, his face masking any trace of emotion. The visit was a matter of courtesy. The subject of politics was never brought up, a thoughtfulness which I noticed and respected. The meeting ended with his offer to help the youth of the city with our fund raising events, which we gratefully acknowledged.

Little did I imagine then, that although our paths would briefly cross from time to time while attending formal functions—that the next time we would meet again on a face to face basis, would be towards the end of the century in America. Thirty three years into the future, I again meet Ian Smith where I was his host at a cocktail party and book signing function in Annapolis, Maryland, to promote his book "The Great Betrayal."

One common factor impressed me in my meetings with the different leaders of Rhodesian society; when it came to matters concerning the youth of the country, political and racial barriers seemed to melt away, everyone did what they could to support and help.

Rae swelled with pride that her son had been selected as the Youth Mayor of Salisbury. Motorcar went around telling his friends that he worked for the "Young Chieftain." Chantelle, when we spoke on the telephone, was also happy for me and announced the good news that she intended to visit Rhodesia during her July college vacations that year. I could hardly wait to see her again! Benny, on the other hand, when our paths happened to cross during my visits to Royal Cycles to visit my mother, did not acknowledge the election other than a jab that the post of Youth Mayor was an "insignificant position!"

Anna and I worked well together in our Youth Mayoral duties and with the deputies to bring the youth of the city together. George, the deputy Youth Mayor, and I worked particularly hard to combine black and white youth activities and it was not surprising that in the combined functions, such as inter club soccer, color was quickly forgotten and replaced with friendly competitiveness and rivalry.

George had graduated from the Highfield High School and had been offered a scholarship to attend the London School of Economics the following year. In our combined quest to further understanding between the youth of the city, George invited me to give a talk at the Highfield Black Youth Club. The deputy had approached his former teacher at the school, Robert Mugabe, to be allowed to use the school hall as the venue for my talk to the youth members. Mugabe had given his permission.

Mugabe had recently been released from detention for his political activities against the state. He was one of Reverend Sithole's top lieutenants in Z.A.N.U., the Zimbabwe African National Union, which represented the Mashona tribes' political faction. It was an open secret that they were receiving backing from the Chinese Communists.

I gave my speech to the youth club, speaking about the inter-club activities and emphasized my theme of unity. My talk was generally well received by the audience with one notable exception; Mugabe sat quietly at the back of the hall and showed very little reaction. After the meeting, George introduced me to Mugabe. I noticed George's nervous fear in the presence of the political leader, which in turn made me feel uncomfortable. I began to wonder what George knew about this man that so scared him. I also, could not help but observe that the politician had the cleanest shining face I had ever seen, almost as though his skin had been polished with a glossy varnish—and spoke with a very deliberate Queens' English.

Robert Mugabe and I spoke for a few minutes, during the course of the conversation it became obvious to me that Mugabe wanted more political activity within the youth groups. When I resisted the suggestion, Mugabe cordially but abruptly ended all conversation and went off to speak to one of his associates outside in the hallway. Little did I imagine how diverse and opposing our two paths would take in the future, or that Mugabe would one day unseat Sithole as leader of the Mashona tribal faction and become the country's first prime minister as independent Zimbabwe.

As we left the school, I asked George about Robert Mugabe. I sensed a fear and a very real reluctance by George to talk about the man, so I decided to change the subject and the conversation turned to the planning of future youth activities. My curiosity for information regarding Mugabe the politician, would have to remain unanswered for the time being.

During the many inter club socials, music was usually provided by a pop group from the Sarum Youth Society. One of the group's musicians Andy Harper, played the guitar and was also an active member in the society's committee and on the Salisbury youth council. Andy and I became friends. As our friendship grew, I was invited to Andy's house to meet his family. Andy's father, to my surprise, turned out to be William Harper, a cabinet minister in the Rhodesian government, and at that time, held the portfolio of Minister of Internal Affairs.

Coincidentally, political events were now in the process of moving very rapidly, Rhodesia was declared a republic. Clifford Dupont was "kicked upstairs" and appointed as the country's first President. William Harper replaced Dupont as the Deputy Prime Minister of Rhodesia. Britain took the Rhodesian issue to the United Nations, invoking Chapter Seven of the U.N. Charter, which declared that the situation was a "threat to world peace," world wide sanctions and embargoes were imposed against the country by the United Nations.... Rhodesians in the meantime, were left puzzled as to who exactly they were supposed to be a threat to?

The Rhodesian government for their part imposed censorship on the news media of the country. So while the rest of the world had a fair idea of the events occurring in the country, Rhodesians were kept in the dark as to some of the developments around us. I looked forward to my visits to the Harpers, as I would sometimes hear news unavailable through the newspapers and radio.

When I would drive to the Deputy Prime Minister's official residence in North Avenue to visit my friend, it always amazed me, how little security was visibly provided for the protection of such a high ranking politician. At the open gated entrance to the driveway stood a solitary armed black police officer. This in my mind, was certainly no deterrent to anyone wishing to launch an attack on the vulnerable government residence, particularly as it was situated next door and within easy access to the residence of the Prime Minister.

During one of the evening visits, I was at the residence waiting for Andy to return from a music practice. I was alone in the house with the deputy Prime Minister.

Mr. Harper offered me a drink and we entered into conversation, which gradually drifted into politics. "The real problem the country is facing is not so much a black and white conflict, but a China versus Soviet expansionism situation." Harper told me. "From the documents our security boys and undercover agents have captured, we have the proof that they are both independently and in competition with each other, training a nucleus army of guerrillas to wage bush warfare against this country, far worse than the Mau Mau acts of terrorism in Kenya ever were. Their main training camps are in Russia, North Vietnam, and China. The Chinese are the major threat, as they have a foothold in Tanzania, now they want to move into Rhodesia. Should they succeed in taking over this country, the white population will become an insignificant factor, caught in the middle of the struggle for control between those two communist powers. The Chinese have wedged themselves with the politicians of the majority tribal group the Mashona, and the Russians, the smaller but warrior political group of the Ndebele . At the moment they are no match for our army, and it is important that we keep it that way, for the foreseeable future. We have for our part, started training our own elite group of men specifically to handle counter insurgency and bush warfare!"

"Talking about the army, did you know that almost eighty percent of our personnel is made up of black Rhodesians?" Harper continued, "…and the army as a whole is probably the best disciplined fighting force in Africa and second in strength only to the South African military!"

"Do you think we can avoid a guerrilla war?" I asked. "I don't know son, even if we are able to reach a settlement with Britain, the Soviets and Chinese seem very determined to get a foothold in this country as a base of operations for the next step in their objective, which is, South Africa!" Harper replied.

I was curious about the elite fighting force being trained to handle bush warfare that Harper had mentioned, but before I could ask any further questions, Andy arrived at the house and the topic abruptly transformed to one of that evenings music practice session. So my curiosity was going to have to be satisfied at some later time.

Johannesburg, South Africa was to be the site of that year's International Youth Conference to be held over a long weekend in March, 1966; to my delight, Anna and I were chosen to represent the youth of Rhodesia at the meeting. We were to leave on a Friday morning and to return the following Monday night.

Flying into the South African city, Anna and I were given a cordial welcome at the airport by the Junior Mayor and youth councilors of Johannesburg. The metropolitan area of Johannesburg was a vast spread out area with a population of a few million, the second largest populated city on the entire African continent, next to Cairo. It was also the financial and mining capital of South Africa. The city had the unusual feature of being surrounded by massive gold dumps, man made hills, that were the result of years of gold mining around the area. Anna and I were taken to our hotel in the Hillbrow suburb, which bordered on the outskirts of the city proper. Hillbrow had the reputation of being the most populated square mile on earth, comprising of residential skyscraper apartments equal in height to any of those in New York or Chicago, it also had an exceptionally high crime rate.

Anna and I checked into rooms at the Rondebosch hotel in Edith Cavell Street, and we prepared for the first day's meeting at the conference.

Meeting with other young people from around the world was a unique and enlightening experience for us, especially hearing the other youth leaders views on world affairs and their varied perspectives on the situation on Rhodesia. They all seemed very interested in hearing the first hand experiences from Anna and I of living in our country.

I returned to the hotel just after 9 P.M. that evening. Excited about being in a new city, I decided to take a walk around Hillbrow and do some sightseeing. Outside the hotel, I was surprised to see that for such a densely populated residential area, the pavements were bare of pedestrians walking along the streets. I thought perhaps, the high crime rate was keeping the residents indoors at night and decided to be cautious as to where I went, making sure to walk only in highly lit up streets.

As I walked taking in the sights, I noticed the only other person visible, was a black man ambling along in the block ahead of me. After a few minutes a policeman walking his beat turned into the street. He saw the black man and went to him asking for identification, the man produced his identification, which the policeman scrutinized with his torch. The policeman handed back the I.D. The man attempted to continue walking, but the policeman hadn't finished with him yet, he grabbed the man by the shirt and slapped him across the head. I was walking close by now and could see the fear in the Black man's face. The policeman saw me, and ignored me, pulling the black man into a darkened alley, between two tall buildings. There, I could hear the dull thud of punches being delivered and the man's groans. I felt sickened to my stomach by what was happening and my first instinct was to intervene and stop the policeman, but I knew better than to interfere! I was a visitor to this country, so reluctantly I kept walking on. After a few minutes I looked back to see the policeman emerge from the alley alone and walk in my direction. As he passed by, I saw that he had a smile on his face.

Anger swelled up inside me. Anger, because the man who was wearing a police uniform had seen fit to abuse the law and his position, using his authority to beat up another man for no apparent reason. If this was his way of instilling fear into the minds of any would-be-criminal perhaps, it was sickening! Anger, at myself, in that I had stood by as an observer, feeling helpless to do anything to stop the beating. I decided that my sightseeing was over for the night and headed back towards his hotel, as I did, I glanced back to see the black man staggering out of the alley.

The next day it was my turn to give a brief speech to the conference. I spoke on the need we had as the next generation to promote understanding and cooperation between the youth of the different nations, I also, emphasized the need to communicate to the young men joining the police forces that they were a tool to maintaining stability and peace in a community, not a weapon to instill their own brand of authority or fear amongst the peoples they served.

After my speech, one of the delegates congratulated me, "You gave that talk with a lot of passion and fire in your words, you must believe very strongly in what you said?" he asked. I reflected back to the event of the previous night "I do!" I replied, and repeated the words, "I do!"

Anna and my visit was comprehensively reported in the South African Sunday papers as well as the Rhodesian newspapers, which carried our photographs and an excerpt of my fiery speech on the role of the police. The visit to South Africa drew to an end with our meeting and making many new friends from the different countries, also, we extended an invitation to the Junior Mayor of Johannesburg to make a reciprocal visit to Salisbury later that year.

Flying back to Salisbury, Anna and I talked about the interesting people we had met and the likelihood of some of them maturing into future leaders of their respective nations. "Are you interested in taking up a career in politics?" Anna asked. "No." I replied, laughing at the thought, "Politics is probably the furthest thing on my mind right now, I have never lost my interest in the law, and I still dream of one day finishing my studies and becoming a lawyer." Anna gave me a warm smile and leaned over to my side of the seat giving me a kiss on the cheek, "I hope your dreams come true!" She said.

Back in Salisbury, I settled into my now usual active life, running the businesses during the day and organizing youth affairs at night. A few days after my return, Benny phoned, saying he had an important proposition to make and that he wanted me to meet with him at Royal Cycles. Intrigued that Benny wanted to actually talk to me, I agreed to the meeting.

When I entered into the office, Benny was sitting behind his desk, he looked up and was wearing the familiar phony smile, I shuddered at the sight. "Come in, make yourself comfortable! Can I get you something to drink?" Benny offered. The unusual display of courtesy puzzled me and immediately put me on my guard. I sat down, "No thanks." I replied eager to get to the point of the meeting, "What did you want to see me about?"

"Your mother and I have come to an arrangement concerning Royal Cycles. She has offered me forty percent of the net profits in the company as an incentive to keep me on as president of the business!" I could already feel the anger building up inside me as I sensed a touch of gloating in Benny's voice. Benny continued, "Which brings me to the point of this meeting, we have an opening in Fort Victoria for the position of manager for The Eastern district of the country. I think that you have proved that you can sell bicycles, so I am offering the position to you, starting the first of next month!"

"Oh, Really?" I replied, "And what am I supposed to do with my two present businesses?" Benny's smile broadened, "Royal cycles will take them over!" He said. "For how much?" I asked. " Surely, you don't expect your mother's business to pay you anything for the two businesses that have only been in existence for a few months, now do you, Ivan? You have already made a nice little profit from them, let it go at that!" Benny said, matter of factly.

I was now convinced that Benny must have become irrational with greed! Playing along with the situation, I asked; "What about my responsibilities as Youth mayor in Salisbury?" Benny had an answer, "That position runs out with time at the end of one year, someone else can take it over for the remaining period you have left!"

"I don't understand…why are you telling me about my mother giving you forty percent of the net profit of the business, and why are you offering me a Job?" I asked. "Very simple, in consideration of the job offer, I want you to sign this agreement my lawyers have drawn up!" Benny replied, placing a four page document in front of me. "What is this?" I asked, picking up the document. "Have you read your Father's will?" Benny queried. "I have never read the contents, but I know that everything was left to my mother!" I stated. "Yes, everything has been left to her, but in a Trust! After she passes away, the named sharing beneficiaries are yourself, your brother and sister. You personally will receive the controlling share of fifty one percent of the company. This agreement ensures that the arrangement concerning my share of net profits will continue indefinitely!"

Suddenly everything became crystal clear. The man was being irrational all right, irrational like a fox! "What if I refuse to sign the document?" I asked. "Then I will tell you the same thing I told your mother, I will walk away from this business and bring it tumbling down like a house of cards!" Benny threatened, his smile broadening into a smirk.

"Then do it!" I retorted.

"What!?" Benny questioned. I picked up the document he had put before me and tore it up, "I said, DO IT! Nobody is barring your path to the door. Do it!"

Suddenly, Benny was no longer smiling and the smirk had gone from his face. "You obviously do not care all that much about your mother's financial security and her peace of mind with the business!" He said accusingly.

"The emotional blackmail, taking advantage of my mother for your own financial gain, I suppose, is an indication of just how much you care for her?" I jabbed back. "Frankly, Benny, I think you need this business more than it needs you! You have threatened to walk out and bring the business down like a house of cards, if I don't sign your agreement? Well I am telling you that I will never sign any such agreement, so why don't you walk out right now!" Benny sat in his seat staring at me, he made no movement.

"I didn't think you would!" I said standing up to leave, and added; "Benny, apart from being cousins, the only thing we have in common, is that we both hope my mother has a long and healthy life, otherwise, you would have me to contend with!" As I walked out the office, I glanced back and noticed that Benny was still not wearing the phony smile.

Leaving Royal Cycles, I felt the anger surging up inside as I thought of Benny's cheap attempt to manipulate me, as he had done for so long to my mother. I needed to find a place where I could just walk and clear my mind. I drove to the city center, parked the car and attempted to lose myself amongst the throng of pedestrians and shoppers. Almost like a magnet, I was drawn towards Manica road and the place where my father had opened the original bicycle retail store shortly after moving to Salisbury. The business had been sold a few years previously, with the expansion into the Manufacturing side of Bicycles. The business had been bought out by an old friend of my father, John Osborne, the store now traded under the name of "Osborne Cycles."

I stood outside the store window looking in and remembering as a child visiting the shop almost daily, my father busily serving customers, yet always taking the time to talk to me. When the shop got very busy, I would go behind the counter and help with the sales, seeing from time to time a proud glance from my father, at my polite and sometimes nervous sales to customers.

I ventured inside the store and looked around at the stack of bicycles and spare parts on display. "Checking out the competition are you, son?" A voice Teasingly challenged me from behind. Turning, I saw that it was Mister Osborne. "How are you, Sir?" I Asked. "Not too bad, Lad. From the business aspect things are going well." He said. "I really was not trying to check your business out!" I said, trying to explain my presence in the shop. "That's all right lad, matter of fact, I was thinking of contacting you! I haven't been doing too well with my health lately, the doctors seem to think it may be cancer! My wife and I have talked about my situation, and I am thinking about retiring in about six months— would you be interested in buying the shop from me?" Osborne asked. The suggestion came as a total surprise. "This was my father's original bicycle shop. Of course, I would be very interested in talking about it, but I don't Know that I can afford to buy the shop!" I replied.

"I can make the purchase easy for you, lad, everything I have in the store is already paid for. So, if you are prepared in six months time to put in a small cash down payment, I will allow you to complete paying the balance of the purchase price in monthly installments from the profits you make from sales. The price I am asking is for the cost of the stock plus a small goodwill amount. I will reduce the present goodwill asking price from twenty thousand to one thousand five hundred pounds! Does that make it attractive enough for you, Ivan?" "Very attractive!" I said without hesitation. The thought of buying back my father's original bicycle business was tremendously appealing to me.

That evening I discussed the days occurrences with my mother, I told her what had happened with Benny, and the surprising offer from John Osborne to buy out his business. "Thank goodness your father left the ownership of the business in a trust. Otherwise, Benny would have tried to force my hand into giving him forty percent of the company shares, rather than having to settle for forty percent of the net profit!" She told me. "Why do you let him get away with it, Mom?" I asked. "Because, all I want is peace of mind, he recognizes that, and takes advantage of that fact by manipulating me with his threats of bringing the company down if I don't agree with his demands!" She replied. "For goodness sake Mom, why not call his bluff, the man is just hot air, he didn't walk out when I refused to sign the document he put before me today. Put your foot down on his demands and I think you will find that you will have a lot more peace of mind, once he realizes you are the boss and he can't bully you anymore!" I advised.

"Perhaps, I will do just that!" My mother replied. "Are you going to buy the store From John Osborne?" she asked. "Yes Mom, I am, the terms are very attractive and it is a golden opportunity to have a shop in the center of the city." I replied. "Then Ivan, I suggest that you keep that news to yourself for the time being, even though it is none of Benny's business as to what you do, you can expect him to try to interfere and stop you if he can!" She warned. "Don't worry Mom, at the moment, that information with the exception of yourself and Motorcar, is strictly between Mr. Osborne and me." I said.

The next day I told Motorcar in confidence of my intention to buy the new store in a few months. Motorcar received the news with approval and the quizzical comment "It is good that you are buying your father's shop back, but how are you going to run all three stores?" "With the help of managers, Motorcar. I have the time, and the breathing space of six months to look for the right persons!" I replied.

Rumors were beginning to circulate around Salisbury that Ian Smith and the British Prime Minister had started a new dialogue and round of negotiations aimed at solving their political differences. Apparently, they were on the brink of finding a settlement to the "Rhodesian Issue." A few weeks later, it seemed as though the deadlock had been broken with the announcement that Ian Smith and Harold Wilson were to fly out for a meeting on neutral territory off the coast of Gibraltar, aboard the British aircraft carrier, H.M.S. Tiger. Smith was gone for several days, reportedly in hard negotiations, before flying back to Salisbury with the news that a tentative agreement had been reached, subject to approval by the Rhodesian cabinet.

The agreement called for the setting up of an interim government consisting of a combination of some present white government leaders and opposition black and white politicians. They were to lead the country to eventual majority rule and Britain's grant of legitimate independence.

One of those named from the black opposition, was a religious figure-head, Bishop Abel Muzerwa, he had been seen coming to the forefront politically, as he had gained some ground in uniting the Shona and Ndbele factions. Less radical than the other black politicians, he presented a hope for peaceful transition.

The prospect of a pending settlement had some Rhodesians prematurely sighing with relief at the thought of a solution to the country's political problems, we looked forward for a return to normal life. Many of the Cabinet Ministers had given open support to Smith's deal with Britain and confirmation by the cabinet appeared to be a formality.

The Rhodesian Cabinet met the morning after Smith's return to the country to discuss the issues, and put to a vote the acceptance of the deal. Rhodesians waited with baited breath for the results of the voting. Deliberations within the cabinet inexplicably dragged and went on for many hours without an announcement.

That evening, I was due to attend a Youth Mayoral function, before leaving, I listened to the news, the cabinet was still locked in discussions. My function ended a little after ten thirty that night, and I eagerly headed to the car to listen to the radio. The Cabinet was still locked behind closed doors in discussions at the Prime Minister's office, there were still no results of the meeting.

I decided to drive by the Prime Minister's office, which was situated near the city center opposite the Parliament buildings on Union Avenue. There, a throng of international journalists and cameras, as well as a small crowd of interested Rhodesians, were milling about outside the doors to the office waiting for news to break. I parked my car and joined the crowd.

Upstairs, on the second floor facing the street, was a lighted open window, where men moving about in discussion could be seen. Occasionally, Smith and other cabinet members were drawn to the window to look out of the office at the crowd expectantly waiting on the street. One of the members of the crowd had a portable radio turned on, and was listening to a commentator describing the scene where we were standing. The deliberations continued.

Shortly after midnight, Smith emerged, leading the other Cabinet members onto the street. Cameras floodlit the area and reporters pushed against each other to get closer to hear the decision, Smith stopped in front of them to make a short announcement that the deal with Britain had been rejected! Waving a clenched fist, he loudly proclaimed "THE FIGHT GOES ON!"

With no agreement having been reached, Rhodesia was hurled back into being an outcast nation. Sanctions by the rest of the world tightened, Foreign currency ran low with tight government restrictions strictly imposed and prosecuted, quotas on imports into the country were increased to the point where businesses were restricted to bringing in a far smaller percentage than they had been able to before U.D.I. A stranglehold was closing around the Rhodesian economy.

Like all economic sanctions, the people who suffered the most were the poorest. The tribespeople, many of whom had no idea of politics, suddenly found themselves having to tighten their belts even further with the loss of available jobs and a slowing economy. The wealthy became wealthier, merely by circumventing the sanctions and supplying an ever increasing demand for less available goods.

Rhodesian businessmen were a resilient bunch of entrepreneurs, bringing to life the old maxim, "Necessity is the mother of invention!" When imported goods and parts ran short, they merely invented substitutes. Businesses, which previously would have stood no chance of competing against imported goods were springing into existence to meet the demands of a product starved nation. When spare parts to repair bicycles ran out, I joined the ingenious group by having my mechanics hand make replacements to do the job. Life was becoming as "normal" as could be, under the circumstances.

A short while after the negotiated settlement with Britain had failed, I visited Andy Harper. We talked about how life had changed under U.D.I. "Pity that we were not able to reach a final agreement with the British. Your father must have been disappointed with all of Smith's work ending in a negative vote by the cabinet." I commented. "On the contrary!" Andy replied, "The cabinet was actually prepared to accept the agreement between Smith and Wilson, it was my father who was against it, he did not think it was a good pact, that is why they took so long to reach a decision. It took him hours to persuade the other cabinet ministers to eventually reject the agreement!" I listened to what Andy said, although I offered no comment, the thought crossed my mind of questioning the wisdom of what had happened. I hoped the decision Harper had so influenced, would not come back to haunt Rhodesia.

The Month of July was approaching, with it would come the much awaited arrival of Chantelle. We spoke to each other often on the phone, each time we talked I could feel the excitement building between us at the expectation of being together. I could hardly wait to see her again, to hear her speak in person, to hold her and feel those beautiful lips against mine. Over two long years had passed since we had last seen each other and the wait had felt like a lifetime.

Fewer imported cars were able to make their way into Rhodesia, more for the reason of exchange control quota restrictions imposed by the government to stop foreign currency leaving the country, than the result of sanctions. The few cars that were being imported, were starting to fetch increasingly higher prices because of the shortage. I had some extra cash available and decided to buy a new car before prices rocketed to prohibitive heights. I liked sports cars and decided on a new British M.G.B convertible sports car, with a blue colored exterior and black interior leather seats.

On purchasing the car, I drove it out of the dealership and decided to take a drive into the countryside. I took off towards Lake Macillwaine game park, twenty miles away, where there was a large dam to supply Salisbury with it's water and a game preserve. I had the top down and felt the exhilaration of the fresh clear wind blowing against my face and hair as I drove along the road.

Arriving at the lake I turned and drove down one of the smaller side roads, towards the game park, coming to a pan of water where some Eland and Zebra were lazily basking in the sun and casually drinking from the muddy water. It was late afternoon and the time of day when the many varieties of animals would soon be drawn to the watering hole. This was nature's ritual before the animals settled down to rest in the waning hours of dusk and to seek the safety of shelter, as darkness enveloped the African sky.

A couple of black rhino broke out of the thick grass and ambled nearby. Oblivious of me due to their extreme shortsightedness, they made their way unperturbed towards the water to drink.

I alighted from my car and sat underneath the shade of a tree to watch the tranquil scene unfolding in front of me. A small herd of buffalo came into sight, cautiously checking out the safety of the pan before venturing to drink from the water. They were slightly startled by the emergence from the underbrush of a family of warthogs grunting their way to the water. I too, was startled by the sound of rustling from the grass behind the tree where I was sitting. A baby deer emerged from the bushes, sniffing around him the little animal was cautious, but seemed to have little fear of the human by the tree. The fawn approached me slowly, I pulled out a piece of sugar candy from my pocket and offered it to the animal, which it gently took into his mouth and munched at it. The fawn's mother a large doe walked into sight and the baby scampered off to join her heading in the direction of the pan, also to drink.

For the moment, in this tiny patch of the world, there was a peacefulness, the type that nature may have originally intended. Away from man's competing ideals of politics, business and lust for material gain. Here everything was equal, there was no concept of man's artificial devices, driven only by the instinct to eat and survive, the animals and nature were in harmony and at peace with each other. I for this brief moment with the wild, also felt in tune with nature, it was a time that I treasured.

Looking at the pan, I watched the two black rhinos quietly drinking from the edge of the water. They were some of the remaining few hundred of their species left in the world, almost driven to extinction by poachers in search of the lucrative payment for their ivory horns.

So much of the population of wild life had shrunken in size with the advancement of man's concrete jungles in my short lifetime; that I wondered how much man would leave of this precious African heritage, to enjoy in the coming years.

As dusk started to set, I reluctantly stood up to leave, taking a last look around at the tranquillity, I thought this was a place I wanted to show Chantelle. I hoped that she too, having been born in Africa, would enjoy this gift of nature.

Driving home, my mind filled with thoughts of Chantelle's visit. I had attempted to be diplomatic because I lived at home with my mother, to book and pay for Chantelle's accommodation during her proposed stay of three weeks, at the newly constructed Monomatapa hotel. The hotel was a grandly built modern building, comprising of twenty three floors of suites and had a magnificent overview of the large floral rich Salisbury gardens on the one side and a view of the city center on the other. When I had mentioned this to my mother, she had questioned me, "Didn't you stay with Chantelle in Brussels when you visited?" "Yes." I had replied. "…And this is the girl that you intend to marry, one day?" she asked, again I answered "Yes." "Well then, she is welcome to stay in our home!" With that comment, she had swept away the need for diplomacy and accommodation. Chantelle had happily received the news, and gratefully accepted the invitation to stay at the family house.

I thought of the time we had spent together in Brussels and wondered if she had changed much, how would she take to life in Salisbury? Those questions were soon to be answered.

The day of Chantelle's arrival, I drove to the airport to meet her. She was coming in on Sabena, the Belgian airline, fortunately for both of us, one of the few air carriers still flaunting sanctions and continuing to fly into Salisbury. I saw her come down the steps of the aircraft, she was wearing a simple white blouse and a pair of jeans. Although I had not thought it possible, she looked more beautiful than ever.

Chantelle saw me in the arrival lounge, waved and ran into my open arms. We kissed and I felt her soft body melt into mine. We locked in the embrace, reluctant to let go of each other. She whispered, "I missed you so much, cheri!" I acknowledged her words with a smile and kissed her again, "You have always been in my heart and thoughts Chantelle. I missed you too!" I replied.

We chattered away as we drove towards Salisbury and I detoured, to give her a brief view of the city. As we drove through the town Chantelle seemed fascinated by what she was seeing and commented, "It is such a clean city, I never had the chance to see much of it when my parents and I came through, when we had to flee from Zaire. The newspapers and T.V. have painted a totally different picture from what I am seeing so far! The media have lead us to believe that there are armed militia along the roads, and I have seen none. They report tensions between the peoples and rioting in the streets that keeps people indoors, afraid to walk in the open. Yet, there are many people in the streets, they are walking about casually with smiles on their faces! Everything seems so peaceful and harmonious, is it usually like this?" She asked. It was interesting to hear the images that were being portrayed of the country by the media to readers and viewers overseas. "Yes, Chantelle, this is what it is normally like here, every day." I replied. "Then it's beautiful!" She stated. "I have brought my camera and plenty of film. Will you help me to photograph some of the local scenes, with the accent on the way things really are? Perhaps I can get them into magazines that I have started doing free-lance work with!" She said. "Yes, of course. I intend to take you on a few sightseeing trips, I am sure you will find ample settings of interest to capture with your camera!" I replied. "Thank you, Ivan." She said stretching over her seat and planting a kiss on my lips.

Arriving at the house, I introduced Chantelle to my mother. The two seemed to take to each other instantly and entered into conversation switching intermittently between speaking english and french. Motorcar came into the driveway riding his bicycle, and I called him into the house to complete the introductions. "It is a pleasure to finally meet you Motorcar, Ivan has spoken often and highly of you!" Chantelle said looking up at the six foot six warrior. "He lied!" motorcar replied jokingly.

I stepped back to enjoy the moment. For the first time, the ones I cared for the most, were here together in the same room.

My mother had prepared a sumptuous dinner which we sat down at the table to enjoy. We talked and caught up on the events that had happened during the two years that had passed, laughing at some of the amusing incidents that had occurred to each of us in that period. I suggested to Chantelle that we go downtown and take in some of the city's nightlife. Chantelle agreed and took her leave to shower and freshen up. She returned a short while later looking stunning in a simple but elegant turquoise silk evening dress and jacket. Her appearance was so exquisite, that I felt an increased level of desire to make love to her.

We traveled downtown and took in the sights, stopping in at one of the nightclubs to dance, finally, arriving back at the house shortly after midnight.

We quietly tiptoed to Chantelle's room. "Alone at last, cheri!" she whispered, sliding her arms around my neck, bringing up her face and lips to meet mine. We kissed with a passion, and pure electricity seemed to flow between our bodies. I looked into Chantelle's green blue eyes. "I wish this moment would last forever!" I said. A tear of happiness dropped from one of Chantelle's eyes running down her cheek, I wiped the tear from her face and gently lay her down on the bed. We each took off the other's clothes, hugged and gently caressed, before making love.

The next morning was a Saturday and the shops were as usual, to be open for the half day, from eight in the morning until noon. I gave Chantelle the opportunity to lay in bed and catch up on her rest from her journey and the late night. She insisted on rising early and coming to help me at the shop in the Avenues.

It was a busy morning, Chantelle had no problem going behind the counter and was soon involved with helping customers. I continued to be increasingly impressed with Chantelle, she was an international model, yet as I observed, equally content to serve behind a counter to help me. She had a warm, confident, friendly air about her that put people at ease and radiated an aura of charisma with her manner.

That afternoon, I had arranged for us to meet with Andy Harper and some friends at Lake Macillwaine. One of those friends had a power boat moored at an inlet in the lake and we went for a cruise on the water. With the recklessness of youth, despite the known presence and danger of crocodiles and hippo's in the vicinity, we each took turns at water skiing. When a skier fell into the lake, the person driving the boat would frantically open up the throttle and get back to the swimmer, pulling them out of the water as quickly as possible, in order to minimize the danger of being taken by a crocodile. Though it was July and mid winter, it was a warm sunny day and the temperature moderated enough to be frolicking in the water.

Late that afternoon we took leave of the friends, and I drove Chantelle down the side road to the game park and pan that I had recently visited. There the animals were strolling in all their splendor to drink at the water. Chantelle had her camera working incessantly, capturing the different species and poses of the wildlife from giraffe to zebra, as they ambled into view by the pan. "It has been so many years that I have been away from Africa,…that I had almost forgotten how beautiful it is to be in a place like this, so close to touching nature!" she said.

I put my arm around Chantelle's shoulder and we stood there watching, two humans amongst the grandeur of nature, taking in the sights of the panorama in front of us. As the sun set, we embraced in a kiss. With the darkness closing in around us, we held each other. Reluctantly we left the vista, and headed back to the city.

The first week of Chantelle's visit seemed to fly by quickly.

During the day she would accompany me to work, sometimes helping out in the shops, other times borrowing the M.G. to drive into the countryside to photograph interesting spots and stopping at the tribal villages, capturing the flavor of local life on film. She would return later and with enthusiasm, tell me of the different accents of life that she had been able to record on film that day.

The Evenings were taken up with dinners at Salisbury's many and varied restaurants, sightseeing, and Youth Mayoral functions. It was an exhausting time, but we felt so much alive with all the activities. Discreetly ending the nights by tiptoeing into Chantelle's room to make love.

The second week coincided with the Junior Mayor of Johannesburg's reciprocal visit to Salisbury for the weekend. The Mayoress Anna and I had planned a charity ball for the Saturday Night in his honour, the visit was a good excuse to raise funds for the needy. Chantelle, Anna and I drove out to the airport Friday evening to greet his arrival into the city. I introduced him to Chantelle and the young man's jaw literally dropped at the sight of her beauty. His unexpected reaction drew chuckles from Anna and me, prompting a wisecrack from Anna; "You can close your mouth now, she's just one of the regular girls in Salisbury, wait till you see the beautiful ones!"

With the arrival of the Junior Mayor, came the start of a more than hectic weekend for all of us. The schedule included T.V. interviews, social lunches with the different clubs and public functions, highlighted by the Saturday night charity event, where Chantelle looked radiant and undoubtedly was the belle of the Ball.

When Monday arrived after a tiring weekend, Chantelle and I were filled with exhaustion, it was almost a relief for the two of us to take the visitor back to the airport for his flight to Johannesburg. Chantelle had a week of her visit left and we planned to spend much of the remaining time just sightseeing and being together.

I persuaded a friend, Harry Miller, who had his own Cessna aircraft to fly us to the Wankie Game Reserve, so that Chantelle could see and photograph the wildlife from the air.

Flying above the immense game park drew a wondrous new perspective on the vastness of the plains, and the size of the herds of animals roaming the range below us. We swooped over a large herd of elephant that numbered in their thousands feeding off the trees and grasslands. Some of the elephant turned their heads to look up at the overflying aircraft in the same fashion people looked at an annoying mosquito buzzing around them, then turned back to their sluggish grazing. We flew by a huge herd of antelope feeding by a stream, their fawn colored movement blended with the brownish grass around them, giving the illusion of waves rippling against the earth as the herd moved along the ground below. Stalking and camouflaged in the trees behind the antelope were a pride of lionesses, waiting for the right moment to advance and commence the chase against their prey. A herd of zebra and water buffalo stampeded at the intrusion and sight of the low flying aircraft, kicking up a storm of dust that enveloped them and clouded the view of the animals below.

Chantelle let out a cry of excitement, as she pointed out a leopard perched and sleeping in one of the high tree branches below us. We had been in the air for several hours when Harry looked at the instruments and mentioned that we were starting to run low on fuel, he throttled the plan upwards for a high, last panoramic view of the game park, before turning the plane to head back to Salisbury.

With only a few days remaining of Chantelle's stay, she and I crowded as much activity as we could into the remaining time that was left to us.

We also picked a quiet moment while we were alone to discuss our future. It was not an easy future to plan. Chantelle had one year left to go with her studies. She then planned to work free-lance, as a photo journalist covering stories from around the world for newspapers and magazines. This was a dream that she had always wanted to accomplish and she asked for my understanding, I could see from the pleading look in her eyes that the situation did need my understanding and how important this was to her. Chantelle explained her dilemma was that she also very much wanted to return to Rhodesia to be with me, a fulfillment of our earlier promise to marry and have a family life together. Recognizing how important this was to her, I decided for the sake of both our futures to encourage her dreams. 'Chantelle follow your goals, we have a lifetime of future to look forward to, so I will be here waiting for you!" I said, putting up a brave front to the situation.

I realized this would mean we would spend a fair amount of time apart. But comforted myself in the knowledge that this was the right path for both of us! If I tried to influence her to settle down and get married before she had the opportunity to fulfill her goals she would one day resent me for that. So, I put aside my inward unwillingness and agreed to what we both believed to be a temporary delay to our ultimate marriage. We also planned to take the opportunities, as circumstances allowed, to be with each other as often as possible during that intervening time, before we settled down to a married life.

The last day of Chantelle's visit I presented her with a pendant, a cross, channel set with precious Rhodesian Sandawanah Emeralds. Chantelle was delighted and then burst out laughing. "What's so funny?" I asked. "Well Ivan, I have a gift for you too!" She said, and handed me a gift wrapped box. In it, was a gold Star of David pendant encrusted with small diamonds. "I was laughing because we both decided to give each other similar gifts, religious emblems, to take with us on our treks over the next few years." She said, putting on the pendant. "I will always wear and cherish this as a reminder of you, my love." "As will I!" I replied, we embraced each other and sealed our promises with a kiss.

I took Chantelle to the airport, it was a tearful farewell. I stood in the airport lounge and watched her board her aircraft. As the plane took off into the sky, I felt as though a part of me was flying away with her too. Slowly, I made my way back to the car and to life for the time being, without her.

Chapter Ten

I found it difficult adjusting to life without Chantelle, but took heart in the fact that we had a future together to look forward to in the years ahead, so I focused on developing my businesses and threw myself into the youth activities. This helped to ease the pain of not having Chantelle there to share my life and having to love her from a distance.

Amos called in to the Avenues shop, I was happy to see him again, commenting that it had been over three months since Amos had last visited and that he had missed meeting Chantelle.

I enquired if everything was going well? "Very well!" Amos had replied and proceeded to tell me the reason why he had been away for such a long period. "There is a new special operational force unit being trained, only the best, toughest and fittest of whites and blacks are being selected for training with the group. After initial training, we are dropped by air at night in the middle of nowhere in different locations in the Bushveld, at least one hundred miles from base with no equipment or food, only a skinning knife for protection against the animals and to use for survival off the land for food. The test is to see how many men can make it back to base camp without any help in three days. Those few who pass the test are considered for further training!"

I thought back a few months, to the time William Harper had started to speak of the elite counter insurgency force that was starting to come into existence, and wondered if this was the same group that Amos was talking about.

"That is quite a rigorous test! How far have you progressed on the course?" I asked. "I made it back to the base camp within the three days! It was awful, in order to get food I had to kill and eat snakes, worms and lizards." My stomach turned at the thought, Motorcar who was standing nearby listening, grimaced at what he was hearing. Amos continued, "Occasionally, I was lucky enough to find wild berries to eat. Having passed that test, I have now moved on to the next stage of the training."

"What is the name of this special force?" I asked. "The Selous Scouts, we have been named after the famous African explorer, hunter and tracker, Fredrick Courtney Selous." Amos said. "Does this mean that you will be transferring to the army?" I queried. "Not really, the unit is comprised of men from the army, police and special air services, as well as the men working full time for the Selous Scouts. We will continue with our regular branches, but be called together for special missions." Amos replied. "Sounds very intriguing! I hope all goes well with the remaining training that you have ahead." I said.

Amos nodded his head, "That is going to be the tough part from what I have heard! We have been told not to discuss with anyone what happens during the last part of the training, it will be at a secret base camp!" he said. "When do you start?" I asked. "Tomorrow! We will be trucked to the secret location, I know that it will be somewhere deep in the bush, so we wont be able to contact anyone outside the base for six weeks, that's why I wanted to come and see you and Motorcar before taking off for my ordeal!"

Motorcar interjected at this point, "Don't worry, Amos, I am sure that the women will all still be waiting for you when you get back…maybe one of them will even cook up a can of worms for you when you return!" He said, with tongue in cheek, drawing laughter from the three of us. Amos said farewell to us and left amongst our good wishes for his success.

From time to time, rumors would circulate about the existence of the elite force, with stories of it's strenuous selection procedure and it's purpose. When questioned on the subject by the media, government officials would make no comment, neither denying or acknowledging the unit's existence.

Motorcar and I knew that the group existed!

The time was drawing close for my purchase of Osborne Cycles, and I phoned John Osborne to make the final arrangements. Mr. Osborne sounded very serious on the other end of the line. "I think It is important that we meet, Benny was here yesterday and said some disturbing things, can you come down to the shop, so that we can talk?" He asked. "Yes of course!" I replied.

At Osborne Cycles, Mr. Osborne led me into his office and once we were seated, he asked "Does Benny own part or have a say in your businesses, Ivan?" I thought that a strange question to ask me. "No, we have nothing to do with each other! He is the manager of my mother's business and that is where it ends! Why do you ask?" I inquired with my curiosity peaking. "Well, Benny made a sales call on me yesterday. I mentioned to him that I would not be making any new purchases, as I was selling the store. He asked who the new owner would be, and I told him that you were buying the shop! Well Ivan, Benny exploded with anger, telling me that you had no right to buy my store and he threatened to bankrupt you, if you did!" Mr. Osborne stated. I shook my head, "Mr. Osborne take my word for it, Benny has no right to interfere in my business. Frankly, he is a bag of piss and wind and I intend to buy the business as agreed…also I intend to go and see Benny to sort this nonsense out!" I stated angrily.

I drove to Royal Cycles and stormed into Benny's office, it was empty! I marched to my mother's office. Rae was seated behind her desk. She looked up to see the anger in my face. "What is the Matter?" she asked. I told her of Benny's visit to Mr. Osborne and the hollow threat to Bankrupt me. "Please Ivan, calm down. Let's not have any more trouble!" She pleaded with me. "Mom, I am sick of that little man interfering and attempting by any means, to put obstacles in my life. Now is the time to confront him!"

At that moment Benny walked by, noticing me glaring at him, he stepped in to the office. "What's the problem?" He demanded. "You are the problem!" I retorted and challenged; "How dare you interfere in my business and threaten Mr. Osborne that you will bankrupt me if I buy back my father's retail cycle shop!" "I dare what I please!" Benny arrogantly replied, momentarily forgetting that I was now a grown man and no longer the little boy that he could bully, he swung a punch and hit me on the chest. I vented my anger, retaliating with a punch that hit Benny in the midriff, knocking the wind out of him and sending him reeling over my mother's desk. Benny picked himself up and charged with his fists flying at me. I sidestepped and connected another punch on Benny's Jaw, again he went reeling backwards ending up sitting spread-eagled on the floor. "If you are wise, you will stay down!" I told him. Benny attempted to raise himself, before flopping back onto the floor. "You have broken my jaw!" Benny accused. "I am sorry Benny, but you asked for it!" I replied. "I'm going to ruin you!" Benny threatened. My mother intervened "No, you wont! I have put up with your greed and hurting my family long enough! She said. "Now you heed this warning, if you do anything to interfere with or hurt Ivan again, I will fire you, I don't care if that results in the business going to blazes. Since you joined this company you have done everything you could to grab what you can and hurt my family in the process! That is going to stop! Is that understood?" She said standing over the disheveled Benny." Yes aunt." he meekly replied. "Now get up Benny, your jaw is not broken, and get back to work!" She told him. Slowly, he got up from the floor and went back to his office.

My mother looked at me and said, "Normally I don't agree with violence, but you know, in this case watching Benny get his dues actually felt good! Let's hope that what happened has it's desired effect." Then with a wink, she said, "Why are you still here, don't you have some businesses to run?" "Yes Mom, I do!" I said with a smile, as I turned to leave Royal Cycles.

I drove to my Borrowdale store and phoned Mr. Osborne. I tried to put Osborne's mind at ease by telling him that I would be proceeding with delivering the initial payment for the business in a couple of weeks, "…and do not be concerned about being threatened or bothered by Benny again with regard to the sale of the shop, as that situation has now been 'resolved!'" "Glad to hear that, Ivan. It always pays to communicate, to resolve differences." Osborne replied. "Believe me Sir, in this case the message has been communicated!" I stated.

During the next few weeks the sale and transfer of the new business went smoothly, with no further hitches. I introduced hardware into the inventory, changing the name of the shop to the same as the other two, "Ivan's Cycles and Hardware." I was also, fortunate enough to find a good former cycle salesman to manage the store. Though, with three businesses to run, I found myself busier than ever, traveling constantly to each of the stores, ensuring that they were operating smoothly.

I also noticed that since my confrontation with Benny, that the man had appeared to mellow and tone down his hostile attitude towards me. "Perhaps there *is* a chance that life will be a little easier from now on?" I thought, hopefully.

As the next few months passed, very little of Rhodesian life changed. The political stalemate continued. Business generally in the country remained linked to the political situation and was slow. Surprisingly, going against the grain, my business remained steady and grew.

Christmas approached and many Rhodesians seemed to tire of tightening their belts because of a dragging economy, they let loose and splurged on gifts, buying whatever luxuries and goods that became available on the market. It was almost as though there was a prevailing attitude of "We don't know where we will be tomorrow, so let's live life to the most today!" It turned into a bumper sales season for me and in particular I had a busy time keeping up with the requests and demand for children's cycles.

With the year coming to an end, so was my tenure as Youth Mayor. It had been a very successful term for the youth societies and the Youth Mayoral group as a whole. I was requested and encouraged to run again by many of the youth leaders, but turned down the offers of nomination, deciding that I needed to concentrate on my businesses and take a rest from the many demands of coordinating youth activities.

I met with Anna, George and Helas for the last time in our official capacities, at the Youth Mayoral Ball in January. The four of us knew that we had made lifelong friends in each other, aware the posts we were relinquishing that night would live on in our memories with honor and be remembered with pride for the rest of our lives. After privately drinking a toast to each other at our table, I went to the podium and gave the farewell speech on all our behalves. I welcomed the incoming officers and wished them success at this time of the city's history.

Without the Youth Mayoral responsibilities and activities, life seemed to have become more subdued. I found this took some getting used to, although still kept busy with my growing businesses. The added free time also gave me the opportunity to reflect on the direction my life was taking. It seemed that I was gradually drawing myself deeper into the world of commerce. The goal I had of becoming a lawyer, seemed to be slipping away, a little more each day. Though, I still felt a hunger to improve myself with knowledge and thirsted for the education of becoming a lawyer. I looked ahead to the future and wondered if it was going to be my lot to spend my life behind a counter selling bicycles and hardware.

Mid February arrived, and with it, a twist of fate that would alter my life. I had been at the Avenues shop attending to customers with Motorcar, when I noticed an elderly man gazing through the shop window watching the activities going on inside. The man stood by the window for a couple of hours before entering the shop and looking around, Motorcar asked if he needed assistance, the man shook his head and said "No thanks, I am just looking!" He then left the store. The man returned the next day and did the same thing, standing outside the window watching the customers entering and leaving the shop.

A couple of days later, the man returned and entered the shop. He spoke to me, asking questions about the businesses. I was becoming convinced that I was dealing with a person who had a few loose screws. "My name is Jim Mitchell!" The man said, extending his hand to me, "How much would you accept to sell all three businesses?" He enquired. I threw out a ridiculous figure, which included a fifty thousand dollar profit just for the goodwill of the shops. Thinking that the excessive amount would scare the man and get this oddball to leave the shop. Jim Mitchell pulled out his cheque book and began to write. "What are you doing?" I asked. Jim Mitchell looked up at me and responded, "I asked you how much you would accept for the businesses, you gave me a figure! Now I am writing you out a cheque, to buy them!" He calmly stated. "Are you crazy? You haven't seen my books, you don't know what the inventory is worth, you have no idea of the business turnover, there is no contract of sale…and you are writing out a cheque to buy me out?" I asked. "Yes!" Mitchell simply stated. "If you are concerned that my cheque may not be any good, take it now and deposit it. I will return in two days once the cheque has cleared and we can close the deal!" I had difficulty in believing this was really happening! "You really are serious about this?" I questioned Mitchell. "Yes, Ivan I am, you see I made my money in buying and selling property, then I retired a couple of years ago and the boredom has started to get to me. Also, my son has been looking for a business to invest in without much luck, most businesses are not doing too well. Yours is one of the few that is growing. I thought if I bought your shops it would give me the opportunity to work together with my son and bring some challenge back into my life. Besides, I have had a recent windfall, a ticket I bought in the Rhodesian

Lottery won the first prize of $50,000, which has left me with more cash than I know what to do with!"

The wheels in my mind started to turn, if Jim Mitchell was for real, selling the businesses would free me to return to university to pursue studies to become a lawyer, which was what I always had wanted to do! The University of Cape Town commenced its academic year during the first week of March, only a couple of weeks away. I would have to move fast to try and gain acceptance by the university, for that year. I explained my thinking to Mitchell; "I will send a telegram to the Registrar in Cape Town, if I can gain admission for this year, we have a deal! I should have an answer within a few days, is that acceptable?" I asked.

Mitchell agreed to return in a few days, leaving the cheque with me to deposit and satisfy myself that the funds were available.

The next few days were a whirlwind of activity, I sent a telegram to the university in Cape town, requesting urgent attention to my application for admittance. A reply came back two days later granting acceptance. I had also been to see one of the city's finest attorney's, Jay Patanak, who drafted a contract of sale for the business delivering the transfer of the shops on an "As is," basis.

I discussed the situation with my mother and felt comforted when she supported my decision to return to my studies and stilled the concerns I had about leaving her on her own. She insisted that everything would be all right in my absence, as the situation at Royal cycles was now firmly under her control.

I explained my intentions to Motorcar and offered to have his employment guaranteed with the new owner. Motorcar took the news surprisingly well, telling me that he had been thinking of retiring, perhaps, now was the time to do that. He wanted to return to his land in Inyanga and spend his remaining time with Sheila and their children cultivating crops. I promised to help and support whatever decision Motorcar came to.

Mitchell's cheque cleared the bank and the funds went into my account with no problems. A day later Jim Mitchell returned To the Avenues shop, where the deal was finalized.

The government had recently changed the Rhodesian currency system from the Sterling pound, to the metric dollar basis. I withdrew five thousand dollars and met with Motorcar. "What have you decided to do?" I asked him. "Well, young friend, I am going to retire and go back to Inyanga." Motorcar said trying to put a smile on his face, "I will miss you Ivan, but I know you will make a good Lawyer, 'Hamba Gashi' go in peace!" He said. I felt an ache of sadness weal up inside me. I would truly miss my old companion. "I can never thank you enough for your friendship. Motorcar, we will stay in contact even though our paths are moving in different directions, wont we?" I asked. "Yes, we will always be friends!" Motorcar replied.

I gave Motorcar the envelope containing the five thousand dollars, "This is to help you with your retirement, Hamba Gashi, Motorcar." I said and walked away before I choked up.

Two weeks later, I drove the 1,650 mile journey to Cape Town, arriving the day before my classes were to begin, and registered for the B.A.LL.B degree course. I was now ready to start life as a student once more.

Jan Van Reibeck, the Dutch East India company explorer and sea captain, when settling the Cape of Good Hope on behalf of his company in 1652, most succinctly described the area, on seeing it for the first time, when he said it was "The fairest Cape in all the world!"

With the most breathtaking scenery and flora imaginable, Cape Town is set on the picturesque slopes of Table Mountain, a single 3,500 foot high mountain range, which at the top flattens into a plateau, and stretches for several miles along the Cape peninsula. Low floating clouds often settle over the top of the mountain and whisper down it's sides giving the effect of a table cloth covering it. The mountain is endowed with a variety of brightly petaled flowers and fauna, some so unique that they are found nowhere else on earth. Many houses are built all along the slopes of the mountain, enjoying the most spectacular ocean views.

The city of Cape Town is situated at the base of Table Mountain, and flanked by thirty miles of ocean front suburbs on either side. To add to its uniqueness, it is on the Southernmost tip of the African continent and the place where the warm Indian Ocean and cold Atlantic Ocean waters meet. The two currents can be seen coming together and overlapping at Cape Point, thirty miles from the city center.

On the Indian Ocean side, is the added beauty of the suburb of Muizenberg, which boasts the world's finest beach, stretching for miles towards Gordon's Bay in the horizon. The seashore is made up of a fine, soft, granulated sand, gently slopping into the sea, one could wade from the beach a few hundred yards into the ocean, with its gently lapping waves and still only be waist deep in its warm waters, it was a very popular holiday resort with Rhodesians.

The Atlantic Ocean side too, had some excellent, but smaller beaches, in particular the Clifton and Seapoint beaches, which were very popular with the university students.

The University of Cape Town, commonly referred to as U.C.T., in the suburb of Rondebosch, is built into the side of Table Mountain, once part of Cecil John Rhodes' Estate, it now formed a part of his bequest to the nation. The view from the classrooms, of the suburbs nestled below and the Atlantic ocean in the distance, is nothing short of spectacular. To me, this was the most beautiful city on earth!

I moved into a large apartment complex in Mowbray, less than two miles from the university, "Liesbeek Gardens". The building was almost coffin shaped containing a couple of hundred apartments. My flat was a one bedroom unit with a reasonable view of Table Mountain. I spent a little time furnishing the apartment with the basic essentials, before settling down to university life and studies.

I soon made friends with the next door neighbors, a married couple, Alan and Colleen Walker. They were a delightful and interestingly talented pair. Both were artists working for the "Argus" newspaper in the City.

Alan was British born, but had lived in Kenya for several years during his youth at a time when the Mau Mau were terrorizing the country. He had hunted on Safari's in the bush near Nairobi, before moving to Cape Town. Here his artistic talents landed him a job working for the newspaper, where he met and married Colleen. Instilled with the sense of adventure, he still took off from time to time on hunting expeditions in remote regions all over Southern Africa. Painting wild life scenes on canvas and making some world record kills for his trophies, that were regularly listed in the Guinness book of records. Only a few years older than me, he was regarded as one of the few remaining "Great White Hunters" left on the African Continent. Although I did not agree with the of killing animals purely for the sport, Alan's desire and fearlessness to take a risk and get into harmless mischief, appealed to me and we became good friends.

Colleen in contrast, was a lady and an artist, not desirous of taking many risks, she was perhaps, the stabilizing force in Alan's life.

Alan's inclination for mischief often got him into hot water with Colleen and his antics sometimes ended up with hilarious results; on one occasion, Alan and Colleen had just laid out a new shaggy carpet in their living room. They had saved for months to buy it. They invited me over to take a look at their new purchase over a drink. During the course of the conversation, Alan decided to demonstrate to me how to make a small rocket. To do this, he emptied a couple of hundred match stick heads into some thin aluminum foil wrapping, with which he covered the matches, leaving a single match stick exposed as a fuse. Colleen requested that Alan do his demonstration outside the apartment, in the passageway, as she did not want the risk of anything burning her new carpet. Alan and I went outside. Alan left the door to the apartment wide open. He lit the fuse to the rocket and it worked perfectly, except instead of shooting off in a straight line outside the apartment, the rocket did a right angle turn, straight through the wide open door, into the entrance hall, burning its way directly to the living room and over the shaggy carpet leaving an indelible black burn trail down the center of the carpet, before embedding itself at the base of the sofa. Alan looked at Colleen sheepishly, "It wasn't supposed to do that, you know?"

On another occasion, Alan attempted to perfect a larger version of the rocket, using home made ingredients. This time the size of the rocket was much larger, well over six feet tall and about three feet in diameter. He put together a combination of ground charcoal, salt peter, sand and other inflammable ingredients which by coincidence, also happened to be the same formula for making explosive dynamite, as the propulsion system. He invited a small group of friends to come and watch the launching.

As a safety precaution, we drove to Blauberg strand, an empty beach on the opposite side of Cape Town Harbour and several miles, hopefully, of any injury being done to person or property. Alan had a two hundred foot long fuse, the idea being was once lit, the observers would dive behind the protection of a sand dune and safely watch the rocket climb into the evening sky towards the heavens. That in theory, was what was supposed to happen! What actually happened was Alan lit the long fuse and everyone dove for cover. The fuse fizzled out after burning a hundred feet, Alan re-lit the fuse and everyone dove for cover. The fuse fizzled out at fifty feet, again it was re-lit, only to fizzle out again, and again, and again. Until there was only two feet of fuse left. In a feat of bravery, Alan lit it once more, ran and dove for cover. The fuse went out again, inches from the rocket base. The consensus was, that with enough explosive in the rocket to blow up half the beach, it would be too dangerous for Alan to try single handedly to light the fuse again, so we all got together and built a base for a bonfire under the rocket, to cause the necessary ignition. Once completed we took cover and Alan lit the bonfire and ran for cover. I was convinced that the result would be a major explosion, rather than the rocket taking off, and huddled into the sand dune. After a few minutes, there was a "pop", from the direction of the rocket in the same magnitude of a champagne cork popping from its bottle! I looked up to see the burnt out shell of the rocket lying on its side, the "pop" had been the announcement of its demise!

A short time later, another famous couple moved in as neighbors on the other side of my apartment unit. Wilbur Smith and his new wife Danielle. Smith had written adventure novels about Southern Africa that had become worldwide best sellers. It fascinated me that the author of some of the books I had recently read and enjoyed, was now living next door to me. Wilbur Smith seemed to take off for weeks at a time in his Land Rover, consequently I saw him rarely and the opportunity never arose to become acquainted with the couple, other than, to give each other a passing greeting.

In going back to university, one consideration that I had not seriously taken into account, was how difficult it would be to return to a life of studies. The four years since I had studied full time and the commercial world had made me rusty in applying myself to the academic world. I failed my mid year exams. Although devastating to me at the time, in retrospect it was probably the best thing that could have happened, as the news of my dismal performance shocked me into focusing harder with the studies—I had not given up my businesses to falter with my subjects. The extra effort paid off with my passing the main exams at the end of the year.

I had made a point of driving back to Salisbury during the university vacation breaks, which was once every three months. After the year end exams, I arrived home for the three month Christmas summer vacation. My mother had been holding up well on her own with Benny. Although the problem the business now faced was that the exchange control regulations had cut the import of bicycle parts to forty percent of what it had been prior to U.D.I. Royal Cycles was barely selling enough to make a profit!

Benny's attitude toward me seemed to have mellowed, and I was not sure whether that was due to the physical confrontation we had been involved in, or that with my being away with my studies in Cape Town, Benny no longer considered me to be such a threat to his running the business. Either way it made little difference to me, as long as my mother was being well cared for.

The political situation had stagnated, with the Rhodesian government holding its ground on the political front and refusing to compromise on majority rule. Rumors were strongly circulating of opposition armies being trained by the communists and it now seemed only a matter of time before armed confrontations would develop in the country. The only factor that no one knew, was what form those confrontations would take.

Chantelle had graduated from her university studies and had started doing free-lance work with several European Magazines and newspapers. She spoke on the telephone with excitement about starting her career and her travels to the different European cities to cover stories and breaking news. She promised to visit me in Cape Town the following year during my winter break in July.

Amos visited the house to see me, he had now been promoted to the rank of sergeant with the police. We sat and chatted about different aspects of what had happened to each of us during the past year, though when I asked questions concerning how Amos's role with the Selous Scouts was progressing. Amos for the first time put up a barrier on any conversation on the topic, "Sorry Ivan, I am not allowed to talk about my activities with them!" Respecting that, I moved on to another subject, though inwardly I was very curious about the fighting force.

With a fair amount of free time available to me I took the opportunity to take a drive to Inyanga for a day, to see Motorcar and take in some of the inspiring scenery of the Inyanga Mountains.

I was warmly greeted by Motorcar and Sheila at their village and was invited to visit their hut. Sheila offered me some home brewed beer and we sat and talked for a while. I noticed that Motorcar had put on a little weight and teased him about the easy life he must be having, now that he had retired, and we laughed about that. I enquired how life was treating them, Motorcar looked at Sheila and went silent for a brief period, then he said "Come young friend, let us take a walk by the fields, where we can talk!" Once outside by the cultivated fields, I asked, "What has been happening, Motorcar?" The warrior's face became earnestly serious, "Life has become very difficult for us and the people living in the villages, young friend. Gangs of black political men come by at night and tell us we have to join their cause. They call themselves "Comrades!". They say that we have to contribute money to become members, if we do not give them money, they threaten to beat us up! So we give them money, then we are issued with cards and told that we are now members of "The Party!"

First it was the members of Z.A.P.U., that came, then a rival political group started to come. They too, demanded contributions, and that we had to join Z.A.N.U., their "Party." They told us anyone who joined the other party was a traitor and would be killed. After taking money from us they too, issued us with their "Party" cards. So now, When one group comes we show them their party cards, when they are satisfied and leave; the other group comes and we show them their party cards!

During the day, the police come by to ask if any of us have joined either of the two parties. The police warn us that it is illegal to join those two parties and if we are found with party cards we can be arrested, so we tell the police, none of us are members of either "Party."

Life has became a living nightmare for us in the villages, most of us just want to live out our lives peacefully cultivating our crops, we do not understand all this political tugging and pulling! Now, the political groups have been coming around recruiting the young men and women from the villages to join their cause, those that don't join voluntarily are taken forcibly and made to help them!" Motorcar said sadly. "I noticed that there was an absence of young people around your village, Motorcar, Where are your children now ?" I asked.

"I sent them to school in Umtali, to get them away from here. They are living with Sheila's brother in the city, where they are safe for now." Motorcar answered. "Does anyone know about the five thousand dollars, I gave you?" I asked. "No, the money is hidden in a safe place, Sheila and I are the only ones who know about it. Even our children have no knowledge of the money." Motorcar replied and continued, "Young friend, it is also becoming dangerous for both you and us, if you were to come and visit us in the village again. We are being watched right now as we speak, if you come again we could be accused of being collaborators with the whites, so it is better, if we visit you in Salisbury!"

Sadly, I understood what was happening. "Motorcar, do you and Sheila want to move to Salisbury? I can arrange for you to move into a house in Harare township." I offered. Motorcar shook his head, and said, "No, young friend, this is my home and I intend to stay here!" "Very well, but I will tell my mother of what is happening here and if you should need to move to safety, she will be prepared to help you, while I am away in Cape Town!" I offered. We walked back to his hut in the village and I bade farewell to the two friends.

Heading back to Salisbury, I thought of what Motorcar had said to me. Motorcar's home was only one small village. I wondered in how many of the hundreds of other villages the same scenario was being played over, repeatedly—innocent people trapped in a situation they neither wanted to be in, nor had any say, or control over. Whatever the outcome they, the ordinary people would be the losers, pulled in different directions by the differing ideologues of politicians. The competing political groups whatever their motivation, were determined to impose their will on the masses, as being the right way, the only way.

I thought of the way things were developing, the fear of being considered a collaborator, was throwing divisions into previously innocent friendships. Where color had not been a factor, it now was, as had happened with Motorcar and me. I grew angry at the politics and the cost it was imposing on the peoples of the country.

Back in Salisbury, I explained to my mother the developments that were taking place with Motorcar and Sheila. Rae agreed to help with any steps she could to provide for them, should they find themselves in need of refuge.

With my vacation time nearly over, I drove back to Cape town to prepare myself to enter my second year at the university.

Although South Africa had its political problems, in comparison to the full scale internal developments in Rhodesia, the situation here at least on the surface, was still embryonic and peaceful.

Television had not yet been introduced into South Africa, so I kept abreast of the news and the events occurring in Rhodesia by reading whatever items appeared in the local newspapers. Amongst those items were articles describing the regular abductions of young black villagers and schoolchildren by the competing political gangs. The children were allegedly being taken outside the country to be trained for guerrilla warfare by the opponents of the Rhodesian government. I was concerned for Motorcar, and worried how he and Sheila were faring with this constant threat to their children.

July arrived and with it came Chantelle's visit to Cape Town. I picked her up at Cape Town's tiny airport. She had blossomed into full womanhood, as beautiful as ever, but now she had an added air of elegance about her. "Cheri!" she called out, we embraced and she melted into my body once again, with a kiss. I loved the way she did that, my heart pounded with the closeness of her and her kiss took my breath away. We broke into excited conversation telling each other of our adventures since we had last seen each other. Chantelle chattered with excitement telling me about the stories she had been able to cover and photograph in Europe.

I drove her to Liesbeek Gardens, took her up to my entrance, picked her up and carried her over the threshold into my apartment. "Cheri, does this mean that we are married for the next three weeks?" She teased. "Consider this a preliminary honeymoon." I answered, laying her down on the bed. We undressed each other, and made love with a passion and desire that had been held back since last we were together.

In the days that followed time seemed to lose its meaning. We traveled by cablecar to the top of Table Mountain, on the flat mountain top Chantelle's camera never stopped clicking at the perfect scenery below that laid itself out to be captured on film. We stopped in at the granite built restaurant at the mountain's edge, drank high tea, taking in the view spread out around us. Then, the sun started to set over the Atlantic ocean and Chantelle found a whole new vista to capture on film; the colorful African sunset.

Even though it was mid winter, the temperature was mild and warm enough for us to take a swim in the Indian ocean and walk along the beaches of Muizenberg. We traveled to Cape Point, the final land tip of the African continent and watched the two Oceans meet. With the currents overlapping, the flow created a line of small clashing waves stretching out into the horizon as far as the eye could see.

Day after day was absorbed in new and different scenic travels, we went a few miles inland to the rich and fertile Stellenbosch Valley, to the grape vines and farms, visiting cellars where some of the finest wines were made.

A Little further out we stopped at a game reserve to watch the graceful herds of Eland, Antelope and Springbok grazing in the open ranges. As we watched the herds, Chantelle went quiet with thought, "What's on your mind?" I asked her. "I was just thinking, how little of this the people overseas know about, we give them stories that make the news and of course the politics which generally is not good. But, this is the real Africa that no one hears of, the natural land that we don't bother to tell about!" She said. "I Can see from the look of determination on your face, that you intend to do something about that?" I commented. "Yes, with articles featuring photos of the beauty of the land, I would like to show the real Africa to be seen and understood, by my readers in Europe. That there is a life besides the politics on this continent!"

All too soon, Chantelle's visit came to an end and I once again found myself in the heart wrenching situation of bidding "Au revoir" to her at the airport. This time with no certain arrangement when we would come together once more, other than the commitment to get married and settle, once I had finished with my studies.

I returned my focus on studies and to prepare for the year end exams.

The news from Rhodesia began to worsen, with organized riots in the main cities and African townships increasing and taking on a more violent character, people were being killed in the melee. In Salisbury rioters had rampaged through the townships, with rioting spilling into the bordering shopping districts and some businesses being set ablaze and looted. The cities of Bulawayo, Gwelo and Umtali had similar riots. The police and army had reacted quickly to bring the situation under control and life stabilized for temporary periods, before new outbreaks of violence and disturbances broke out again.

Blacks who were regarded or even rumored to be collaborating with whites were being murdered in the most heinous ways, sometimes in public as a warning to others, by the rival political gangs. One of the ways the executions were being carried out was by "Necktie" where a car tire was filled with gasoline and placed over the head of a bound and gagged victim, and set ablaze.

Military call ups were regularly draining the resources of the business sector, with most of the young able bodied men being conscripted into the army to protect civilians and assist the police in maintaining law and order.

Whites who'd had enough and wanted to leave, felt restricted from leaving the country by stringent exchange control regulations. Whether as an individual or as a family, those wishing to emigrate were permitted to take out the maximum amount of one thousand dollars to start a new life. The middle aged, the older residents and those with families had little hope of leaving the country and starting anew with such meager resources, unless they had families or a job waiting for them outside the country to assist them. Many of those who were leaving were single young people on the threshold of their careers, who were prepared to start a new life from scratch, a further drain on the country of trained human resources.

As a student I received no special privilege, although while in Rhodesia, I had full access to my funds and was able to live well. I was only permitted to take out of the country my tuition fees which was paid directly to the university, and a maximum of six hundred dollars a year. From that I had to pay for my rent, electricity, gasoline and food. With an average of fifty dollars a month to live on, there was no latitude for any luxuries.

Rhodesia and South Africa's neighbor to the East, Mozambique, was also becoming a serious source of concern in the region, as it too, was having more than its fair share of political problems. Known also as Portuguese East Africa, the territory had been administered by Portugal as though it was a provincial part of its own metropolitan area. There was no central elected government and it was ruled by long distance in the form of decrees from Lisbon, which were enforced locally by the Governor-general in Lorenco Marques.

The Soviets had backed the political group known as Frelimo led by Samora Michele, which was leading an armed insurgency against the Portuguese. The insurgents were having a fair amount of success, primarily because Portugal was sending out conscripts from Portugal to defend the area, who had no idea of jungle life and had little incentive to risk life and limb for this wilderness so far from home. This was very different from the situation in Rhodesia, where there was, except for a sparse few, no other country to call "Home!"

News circulated about the poor fighting techniques of the Portuguese troops; When they heard of a guerrilla attack in a particular region, they would travel to the trouble spot, stay on the roads and unload weaponry, blazing firepower from the safety of their positions into the entire surrounding vicinity, barely leaving a twig standing. Before taking off again, without checking out to see if their attack and weaponry had been of any effect.

I like many other Rhodesians, could see the writing on the wall for my country. The situation was unlikely to improve. But also, like most of my countryfolk, tried to remain optimistic that something positive would develop on the political scene, which would pull the country back from the abyss of confrontation. If a solution was not found we faced a direction where many Rhodesians whatever their color could die.

At the end of the year, I headed back to Salisbury for the summer break. Rae was happy to have me back home, but during the first few days, I could see that she was troubled. "What is the matter, Mom?" I asked. "It is the business, Ivan. The exchange control quota's have been tightened so stringently, that we are now only able to import twenty-five percent of our capacity in cycle parts. Which means in order to survive we are going to have to let go several employees that have been with the company for years!" She replied. "Is there anything that can be done to increase the quota and save those jobs?" I asked. My mother shook her head "No, poor Benny, for once he has worked his heart out, he has tried everything to save the jobs and the business; he's been to the authorities to argue for an increase almost every week, written letters, had meetings with cabinet ministers, all with no success. It seems our foreign funds are weak, with the additional burden of most the money having to go to strengthen the defence forces." She said.

Once again, it seemed that while the politicians maneuvered the course of the country from their ivory towers, the real victims feeling the impact of their actions and political fight, would be the ordinary man in the street. It did not seem to matter, that all most civilians wanted to do was to make a living and get on with their normal lives.

I began to think about the future, it was becoming very uncertain for both blacks and whites. If one of the black groups did gain control of the country, it would most certainly be Marxist dominated. In the other African countries that this had occurred, it was invariably followed by a break down of law and order, economic collapse and rampant corruption. Then a chilling thought crossed my mind: Even though Rhodesia was my place of birth and this was my home; would all the whites also be forced to leave in a mass exodus, as had happened in the countries to the North? If that did occur what would I do? I decided that I needed to do something to cover that contingency.

A South African or Rhodesian law degree would do me very little good in countries overseas. What I needed was to obtain an internationally recognized qualification, one, that if the situation did turn for the worse in Rhodesia and I was forced to leave the country, would be recognized in either Europe or the United States. I began to look at the Universities of Oxford, Cambridge and London.

The University of London, had a very strong faculty of law. Recognized by most countries in the Western world, the faculty admitted external students to register with them and sit the exams in their home countries. The caution the university gave to all students was that the course was a tough one, on average seventy-five percent failed the course, with only one out of four students graduating with their LL.B. Degree.

I went to seek advice from the professor of law at the Rhodesian university, who had been on the panel when I was elected Youth Mayor of the city. Professor Christie was a knowledgeable and friendly counselor. He listened to my thoughts of registering with London after completing my undergraduate studies at Cape Town that year. Christie added his own caution as to the difficulty of doing the degree by long distance, but added that he was prepared to assist in two ways; firstly, by giving a letter of recommendation on my behalf to the London university. Secondly, he would put me in contact with the country's Director of Public Prosecutions, Brendan Treacy, with the purpose of being interviewed for a position as a public prosecutor. There was a general shortage of prosecutors and the Attorney General's office was prepared to hire undergraduates to prosecute in the Magistrates courts.

Professor Christie's suggestion to me was; that as I intended to practice as an Advocate in the higher Courts, that this would be an ideal way to gain the experience and build a reputation. It would also provide the practical experience for the time when I graduated and went to the bar. Success at the bar, he explained, relied on a good reputation to handle cases and was a necessity in order to receive briefs from Attorneys. At the same time I would also be able to earn a living while continuing with my studies.

As arranged, I meet with the Director of prosecutions, I was offered a position as an Assistant Public Prosecutor when I completed my studies at Cape Town the following year. I was delighted with the news, and the fact that I would at last be getting to work in the courts. I was starting to realize my dream of becoming a lawyer.

The Sunday before I was due to leave Salisbury to Return to South Africa, The city was rocked with a loud Explosion. A Bomb had been set off in the city center. Fortunately, it had been a weekend and no one had been injured, but the bomb must have been a large one, as almost every single window had been shattered in the twelve storied building next to where the explosion had occurred. I went to the scene, it was one of devastation with fragments of glass, bricks and warped metal everywhere.

The government did its best to play down the explosion as a random isolated incident in which no one had been hurt.

I left to return for my last year of studies in Cape Town. In my own mind, happy that I had made the arrangements to complete my law studies through the London university. It gave me the opportunity to complete my studies in Rhodesia, as well as to be close to my mother and cover for her safety. At the same time, I was providing for the situation where if the worst happened, and we were forced to leave the country, my overseas qualification would put me in a strong position to take care of both of us. I also knew that my brother and sister would help in those circumstances.

Chapter Eleven

In a remote region of North Eastern Rhodesia, in Mount Darwin, near the border with Mozambique in early 1970, a young couple had put their small child to bed and settled in to sleep for the night at their farmhouse. During the early hours of the morning, a gang of guerrillas numbering approximately thirty, who had been watching the isolated family, attacked.

With Chinese made A-K47 rifles the young family was mercilessly gunned down and butchered. The terrorist war in Rhodesia had begun.

A short while later a second attack took place in the same area. This time it was an elderly couple that was murdered. Their farmhouse was struck in the middle of the night and the couple were gunned down in their beds.

After a few days another attack took place near the border with Zambia. There a family that had farmed the land for forty years was attacked, again in the middle of the night and butchered to death with automatic weapons, this time with Soviet made rifles.

The attacks on lonely farms began to occur with increasing frequency. The police and army had moved rapidly in each case, but by the time they arrived on the scene, the terrorists had melted away under the cover of darkness to the shelter of the surrounding hilly slopes and bush region, or, had slipped across the country's borders, making it practically impossible to find them.

If the terrorists intention was to instill fear and disrupt the agricultural life, they succeeded only in instilling fear. The perception of these attacks by white Rhodesians was that of cowardly acts of murder on innocent civilians unable to defend themselves. The killing of innocents, left a feeling of disgust and outrage even amongst moderates who were attempting to work out a solution to the country's political differences, the division between the two races hardened. The white farmers became determined to stay and work on their land and win the terrorist war.

I kept abreast of the developments happening at home, through friends that visited cape Town, my mother's phone calls and letters, as well as the local newspapers. I read of the attacks on vehicles along lonely roads, making it necessary for me now to travel home under the protection of armed convoys.

Some of the terrorist leaders were gaining personal notoriety, using pseudonyms, their activities were reported in the local press. Names such as "Che Guevera", "White Death" and "One eye" appeared with regularity. The name "One Eye" had an unusual ring to me, and I wondered if the terrorist had come by that name through an injury sustained in a contact with the Rhodesian forces.

Occasional references also started to appear in the news about a highly effective counter terrorist force, sometimes referred to as the "Selous Scouts". The reports were that the group was composed of blacks and whites, all able to speak Shona and Ndebele, as well as other local dialects. They had been effective in disguising themselves as guerrillas, infiltrating the terrorist camps, sometimes capturing the members, or, in the case of resistance taking them out in fire fights. I thought of Amos and wondered if the risks he was taking with the Selous scouts were not too dangerous.

The news from Chantelle was encouraging, her career was doing well and moving along. She had sent me cuttings from several magazines, containing her stories and photographs of the beauty of Southern

Africa. She also wrote of her experiences. She was now traveling, covering the developing stories in Vietnam, Cambodia and Laos. Her letters were very descriptive of the guerrilla war raging in South East Asia and the tragedy in the loss of human life. She expressed her concern and hope that the situation did not develop to the same extent in Rhodesia.

I completed my studies at Cape town and headed back to Salisbury at the end of the year. I looked forward to the experience I would gain in the prosecutors office, although I was now going to be earning less than a tenth of the income I had made when in business for myself, in the cycle shops.

I started work in the prosecutor's office under the training and supervision of the Senior Public Prosecutor. The offices I worked out of were next to the Magistrates courts, an old brick building with rickety wooden floors and interior. Built in the 1920's, in Forbes Avenue, it had an aura of almost belonging to a previous century. A new modern facility was being planned for, at a larger site on the outskirts of the city, but that was still in the works and two years away from completion.

For two months I followed the senior prosecutor, and watched the court procedures, before my authority to prosecute was issued by the Attorney general.

As an initiation, the Senior prosecutor, found the most embarrassing case available, for me to try as my first case. It was petty matter, The charge was "Indecent Exposure" against a visiting stripper from Europe, appearing at one of the local night clubs. It seemed from the facts presented in the docket, that under local regulations, while she could bare her breasts, she had to cover her bottom half with at least a "G" string. The stripper had decided on several occasions to "Bare all!" The police had warned her that her act was going too far on a few occasions, but she continued to defy them; hence the charge. The pending case had gained a lot of attention and was widely covered by the press.

On the day of the trial I entered the packed courtroom, accompanied by the Senior Prosecutor. The defence attorney was present, so was the stripper. She was wearing a low cut see through pink blouse, Mini-skirts were the rage of the time, and she was wearing one, a tiny one. She sat in the open dock, she was also wearing see through pink panties, which left nothing to the imagination. She was a beautiful women, but, I doubted that anyone was looking at her face.

Everyone stood as the Magistrate was called in to court. The Magistrate walked in, did a double take at the defendant, turned and walked out of the courtroom. I began to believe I was in a nightmare!

All the lawyers were called into the Magistrate's office, where we were chewed out for allowing an improperly dressed defendant into court. I wondered how I could possibly have any control over what a defendant wore, but decided not to argue the point. The trial started and the stripper was convicted and fined the amount of fifty dollars. The stripper thanked the Magistrate for his leniency, and promptly invited him to see her show for free.

I settled in to the small cases assigned to new prosecutors, which consisted mostly of petty traffic violations, thefts and assaults. I had also, to adjust to the London university timetable, which went by the Northern Hemisphere schedule of sitting exams in May or June and not in November as I was used to. I had decided to study for and write the first year exams that June as a dry run, before making a more serious attempt the following year. To my total surprise, I passed the examinations!

With time and experience, I moved on to more complicated cases, by the end of the first year I was prosecuting, fraud, arson and the more serious assault cases termed; assault with intent to do grievous bodily harm. One case in particular hit the international news media. It was the case of the "Red Fox!" In that case, the accused had returned to Rhodesia after serving two years in prison in Zambia. When he arrived back, he discovered that a parking meter supervisor had been having an affair with his wife. His wife now wished to separate from him.

One night, the "Red Fox" laid in wait for the supervisor outside his wife's home. When the supervisor arrived to visit the woman, the "Red Fox" pounced from his hiding place and proceeded to beat the living daylights out of the man nearly killing him, after which the "Red Fox" rang his wife's doorbell. When she answered the door he picked up the unconscious supervisor and displayed the languid and bloodied body of the man to her, with the comment; "What do you think of your boyfriend now?" She had gone into hysterics and called the police. Amongst other injuries the supervisor had suffered a major concussion, a broken leg and a broken arm.

The "Red Fox" had retained Jay Patanak, a lawyer for whom I had the greatest respect. Patanak was literally a walking legal encyclopedia, whom most prosecutors dreaded arguing cases against, and, if there was any kind of flaw, crack or loophole in a case he would find it and win the trial. He entered a plea of not guilty.

While admitting beating up the supervisor; Patanak entered the defence that this was a crime of passion, that the supervisor was committing adultery with the wife while the "Red Fox" was away helping the country by doing undercover work for the Rhodesian Special Branch in Zambia. He said that the "Red Fox" had deliberately gotten himself convicted of fraud in Zambia to get himself sent to prison as a cover. From the prison with the help of the prison guards he would sneak out at night and infiltrate the nearby terrorist camps, gathering information which he would then relay back to police headquarters in Rhodesia under the code name "Red Fox", by hooking up a wire from his prison cell to the telephone wires running outside the prison. I argued that even if those facts were true, the "Red Fox" admitted the assault, that this was no defence to taking the law into his own hands, and these facts purely went to the mitigation of the case.

The matter was widely reported in the press and raised a lot of sympathy for the "Man who was taken advantage of, and marriage destroyed, while serving his country!" I felt sympathy for the man too, but I had a duty to prosecute the case to its full extent. The police also denied that the man had ever done any undercover work for them and said the whole undercover story was a figment of the man's imagination!

I requested a meeting with the officer commanding Special Branch, at police headquarters. The assistant commissioner that met with me flat out denied any covert undercover involvement with the "Red Fox!" As I got up to leave the meeting feeling satisfied as to the lack of any connection, the police officer shook me by the hand, smiled and made the parting comment "By the way, for future reference, it is our policy to officially deny any individual's involvement with Special Branch!"

As an officer of the court, I had a duty and obligation to disclose that comment, potentially favoring the defendant in court. Patanak seized on those words and the case dragged on for several weeks. More time was spent on the side issues of the "Red Fox's" alleged covert activities for the State, than the assault for which the man was being charged. The courtroom was regularly packed with spectators. The case also made the international tabloids; Leon, my brother sent me a cutting from the London daily paper which headlined that Rhodesia was putting it's own spies on trial! Chantelle who was covering a story in Paris sent a copy of a Parisian paper mentioning my name as prosecuting the "notorious double agent, the Red Fox," for his spying activities, with very little said that the trial was actually about a serious assault.

The Magistrate at the end of the lengthy trial convicted the "Red Fox" of the lower charge of common assault, and fined the man thirty dollars.

That case taught me the power of the press and their ability to take a simple case and hype it up into a media circus! I also learnt a little more about deception and misinformation; Amos, was a regular visitor to the courts, either as a witness or dropping in to say hello to me. A few months after the completion of the case, during one of those visits, Amos said to me, "Do you remember the case of the "Red Fox?" "I don't think I will ever forget it!" I replied. "Well the fact is that he was really a courier working with us in the Selous Scouts. He went to Zambia to collect information from the real spy! You see, all those things he said in court really did happen—except not to him! He was not the one sneaking into the terrorist camps and feeding us the intelligence. That was one of our black officers who got a job at the Zambian prison, and he continued to feed us with the intelligence, while the trial was going on in Salisbury and focused on the "Red Fox," feigning to be the spy!" I looked at Amos dumbfounded.

Amos continued, "I can tell you this now, because the officer is now back and safe in Rhodesia. When the "Red Fox" came back and assaulted the Parking supervisor, we spoke to him after his arrest and he agreed to tell the story we created as a diversion intended for the ears of the Zambian authorities, in case they were starting to become suspicious of the real perpetrator in their midst!"

A short while afterwards I received my military call up papers, but because of the importance of my prosecuting duties, the Attorney General had the military training deferred. Instead, I was seconded to duties in the Court Martial's office, prosecuting army cases over weekends. I was also placed on police reserve duties. Which meant late night duties two to three days a week and over alternative weekends. In order not become involved with matters which could conflict with my role as a prosecutor, I was assigned to walk a beat from midnight to four in the morning with other reservists, to protect the suburbs from terrorist attacks.

Terrorism in Rhodesia was increasing at an alarming pace. It become a staple for most people in the country to tune into the eight-o-clock news to hear the daily reports of the latest attack on a lonely farm, the people killed in those attacks; the contacts between the armed forces and the terrorists, and the lose of life sustained by either side. There was also a mini war developing between the rival terrorist factions, Z.A.P.U. and Z.A.N.U., it seemed that the Soviet and Chinese backed groups were equally determined to wipe out each others forces, as they were to fighting the government forces.

It was always a sad event to hear of the people being killed on a daily basis, and even more heartwrenching to hear the news of a friend or of young people I had grown up with, dying in the conflict. The bar at the Repertory Theater, "Reps Bar", was a favorite place to meet on a Friday evening for a social after work. Now, those Friday evenings at Reps, more often than not was the meeting place for a wake for some friend that had been killed during the preceding week.

The court house where I worked was only a couple of blocks away from Railway Avenue, where the Royal Cycles assembly plant was situated. I would often take a lunch break from the stress of my duties to spend the lunch hour with my mother, Rae. The business was struggling along. There was no improvement in the import quotas and it had become a major task to find sufficient parts for bicycle assembly. My mother was seriously talking of selling out her interest in the business, but ran into the problem of finding a buyer who would be interested in buying this or any other business that could not bring in sufficient parts to operate lucratively.

My responsibilities increased in the prosecutor's office. I was required to sign the Official Secret's Act, and did a tour of duty handling Inquests of terrorist attacks on the civilian population.

The first Inquest I did, caused me to be violently ill to my stomach. It involved an attack by terrorists on a school in Inyanga, run by seven Nuns teaching black children. All seven Nuns had been raped, then shot to death with automatic weapons. Some of the lifeless bodies were dismembered, with parts of their bodies laying in different parts of the school. The children had been abducted, obviously either to do pack carrying for the guerrillas or to be sent on for training as guerrillas themselves. I wondered what kind of animals these people were to carry out such atrocious acts and whether this was a foretaste of their type of "Democracy" that those political factions were going to impose on the peoples of the country. From the reports of the older black workers who had survived, the attack had been led under the command of the terrorist known as "One Eye!"

I wanted to know more about the guerrillas leading these attacks and was supplied the confidential portfolios of what was known of the terrorist leaders in the region. I browsed through the information, reading the background information on the men using the pseudonyms "Che Guevera", then "White death."

I came to the documents of the man I was the most interested in, the man responsible for the brutal slaying of the Nuns, in Inyanga, "One Eye!"

What I read was so unexpected, that it left me with a feeling of complete horror! I read the documents with a feeling of disbelief "This couldn't be true!" I thought. I put the documents down and stared out the window stunned at the information!

After a few moments I picked up the documents and read them again.

"Confidential/Top Secret"

TERRORIST leader: "One Eye" alias: Enock.

Date of birth: Unknown. Origin: Mozambique.

Known information: TERRORIST LEADER OF Z.A.P.U IN THE INYANGA DISTRICT, HOLDING RANK OF COMRADE COLONEL. RESPONSIBLE FOR LEADING SEVERAL ATTACKS ON ISOLATED FARM HOUSES AND THE BRUTAL SLAYINGS OF WHITE FARMERS. HIS METHODS ARE KNOWN TO BE RUTHLESS AND SOCIOPATHIC. HE HAS BEEN KNOWN TO HAVE GUNNED DOWN HIS OWN MEN FOR ANY BREACH OF HIS ORDERS. DISAPPEARS INTO THE BUSH TERRAIN AFTER HIS ATTACKS WHERE HE REMAINS HIDDEN FOR DAYS, TO AVOID CONTACT WITH OUR MILITARY FORCES SEARCHING FOR HIM AFTER CARRYING OUT ACTS OF TERRORISM.

BACKGROUND: JOINED THE COMMUNIST PARTY IN 1961. TRAINED IN MOCAMBIQUE FOR TWO YEARS, BEFORE BEING SENT TO NORTH VIETNAM FOR THREE YEARS TRAINING IN GUERRILLA WARFARE BY CHINESE AND NORTH VIETNAMESE INSTRUCTORS. RETURNED TO MOCAMBIQUE FROM WHICH HE RECEIVES SUPPLIES AND LAUNCHES HIS TERRORIST ATTACKS.

PRIOR TO MILITARY CAREER, KNOWN TO HAVE WORKED FOR THE BENDER FAMILY IN BELVEDERE. HE HAS ACHIEVED AN ACADEMIC LEVEL OF FORM TWO WITH THE HELP OF HIS EMPLOYERS, IN PARTICULAR IVAN BENDER.

HIS ALIAS STEMS FROM THE FACT THAT HE WAS BLINDED IN ONE EYE SHORTLY AFTER BIRTH BY HIS PARENTS IN ORDER TO GAIN SYMPATHY AS A BEGGAR ON THE DOCKS OF BEIRA.

HE IS A HIGHLY DANGEROUS AND SKILLED GUER-RILLA TACTICAL LEADER....

I could not read any more, I felt devastated by the disclosure and put the documents down.

Reaching for the phone, I placed a call to Amos at Police Headquarters in Railway Avenue, requesting that he come to my office immediately. "What's the matter Ivan, You sound upset?" Amos said in agreeing to meet with me. "I will tell you about it when you get here!" I replied and hung up the telephone.

A short while later, Amos entered into my office to see a very serious expression on my face looking across at him from behind the desk. "What do you know about Enock's activities since we last saw him?" I asked. Amos went silent for a few seconds then sunk into the seat in front of me. "I was wondering when you would find out about Enock! I am sorry Ivan, but that was confidential information under the Official Secrets act, I was not permitted to talk about it freely with you!"

Amos stated. "How long have you known that he had become a terrorist?" I asked. "For a few years now! The sad part is to see how really evil he has become. I think he enjoys the killing and the bloodshed." Amos answered and continued with a caution, "You know that you cannot discuss what you have learned about Enock with anyone, including your mother!" He said. I nodded my head, "It is going to be as tough a secret for me to keep, as it must have been for you over the last few years!" I replied.

I approached my second year examinations with the university of London. My work with the prosecutors office and duties with the police and military, had left me very little time for proper preparation. Nevertheless, I wrote the papers in late May, 1972; and failed the exams. The results were a disappointment, but I steeled himself with the news that I had not passed and resigned myself to the fact that I would have to write them again the following year.

Things seemed to have a knack of going wrong all at the same time. The day after I had received the news of not having passing my exams, I was called in for a Saturday sitting of the court. Two white males had been arrested for a series of Bank robberies and were being brought to court for a preliminary hearing and to be remanded to a trial date. One of the accused entered a plea of guilty and was heard separately from his co-accused who was denying the charges. After his hearing he was led back to the cell in the center of the court house. The second defendant was heard and remanded to a separate trial date. After the court adjourned, the second accused was being led to the cell when he bolted from the prison officer and escaped, running past me. I gave chase as the man ran out of the building onto the street, closing the gap between us as we neared the end of the block. I was about to tackle the fleeing fugitive, when suddenly I got tackled myself from behind and was brought crashing down to the pavement. The prison guard in pursuit had mistakenly thought that I was the escaped felon and tackled me. The two of us struggled on the pavement, I yelled at the obstinate guard that he had gotten the wrong person and was seriously tempted to swing a punch at the moron. The felon in the meantime was increasing his distance away from us and would have made good his escape, except he ran into two magistrates who understood what was happening. They tackled the fleeing man, capturing him and handed him over to the red faced guard. The report in the newspaper the next day ran the embarrassing story under the headline: "Magistrates capture fleeing prisoner, while Prison guard captures prosecutor!" This resulted in my having to endure several days of healthy teasing from my co workers, with comments such as "So, have you been captured by any good prison guards, lately Ivan?" Mercifully, with all the different events going on at the courts, the incident was soon forgotten and I was able to put the teasing behind me.

Work was being completed on the new court house. Built on the outskirts of the city center, it was a large, modern, circular, five storied complex. A vast improvement from the rickety old courts in Forbes Avenue, this building had a large fountain in the center hub of the circle. There were eighteen courts on the first floor, housing the junior, senior and provincial courts. The second level consisted of the prosecutors offices. The third level was made up of the Regional courts which handled the more serious cases for the Eastern District of Rhodesia, and the civil courts. The rest of the building accommodated the magistrates, administrative, prison and police offices.

When we eventually moved in to the new premises, I really liked the changes, with my new modern office, combined with the updated facilities and spacious court rooms. I settled in happily and shortly afterwards it was almost a disappointment, when I heard that I had been promoted and would soon be moving to the position of Public Prosecutor for Harari, at the end of the year. The Harari courts were only a few miles away, near the African townships. Those courts handled a heavy volume of cases and received the second largest number of district court case trials heard in the country. More modern than the old Forbes Avenue court house, the Harari courts still fell far short of the amenities of the new courts. With a few months left before the end of the year, I thought that I would at least make the most of my stay in the new building.

The next two months seemed to pass by in a blur with a heavy workload of new cases being submitted by the police for trial at the new courthouse. I settled in to handle my share of the workload. I began to find that between trying court cases, my police reserve duties and the commitment to army court martials's, there was no time left for anything else.

Then, I received the news that shattered my world. After a particularly heavy load of trials one day, court had been adjourned for the daily session. I walked outside the court room to take a breather and found Motorcar's wife Sheila, sitting on one of the benches waiting for me. She was sobbing, looked very frightened and in a distraught state. "Dear goodness, Sheila! What is the matter, you look like something terrible has happened?" I asked, sitting down beside her . "Its Motorcar." she stammered, "The terrorists have killed him!" She said between sobs. Her words hit me like a hammer and I had to force myself to stay in control of my emotions. She continued, "Motorcar told me that if anything should ever happen to him, that I was to come to you Ivan. He said that you were his friend, and that you would protect his family!" I felt a darkness close in around me at the news of hearing of Motorcar's death, and tried to remain rational. "I am glad that you came, Sheila! I am so sorry for you and the children. Please, tell me what happened?"

Sheila continued to sob "In the middle of the night last week, Enock came with seven of his men to the village. They woke us and called us out of our huts at gun point, Enock said that there was a collaborator in the village. He pointed to Motorcar and said that they were going to show us what they did to people who worked with the whites. Enock and his people dragged Motorcar to the middle of the village and began to beat him with their guns. Then they made him stand up and shot him many times, Motorcar fell, dead! Then they drank beer and laughed. When the sun started to rise, they got up to leave, Enock turned to me and said; Now, you can tell Ivan what I have done!'" She said.

"I am so sorry! Motorcar was a good man! I am so sorry!" I repeated. "Where are your children?" I asked. "They are safe at school in Umtali." She replied. "Come up to my office, I will make arrangements for a place for you to stay!" I said. In my office, I phoned Amos who was equally devastated with the news of Motorcar's death. He came to the courts to offer his condolences personally and offered to have Sheila to stay with him at the police barracks. Sheila gratefully accepted his offer.

The next two nights I was unable to sleep because of the emotional turmoil, finally I made up my mind as to what I was going to do! I Called Amos to enquire about Sheila and asked him to come to my office after court, the next day.

"It is terrible what Enock did to Motorcar…" Amos started to say, before I interrupted him. "Yes it was, and I am going to do something about it!" I stated. Amos faced me "What are you going to do?" He enquired. "I am going after Enock in the bush!" I said, matter of factly. Amos stared at me "Are you 'Penga'!" He asked, 'Penga' being the Shona word for "crazy!" "No, I am not 'Penga', I know exactly what I am doing. Can you arrange for me to meet with your superior officer in the Selous Scouts?" I asked. "That can be arranged, but I do not think that will do you any good!" Amos replied. "Please, do it." I requested.

The next day I received a call from Amos, setting up the meeting for that evening in the Special Branch offices at police headquarters.

Arriving at the offices, Amos took me past security, to the operations section. Captain Swartz of the Selous Scouts and police Superintendent Black were seated waiting for me. Swartz came immediately to the point, "Sergeant Amos tells us that you want to go into the bush after 'One Eye' is that correct?" He asked. "Yes, it is, I think I can capture him!" I replied. "By yourself?" The policeman Black questioned. "Yes." I stated simply. Swartz shook his head, "Are you crazy? We have been chasing after him for a few years now without any success. Each time he has struck we have immediately gone in after him, and he has been able to elude us...what makes you think you have any better chance of catching him?" Swartz charged. I was beginning to become irked with the confrontational questioning, "That is the second time that my idea has been called 'crazy' and it is starting to annoy me!" I responded. "Remember, I know 'One eye' probably better than anyone else, with the possible exception of sergeant Amos and I have a very good idea of how he thinks! When 'One Eye' strikes, he knows damn well that the Scouts are going to come chasing after him, so he melts into the bush and stays hidden until the search for him and his men is exhausted. When your men leave, to give attention to attacks taking place elsewhere, he comes out of hiding and strikes again and the cycle begins once again!" I paused, noticing that I now had Swartz and Black's attention. "Go on!" Black said. "My plan is to go in *after* the search for him by your forces has been exhausted and your men have been pulled out! I would prefer to have the help of one of your men that knows the terrain in Inyanga, but I am prepared to go in alone!" I explained. Swartz looked at Black, "The idea is so wild, that it just may work!" He commented with a laugh.

Superintendent Black looked pensive, "We have been in the Inyanga area searching for 'One Eye' for over a week now, since his last attack, when your friend Motorcar was murdered. We are going to look for another couple of days, before calling off the search. Perhaps, that would be the time to set the trap that you suggest, but you would definitely need help, it would be suicide to go in alone!" Amos stepped forward; "I am prepared to volunteer to go with Ivan!" He said, offering to support me.

Swartz turned to me, "Black and I need to discuss this matter! Please, would you and sergeant Amos wait outside in one of the other offices, while we talk about it—I can make you no promises!"

Amos and I did as instructed and waited in a sparse bland operations office for over an hour. Then superintendent Black called us back in to his office. "Sorry to keep you waiting, but we had to go through the appropriate higher channels and discuss this matter with our superiors. Normally, your suggestion would never stand a chance of being approved! However, as you can guess, we want to capture 'One Eye' badly enough to do the unusual—it would be a major morale booster for our forces! In this case, you both know the adversary and while there is only a remote chance of your succeeding, you have opened an unusual opportunity to capture him. So, we have been given the go ahead to help you!" Black Stated.

Captain Swartz took over, "Here is the plan we have come up with to get you into the area unnoticed! We are going to continue our present search for 'One Eye' for another two days. If we do not have a successful contact, we will pull out our troops early morning on the third day. To do that, we will as usual send in trucks to pick them up. In case we are being watched, about a mile from the pick up site, the driver of one the vehicles will have engine trouble near a heavily bushed area. The two of you will be in the rear of that truck! You will slip off into the bush, while attention is being diverted to repairing the truck's engine. Stay hidden in the bushes until the trucks are well out of sight. That is the best we can do to help you get in, so after that time, you will be on your own! Any questions so far?" Amos and I were following his scheme so far and replied that there were none.

Swartz continued, "We will supply you with Ak-47 rifles that we have captured from the terrorists, camouflage clothing and flares to set off to draw attention to your position, if you should need help! Is there anything else you might need?" "Yes!" I replied, "We will need four hundred and fifty yards of khaki spool thread. Also, I would like you to move out all the troops from the vicinity, and without being conspicuous, make it fairly obvious that they are all being pulled out! I am requesting that for two reasons; firstly, I want Enock to think that he has a free reign in the area, and secondly we do not want to accidentally trip over our own forces that may not know who we are and end up in a friendly but deadly firefight!" "We can do that!" Black replied, "Anything else?" He asked. "Yes, I need someone to arrange a pretext for me to be away from the prosecutors' office, for a few days!" I requested. "That part is easy, we can arrange for you be called up on emergency duties!" Black replied. "But remember this; if anything goes wrong, we will deny any involvement with you! Should you be injured or killed, we will put you down as merely another casualty statistic of the war, or if necessary, as loose cannons that went off into the bush on your own!" Amos and I nodded our heads in agreement.

The following two days the security forces continued their intensive search, but were unable to find any trace of "One Eye". Accordingly, preparations for our plan went into effect and I received my "Emergency call up." In the evening as I prepared to leave for police headquarters to await the early morning transportation to Inyanga, my mother knocked on my bedroom door and entered into the room. "Ivan, I can sense that there is something wrong with this particular call up?" She asked. I found it very difficult to lie to her, "Mom, it is okay it is just an emergency call up, I will be back in a couple of days!" I could see that she was not buying what I was saying. "I know you too well Ivan, does this have anything to do with Motorcar's death?" She challenged. I couldn't look at her for the moment, "Now Mom, how could my call up have anything to do with Motorcar's Murder?" I said, and not giving her a chance to reply I gave her a hug and left the house.

I met with Amos at the special branch offices for a final briefing from superintendent Black. We checked our equipment and rations, putting on our camouflage tunics, before settling to get some sleep on the uncomfortable wooden chairs in one of the offices. We were awakened just before sunrise and set off in a Land Rover, towards the military post where we were scheduled to meet with the transportation trucks, a few miles outside Inyanga.

The convoy of trucks was at the ready, and set off to pick up the troops. Amos and I lay crouched and hidden in one of them, it was just after eight in the morning. The convoy traveled for several miles on the main road and then turned off onto a dirt side road to head towards the pick up point of the troops in the bush. In doing so, the trucks entered into an area of heavy undergrowth where the grass had grown to almost the same height as the vehicles. As pre-arranged, the truck in which we were covertly traveling, began to have engine trouble. A smoke bomb hidden under the hood was triggered and billowed out black fumes from the engine. In the resulting confusion, with the vehicles stopped and men moving around us to effect repairs, Amos and I slipped off the vehicle and melded in with the surrounding bushes. A short time passed, The truck drivers "repaired" the engine problem and returned to their vehicles. Amos and I watched from the bushes as they took off. We remained motionless for a good half hour after the trucks had departed the vicinity, in case the scene was being watched. Quietly, we crept forward and farther into the veldt checking for any spoor or signs of human presence.

By early evening we had crawled our way several miles, penetrating deep into the bushveldt. We approached a rocky terrain containing a large series of balancing rocks and caves. Amos and I surveyed the area and concluded that this was one of the ideal spots that "One Eye" and his men might pick as a hiding place to become lost in. We made a note of the spot, then moved on, continuing to search for other likely places that Enock might pick as a base to cloak his presence. We uncovered a handful of other probable areas that offered a suitable refuge for camouflage. A few hours later, we returned to the rocky terrain. After some discussion, Amos and I came to the conclusion that this locality provided the best concealment for Enock and his men. We decided to set up our trap at this site.

I took out the spool of Khaki thread that we had brought along as part of our equipment. I had been surprised that no one had asked me why I had made the request for this item. I was also grateful that as a result, I did not need to explain my intended use for the thread. I unraveled the thin cotton filament and stealthily tied one end to a tree covering the main access into the balancing rocks. Then I unthreaded the spool along the length of several other gaps that led into the rocks for a distance of a hundred and fifty yards. Where the rocky ground ended, I ran the thread around a small bush without knotting it. I moved back about a hundred yards and knotted the thread around the little finger of my left hand. I instructed Amos to go to a position two hundred yards in a straight line away from me, unraveling the thread as he went. I informed him that when the thread ran out, Amos was to tie that end to a finger on his hand. I went on to explain; "If 'One Eye' comes through any of those gaps, he will cause the thin thread strand to yank on my finger before it breaks. I in turn, will pull on the thread that links me to you, so that we can silently communicate from our cover that there is a presence coming through the bushes!"

We settled and crouched into our respective positions two hundred yards apart, separated by the thick undergrowth. I checked my watch, it was near midnight. The adrenaline began to pump throughout my body causing my senses to feel heightened as my eyes scanned the vicinity and my ears peaked for any feet rustling over grass. Other than an owl hooting in a nearby tree, there were no sounds to be heard and nothing moved. Time appeared to slow down and the hours of the darkness lingered. I kept prepared with my finger ready on the safety catch of the AK-47 rifle, geared to spring in to action.

Amos and I waited motionless in our spots throughout the night. Not even a field mouse had stirred through the grass by the time the first early morning rays of light spread across the bushveldt. I relaxed my vigil momentarily, to take in some water and rations.

We remained and waited through the day. I started to get cramps and gently massaged my aching muscles to relieve the pain. With the visibility of daylight I was now able to observe the rocky terrain in its entirety. I noticed that other than some birds in the trees, there were no animals foraging on the ground or in the rocks. I felt sure that this was a telltale sign of the wild life avoiding a human presence.

Evening started to fall again and everything remained quiet. We watched and waited, I fell into a light sleep, occasionally waking during the different times of the night. Sunrise arrived and I awakened with it. We waited motionless, throughout the day. Night came again. Still nothing!

By the third day, I began to give up hope that my plan was going to work. The rations were starting to run low and there had been no signs of any activity around the rocky terrain. I wondered how Amos was doing under these conditions, we had not spoken or moved since taking up our positions. "Perhaps, tonight should be the last night we stay at this place before moving on!" I thought to myself.

Evening began to draw in. It was a clear moonlit night, conditions that were the least likely to bring Enock out on one of his strikes. I moved my body slightly to keep the circulation going and settled in for another night of watchful waiting. After midnight I fell into a light sleep. I was abruptly awakened by a strong tug from the thread on my little finger, the tension on the thread went loose—it had been broken! I yanked on the thread leading from me to Amos and it too, broke. I prayed that Amos had gotten the message! I looked at my watch and was able to make out that it was four in the morning. Quietly, I crept forward for a distance, then I froze! Ahead of me, I could see the outline of eight men walking in my direction. I crawled for cover behind a rock and waited.

The men drew closer and stopped momentarily a few yards in front of the spot where I was hiding. The moonlight was bright and I was able to see them clearly. They wore the Viet Kong style camouflage tunics and carried AK-47 automatic rifles slung over their shoulders. I focused on their features under the moonlight and was able to identify one of the men. It was Enock! I tried to hear what the men were talking about, much of what was being said was inaudible. But, what I was able to understand, Enock, was giving instructions to his men about an ambush they were going to set up on an isolated farmhouse some miles away. The men commenced to walk again closing in on my direction.

As the men drew closer, I decided on a bluff in order to capture them alive. "Drop your weapons, we have you surrounded!" I called out. The men responded by opening fire with their automatic weapons. I returned the fire and saw three men drop. The remainder took off running, heading in Amos's direction, where gunfire splattered from out of the bushes, two more men dropped. The three remaining men, split up, bolting in different directions. If one of them was Enock, I did not want to lose him in the bushes. I fired a flare into the night sky, brightly illuminating the scene, I could clearly see the top halves of the three men running in different directions through the bushes. To my left I recognized Enock and gave chase as the light from the flare dimmed. Enock stopped momentarily, turning to fire shots haphazardly at his rear towards me, before taking off running again. I did not stop to fire back, but kept running to close the distance between us and to block off entrance into the balancing rocks. The moonlight was still bright enough to make out Enock's form and direction that he was running in. Enock made it to a small group of balancing rocks, he slipped into them and from the refuge opened fire at me. I lunged into the grass rolling for cover and this time returned the fire, the sound of shoots being fired from behind the rocks stopped. For a few moments everything went quiet, I listened for any kind of sound. Then I heard the light rustle of running, the sound was moving away from me. I fired a second flare and saw Enock running in the opposite direction away from the rocky area, I gave chase. We were heading towards less bushy surroundings, Enock dodged in and out of available cover, occasionally stopping to fire a volley of shots at me. We reached a clearing, I fired off another flare and the light gave me a clear shot at the man running in the distance, I raised my rifle, and had Enock in my sights, then I hesitated. Everything seemed to blur! All I could see, was an image in my mind's eye of a raggedy waif, blind in one eye, knocking at the door to my home asking for a job! Ahead of me Enock stopped, turned and opened fire on me. The bullets whizzed by my head. One bullet ripped through the tunic above my left shoulder, giving me a flesh wound. I raised my rifle again, but before I could pull the trigger, a burst of gunfire blazed out of the bushes to my right. Bullets ripped into Enock, he slumped forward and fell to the ground dead.

Amos emerged from the bushes, I turned to him gratefully, "Thanks Amos, you very likely saved my life!" He remonstrated with me. "Why did you hesitate Ivan? You had a clear shot at Enock. He could have killed you?" Amos asked. " I don't know! Perhaps some day, I will be able to answer that question!" I replied, shaking my head. sadly at the sight of Enock laying still in the grass. Amos observed the blood dripping from the wound on my shoulder, "Are you badly hurt?" He asked. " No, it is just a flesh wound, I will be fine!" I replied.

We walked over to the motionless body of Enock, the sun was beginning to rise and the birds were starting to chirp in the trees, a new day was being born. I was saddened by the thought that neither Enock or Motorcar would see this, or any other day. We searched Enock's body and amongst his possessions found two pouches tied to his armaments belt. I opened the pouches, "Son of a gun! He did it!" I exclaimed. "What are you talking about?" Amos asked. "Rubies, the pouches are full of rough rubies! Remember long ago by an evening campfire, when we were talking about what we wanted to do in the future. Enock told us that he had heard rumors of a hidden ruby mine in Mozambique. That one day he would find it. He did, there must be at least fifty thousand dollars worth of rubies in each of these pouches!" I said, handing a pouch to Amos to examine.

I sat myself down on a small rock and addressed my friend; "Amos, we don't know how this war is going to turn out, I suggest you keep one of the pouches for yourself. Give the other to Sheila! That way you will both have a secure future, no matter what the outcome of this conflict is, you will have those gemstones to cash in if you need to!" Amos looked at me, "What about you?" he asked. "We have avenged Motorcar's death and probably saved lives in the future." I answered, "That is all I came here to do, I want nothing else! Besides, I have the money left from the sale of my businesses."

Amos and I started to trek back towards Inyanga. An hour into our walk, a military helicopter came chopping into sight. We waved at it and got its attention. The helicopter landed in a clearing nearby. Captain Swartz emerged, "Thank goodness, you are both all right! We had reports of flares being fired into the sky early this morning, we feared that you had gotten into serious trouble, so we came out in search of the two of you!" Swartz then questioned, "Did you two get into more trouble than you had bargained for?" He asked. "On the contrary!" I replied, "One Eye and five of his terrorists are laying dead over there!" I said pointing to the balancing rocks in the distance behind us. "WHAT!" Swartz blurted out. The unexpected reaction from the Selous Scout captain was almost laughable.

The military helicopter dropped Amos and I near a waiting Land Rover. We drove back to Salisbury for a debriefing session in superintendent Black's office at the main police station. Black portrayed the same surprised reaction as Swartz had shown with the news of the success of our mission. After showering, cleaning up my wound and changing into my regular clothes at police headquarters, I was back home by mid afternoon. Exhausted, I slept for a couple hours, awakened by a hug from my mother. I sat down to have dinner with her that evening. We listened to the Eight-o-clock news; the announcer read the military release, " In contacts with security forces early this morning, six terrorists were killed, one of them being the notorious renegade leader known as One Eye. Security forces suffered no casualties during the contact!"

I could still feel the adrenaline pumping through my body. The emotional trauma of Enock's death was also starting to impact on me. I needed to get out for a little while and drove to Reps bar. Avoiding social contact, I sat quietly at a back table having a drink. Without realizing it, I rapidly downed several Brandies, the pain seemed to ease a little.

Closing time of Eleven-o-clock approached and the bar thinned to a handful of people. One of those remaining was a man named Kloppers. He was a captain in the regular army, and had been sitting at the bar drinking more than he could handle of Vodkas. He called out to me, "Hey, Mister prosecutor! Can I come over and join you?" I beckoned him over. We sat together and swigged down a couple more drinks. Kloppers turned to me and slurred, "I really envy your cushy job with the courts, while the rest of us are out there risking our lives!" I smiled and nodded in agreement. Kloppers then passed out, onto the carpet. I walked over to the bartender and paid for the drinks, "Tell Kloppers, when he wakes up that the prosecutor with the cushy job, paid for his drinks!" with that I left the bar.

I had held the rank of lieutenant in the army for the purposes of conducting court martials. Unexpectedly, I was promoted, to the rank of Captain. I wondered, if this was a discreet reward for the mission.

Chapter Twelve

As scheduled I started my duties as Public Prosecutor for Harari at the end of the year. Rioting was starting to become a frequent occurrence in that district. As a result, during my daily drive to work each day I would be accompanied by a sense of apprehension, never knowing whether to expect a disturbance along the way, or when I arrived at work. The knowledge that the Harari courts could become a prime target for attack, by either rioters or terrorists did not help to ease my concerns. Sometimes driving to the courts, which were adjacent to the city's largest black township and the busy industrial sites, I would see remnants of the previous nights disturbances. Streets would be littered, shop windows smashed with the occasional store looted of its contents. At times, after a night of heavy rioting I would pass by the smoldering remains of a burnt out building.

Black on black violence was on a steep increase, mainly because of the competing ideals of the black parties and each's intolerance of the other's views. Consequently, the majority of cases heard at the courts involved assault proceedings at differing levels of gravity. The remainder of the cases, consisted of an assortment of preliminary hearings for murder, terrorist trials, theft, arson, fraud and a staple of negligent or drunken driving cases.

My duties were mainly in the "Set Down" office where cases received from the police were reviewed for their suitability for prosecution.

Based on the law and the evidence, a decision was then made as to whether or not to proceed to trial. Once the decision was made to proceed, it was a matter of evaluating the severity of the crime and setting cases down before the appropriate courts. The case load often became overwhelming!

A short while after I started my duties at the Harari courts, terrorists set off a massive bomb inside a nearby Woolworth's store. The shop was mainly frequented by black shoppers from the nearby township. The explosion occurred during the peak shopping hours, resulting in seventy-one people seriously injured and five deaths, all black people. The documentation presented to the courts showed a scene of total carnage, the explosion had ripped through the entire premises and it was by sheer good fortune that more people had not been killed. I wondered what the purpose was in the terrorists killing these innocent black shoppers.

A couple of months later one of the terrorists responsible in planning and planting the bomb, was captured. The man was brought to the Harari courts for the preliminarily hearing. The case was to be heard in camera, which meant that apart from the presiding magistrate, the defense attorney and myself as the prosecutor, the public were excluded. The press were barred from reporting the details of the case, in the interests of State security.

The "Warned and Cautioned" statement made by the accused gave details of how he and five others had received instructions from their hierarchy to bomb the store. The planning and planting of the bomb was also detailed. During the discussions that took place between the defense attorney and myself as to which points were undisputed and to be entered in as evidence, the accused was present. To my surprise, the accused seemed to have no problem in entering the discussions as to the events. One factor stood out, he had no remorse for the deaths he had caused. He also seemed to have little comprehension as to the damage to lives and families for which he had been responsible. When questioned as to why that particular store had been chosen, he merely shrugged, those had been his instructions and that is what had been carried out. With the defense attorney's permission, the conversation continued off the record. I asked the man's political beliefs; he had none. He had been abducted as a child by guerrillas, carried packs for them for two years and later trained as an urban terrorist.

After the preliminary hearing, the defense attorney who was himself black, joined me for tea, in the set down office. "You know when this case gets heard in the High court, there is very little doubt that he will be convicted and sentenced to hang!" He said. I responded; "I think you are right, though normally I am against the death sentence, in this case with so many innocent people killed and injured, I do not think he deserves any kind of clemency!"

The man was tried and convicted in the High court, where he was sentenced to death. He was later hanged, his, was one of the few death sentences that were actually carried out in Rhodesia at the time.

Official government censorship, barred the press from reporting some of the political events taking place in the country by the political parties of Z.A.P.U and Z.A.N.U., and the fact was that many of the black political leaders were being detained without trial under the country's proclaimed State of Emergency. One fact that the public was starting to hear about was that the parties were starting to loosely unite under the leadership of Bishop Abel Muzerewa in an umbrella party calling itself the African National Union, or A.N.U.! Despite many of the white's dislike for the new "troublemaker!" Muzorewa was a man of religion, a Methodist minister, who leaned more to the West than was the case with the other Marxist backed leaders. With Muzorewa at the helm, there seemed to be an opportunity to work out some form of reconciliation.

Ian Smith, The Rhodesian prime minister, entered into negotiations at this time with the British and an agreement was reached with them. The proposal was to gradually increase black representation in the government. The agreement was subject to approval by the black Rhodesian leaders. To gauge this acceptance Britain sent out a commission, headed by a British Peer, Lord Pierce. The black leaders of Z.A.P.U. and Z.A.N.U. who had been detained were reluctantly released by the Rhodesian government, as part of the agreement package.

The A.N.U. umbrella group orchestrated riots and protests to show that the agreement was not acceptable to them. I found that the overloaded case load I had been dealing with at the Harari courts, suddenly tripled! Truckloads of rioters and protesters were being brought in. As there was no way that the remand prison could handle the volume of people arrested, the solution was to detain the rioters for a few hours and bring them to court for immediate processing. The people charged were generally treated with a slap on the wrist receiving fines ranging from ten dollars for those involved in minor disturbances to fifty dollars for the more serious cases.

The disturbances, combined with the commissions meetings with the black political leaders, lead the Pierce group to the conclusion that there was a resounding "No!" verdict by Rhodesian blacks to the proposed agreement and Britain backed away from the settlement. Many of the previously detained black leaders left the country and became heavily involved in directing the guerrilla and terrorist war from "Exile." Amongst them was the Z.A.N.U. lieutenant Robert Mugabe. The war escalated dramatically from this point forward.

Amos when he returned from his police and Selous scout duties, was a frequent visitor to the Harari courts and sometimes he and I would take a lunch break, and sit under the shade of an oak tree on the court grounds. On one of those occasions I enquired whether Amos was being kept busy with Selous Scout activities, expecting as usual a short non committal reply. This time it was different, Amos seemed to almost welcome that I had asked the question. There seemed to be something he wanted to get off his chest. "Yes, we have been kept very busy. Both black and white members have been very effective with disguising ourselves as terrorists and infiltrating their guerrilla camps. What is surprising is that a large number of terrorists once captured, have joined our side, that, is making us even more effective!" Amos said. I had a question which I had long wanted to ask, "How do the white officers get away with being accepted as terrorists by the black guerrilla groups?" I enquired. "Apart from us being fluent in all the dialects, and using captured AK-47 weapons, the white members of our group cover themselves with an indelible brown solution, which makes them look the same pigmentation as the rest of us. Sometimes, if the white has fair hair we shave his head, which is what a lot of the terrorists normally do anyway, and our people are able to blend in with them." Amos replied.

There was silence for a few seconds, then I said, "Normally you do not talk much about what you do in the Scouts, is there something troubling you?" Amos nodded his head, "Yes, there is, it seems we have been too effective in disguising ourselves, we recently had a successful contact with a group of ten guerrillas, we call them "Ters", in which we were able to capture the whole group. We brought them back to a pre-arranged meeting point by the side of a river where the prisoners were picked up by waiting trucks and brought to Salisbury. One of the white officers Andre Rabie, stayed behind and was sunning himself by the river bank, when he was seen by our regular army troops on patrol. They observed what they thought was a black man, wearing "Ter" camouflage and an AK-47 rifle by his side. The troops opened fire and killed him!" "Shit!" I exclaimed, "You mean he was shot to death by our own people?" Amos nodded, "It seems we are running the risk of being hit by our own troops as well as the "Ters" now, because of the disguise!" He said. "I can see why you are upset! There must be some way from preventing that from happening again?" I remarked. "There is, I just hope the new plans being made come into effect before more tragic accidents like that, happen again." Amos commented, as the lunch hour ended.

It became the policy of the government to give prosecutors a police and military briefing on a regular basis as the armed conflict in the country developed, in order to be better prepared for questions that might arise in court. Initially, the officers giving the briefing were very reluctant to even make mention of the role being played by the Selous Scouts. Eventually, that attitude softened and the subject was talked about openly.

At one of those briefings, I specifically brought up the circumstances of Andre Rabie's death. The Briefing officers took turns at explaining how the incident had transpired and the plans they had effected, to avoid the occurrence of that tragedy from happening again. "As you can appreciate we cannot go into details, for security reasons, on how the Scouts operate. They are however, responsible for close to ninety percent of all the captures or kills of "Ters" in the war so far. The plan that we have formulated is, that we have segmented the country into several military sectors. Whenever there is a call for the Scouts to go in to an area, we pull all the regular troops out of that sector and make it a blanket "No go" zone, for as long as the Scouts are in that region." A police superintendent told us. I understood what he was saying and thought briefly back in time, to my own request for all troops to be pulled out, while Amos and I had gone into the bush in chase of "One Eye!" I recognized now how similar that was, to the new military course of action.

The army major took over the briefing, "The 'Ters' have continuously carried out attacks on lonely farms. Striking in the dead of night. Militarily, this achieves them nothing, the only purpose of these attacks is to scare the farmers into abandoning their farms and the widespread publicity it gets them! I believe one of the other purposes is to give the impression that they are more effective than they really are, because they know that they would not stand a chance against our black and white armed forces in the field of combat. At the moment the guerrilla leadership of the two political parties are headquartered in two neighboring countries; Nkomo's group Z.A.P.U. are basing their operations out of Zambia. While Sithole's is in Mozambique. As you already may have heard the Portuguese are not doing a good job of defending their territory in Mozambique and our troops have on occasion been called in to give assistance. Confidentially, we do not see the Portuguese holding on to the territory much longer before it is taken over by the rebels and given Independence. In which case we expect it to go the same way as Angola, with civil war breaking out between the rival communist backed guerrillas. Angola, already has a large Soviet presence and the Russians have started to import large troop numbers of Cuban forces to help the party they are backing to overcome the rival opposition." He said.

One of the prosecutor's asked "Do you think the Cubans would attack us?" The Major thought for a while before responding;" "Frankly, I do not Know, we have contingency plans for that event, but I doubt that the Soviets would risk an overt international incident, which would make Britain quickly forget their squabble with us and bring in the Americans and South Africa on our side to stop them!" he replied.

"Why don't we just go in and knock the countries harboring terrorists out, like the Israelis did with their adversaries in the six day war?" The prosecutor asked with almost a sarcastic overtone. The Major smiled, "For the very simple reason that we do not have any hostile intentions towards our neighbors! Yes, in theory we are militarily strong enough to conquer Zambia, Angola, Zaire, and a few other countries to our North in one swoop. The campaign would be over in a matter of a few weeks, but then we would have the reverse situation that I explained with the Cubans attacking us, and the Soviets using that as an excuse to come into this region with their forces." He replied and added, "I am afraid that we are stuck with attempting to solve the terrorist incursions and attacks from within the boundaries our own borders for the time being!" The Major ended the briefing with a somber note, "For those of you who are followers of history, you might like to know that since the modern inception of the idea of guerrilla warfare, no country or government on which this type of war has been mounted against, has ever been ultimately successful in beating back the rebels. The insurgents have always won. Obviously, it is our intention to win this war, but if we do, it will be a first!"

Shortly afterwards, I received the news which included a development that I had long waited and hoped for, it was from Chantelle. She phoned from London, to tell me that she had joined the Reuters News agency. She had been able to convince the group to assign her to cover the Rhodesian story. Chantelle told me that she would be arriving in Salisbury in the middle of June,1973 which was only a couple of months away! "How long will you be coming for?" I enquired. "Cheri, the assignment is for at least six months, possibly a year." She said. "Then what?" I asked. "Well Cheri, I am not usually in the habit of proposing to a man, but, how about getting married?" She asked. "Funny, but I think the world just become a whole lot more rosy! Yes!" I answered. "Good!" She replied. "Because I would love to have your babies!"

I wrote my second year exams with the university of London at the end of May. This time I was successful in passing the tests and had one more final set of examinations to pass to obtain the LL.B. Degree. "One more year, and I will be able to leave the prosecutor's office and go into private practice as an Advocate!" I thought.

To celebrate the passing of my examinations, I invited a number of Harari colleagues out to lunch at the newly renovated five star Meikles hotel lounge, in the city. As our group walked down Manica Road towards the hotel, one thing was apparent the atmosphere in the city had changed dramatically. Gone were the once happy, smiling, relaxed faces of the blacks and whites that once walked carefree along the street. They were replaced by the fewer and more somber expressions of people that seemed to have something weighing heavily on their minds. The once easily accessible stores now had security guards at the entrances conducting body and bag searches on anyone wishing to enter. Many of the once familiar men's safari suits had been exchanged for military camouflage tunics. There was also a slight paranoid feeling in the air, with the fear of when and where the next bomb explosion may occur, to take more innocent lives.

We passed by the bicycle shop that I had once owned. I stopped to look in through the window. The store was empty of customers. The manager I had once employed was still working there, only now it was for Jim Mitchell, he was standing behind a counter, marking time. Recognizing me, the manager waved at us, as the group moved by.

At the hotel, all the prosecutors went through the procedural body search at the entrance before being allowed in. Finally, we sat down to enjoy the meal that was to be my treat. As we ate, the music in the lounge played the tune "Where have all the flowers gone?" The sad melody, written for Americans going off to fight in the Vietnam war, had a sobering effect on all the prosecutors sitting around the table "How appropriate for our times, that song is!" Someone commented. The rest of us somberly nodded in agreement.

With the arrival of Chantelle in June, life for me, seemed to turn around and become more complete and fulfilling. Just being together with her, seeing her warm gentle manner, looking into her smiling sparkling green blue eyes and feeling the soft touch of her skin made me feel good. Moreover, I always recognized, that behind her softness and beauty was an intelligence and strength of character which I respected and admired.

When she first arrived, Chantelle stayed at our house. My mother as always was the good host and the two got along well. The second day after Chantelle's arrival, I spoke to her about the plans I had in mind for the future. "I have waited a long time before buying a house. I wanted you to be here so that we could chose one together, one that we both like and be happy to live in!" I told her. "You mean our own little home!" She exclaimed with excitement, "Oh Cheri, that would be wonderful, I know that we have both waited a long time for this moment, when can we start looking ?" She asked. "Is tomorrow too soon?" I replied. She snuggled in to me, "Thank you my love, for your patience in waiting for me. No, it is not too soon!" She said, planting a kiss my lips.

We looked at many houses over the course of the next several days and settled on the one house we both fell in love with. It was a three bedroomed, white bricked home on an acre of land with an exquisitely arranged garden of roses, hydrangeas and hibiscus. It contained a carefully manicured lawn with a large jacaranda tree in the center for shade. The property was encircled by small orchards of fruit trees, among which were mangoes, apples, peaches and avocados. Situated near the University, in the suburb of Mount Pleasant, it was in one of the better Salisbury neighborhoods.

My mother had been very understanding about us wanting to move into a place of our own. She had mentioned that the present house we were living in, was getting too big for her to cope with and that she would be comfortable moving to an apartment. I knew she was saying that to make it easier for Chantelle and me to make the move without feeling guilt for leaving her on her own.

Within a matter of weeks we started to move into our new home. Chantelle excitedly went shopping for furnishings and had the extraordinary touch of decorating the interior of the house so that it took on an air of charm, elegant style and yet felt very livable.

One Saturday morning we went to a pet shop to buy a dog, to add the final touch to our new home. Uncertain what type to get, we looked at Collies, an Alsatian and even a husky with a thick fur coat totally unsuited for the warm African climate. In one corner of the shop surrounded by a pen of chicken wire, was a little puppy, a cross between a Chihuahua and a miniature Whippet. The little fellow would stand on its hind feet and dance a pirouette each time Chantelle and I walked by him. We stopped to pet him and his tiny tail wagged incessantly loving the attention. "Aren't Chihuahua's usually bad tempered noisy little dogs?" I asked. "Not this one! He has the friendliest most gentle quite nature, I have ever seen in a dog!" The store owner replied. Chantelle and I looked at each other, "This is not the medium sized guard dog we had in mind and he is a mongrel!" I said to her, as the puppy did another pirouette for us. "Yes I know, Ivan, but just look at him he is just so adorable!" She replied, as if on cue, the puppy licked my hand and cocked his head in an inquisitive stance as if waiting for an answer.

As we walked out of the shop with the puppy, I commented "He must only weigh about two or three pounds, he is so tiny!" Chantelle smiled, "That is the perfect name for him, let's call him 'Tiny'." She suggested. I nodded in agreement. "Well, that name certainly took a lot of imagination to think up!" I kiddingly answered.

The little dog fitted in perfectly in our new residence. His good nature actually become a source of even more love to share in the home.

A few nights after moving in, Chantelle and I were seated by the fireplace. A gentle glow radiated from the log fire that was burning to warm the cold July winter's evening. Tiny had settled himself between the two of us for a snooze. I poured out some Rhodesian white chardonay wine, it was not exactly "Dom Perignon", but certainly palatable in view of the fact that there few wines coming into the country because of sanctions. We toasted each other and our new home. It was one of the few nights that we had been able to sit back and relax, away from both the pressures of work and moving into the house. Finding the free time to make the move had been complicated for both of us. With me it was my usual heavy court work load, being on reserve police duty as well as the occasional courts martial. Chantelle's life had been equally active, starting her new position, getting her office together and keeping up with the late breaking stories to be telexed to the head office in London.

As we talked, our conversation eventually turned to our work. Chantelle told of her experiences covering the war in Vietnam. She told me of the horrors she had seen and had to report about. The young American soldiers dying so far away from home. How she had covered the fighting as it spread to the neighboring countries of Cambodia and Laos, before Nixon, as President, had been able to negotiate a cease-fire in January of that year.

She told me, that she had as a reporter, been allowed to conduct interviews with both the South Vietnamese and American armies. One fact that she had found interesting was in her interviews with the Green Berets, many were aware of the conflict brewing in Rhodesia and had expressed their interest in coming to fight for the Rhodesian army now that they were being withdrawn from Vietnam, rather than returning to their civilian lives in the United States.

Although I could not say anything, I was already aware that a trickle of ex-Green Berets had started making enquiries to join the Selous Scouts in Rhodesia. "What are your plans as far as reporting stories for the news agency?" I asked. "Generally, the day to day situation as it develops here!" She said. "But more specifically, I would love to get the scoop on the Selous Scouts, which no other reporter has been able to do yet!" She looked at me, "You know quite a bit about them, would you help me get my scoop?" she asked. I went quiet for a few moments, then I told her, "Chantelle, there are some topics that I am never going to be able to talk to you about. One of them is the Selous Scouts. If I were to say anything, I may be inadvertently putting some young men's lives at risk, it really has little to do with loyalty to country, but more to do with jeopardizing peoples lives! I just can't do that, to help you with a story!" I said. "I understand, Cheri! I wont ask that again." She said apologetically, and changed the subject. "You know, the big contrast that I have noticed between the situations here and in Vietnam, is that here apart from those actually involved in the fighting the ordinary blacks and whites in the street actually seem to like each other! I have seen sadness amongst the people, but no bitterness or hatred. That surprises me because of the circumstances, I would have thought there would be open racial hatred. I haven't seen that!" She stated. "Perhaps, that is because this has been the home to both races for quite a few years now, and the ordinary people don't want this war and the killing that goes with it! Perhaps, just perhaps, we have gotten to Know each other over time." I replied.

Chantelle loved word games and we settled in to spend the remainder of the evening away from the issues of the world, enjoying a game of Scrabble.

Over the next eight months both Chantelle and I maintained our busy schedules. My mother, Rae, was a frequent dinner guest, whenever our timetables allowed us to be at home to cook a dinner that we could sit down to enjoy together. There was no improvement with the importation of bicycle part quotas and Royal Cycles was limping along, barely holding its own. Chantelle had on occasion traveled to Zambia and Angola, to conduct interviews with the guerrillas operating out of those countries for her news agency. The stories she wrote were censored from publication in the Rhodesian press, so I as well other Rhodesians never got to read her articles which were published in the overseas press. Out of respect for the confidentiality of both our jobs, I never asked what she had observed of guerrilla activity while in those countries.

Early in 1974, the war in Rhodesia had increased progressively. The guerrillas were continuing with their tactics of terrorist attacks on lonely farm homesteads, but now in an ever increasing widespread area, and more frequently. Casualties were mounting on a heavier scale. For the whites it was in the number of deaths suffered at the hands of terrorist attacks on the farms. For the guerrillas, their casualties were in the aftermath of those attacks on the lonely homesteads with the Rhodesian forces chasing after them and engaging them in contacts. There was also now, the added dimension of the instructions by the government to the Rhodesian armed forces to continue the chase of terrorists into neighboring countries and engage in contacts there, under the policy of "Hot Pursuit!". Under that guise, the armed forces were able to hit terrorist bases and inflict severe casualties on the guerrilla camps that were based in Zambia and Mozambique.

Thinking that they would be safe in setting up terrorist bases in Angola, by having the country of Zambia as a buffer zone between them and Rhodesia, the guerrillas began setting up base camps in that country, with Cubans as their protectors. They started to receive military weapons shipped in by the Soviets through the port of Luanda. The weapons were then transported overland near the border, to the base camps of the guerrillas. To counter this a group of two hundred Rhodesian paratroopers were ferried in, flying in low over Zambia with helicopters of the Rhodesian air force. They engaged in a surprise attack on the guerrilla bases in Angola, effectively knocking out the majority of camps, capturing the large cache of weapons, as well as putting the Cuban troops on the run. When the news was reported back in Rhodesia, it was received with astonishment, there had been so much achieved, with so few men. It was a tremendous morale booster and had many Rhodesians believing that they had the best fighting men in the world!

Chantelle's news agency had rented permanent space at the Monomatapa hotel. It was a small conference room on one of the lower levels of the building. From there she conducted many of the interviews she had with the continuing flow of dignitaries and diplomats entering the country to meet with Rhodesian government officials, many of them searching for a solution to the fighting. Often those interviews would go into the early hours of the morning. Taking place after the diplomats had completed their daily heavy schedule of negotiations and only then, agreeing to meet with her and other members of the press corps to give an update on the way the talks had progressed.

After the interviews, Chantelle would continue to work through the night preparing her stories for transmission to her central news office. Often she arrived home just in time to get into bed and snuggle into me before the early morning sun arose. Even that, was sometimes conditional that I too, was at home and not out on patrol with my reserve police duties, before going to court.

One of those nights, I had been on patrol of the suburbs. It had been a quiet night and having finished with my duties I returned to the house. The sun was starting to rise as I entered the driveway, looking at my watch, the time was just after five in the morning. Suddenly, there was the deafening sound of a blast coming from the direction of the city which was situated three miles to the south. The force of the sound wave was so violent that the windows of the house shuddered. Looking in the direction of the city, I could see a plume of flame rising to the sky. The terrorists had set off another bomb.

I hurried into the house, calling for Chantelle. There was no answer! In the bedroom the bedcovers were still tidily made and the bed had not been slept in. I ran to the garage, her car was not there, I surmised that she had been working late at the hotel. Still wearing my police uniform, I jumped into my car and raced downtown towards her office at the Monamotapa hotel.

My worst fears became realized when I got there, and saw the hotel building in the process of being surrounded by the arrival of police cars, ambulances and fire engines. I stopped my car and dashed towards the hotel, stopping momentarily to ask an arriving police vehicle what had happened. The policeman recognized me as a prosecutor, and said that the report over his radio had stated that a bomb had been detonated in a church next to the Monomatapa Hotel. I resumed running towards the hotel entrance. Smoke ominously wafted in the air and there was a clutter of debris everywhere! Jumping over still burning fragments, I entered the hotel lobby and ran up four levels to the conference room. Flinging the door open, I caught sight of Chantelle. She was laying semi-conscious on the carpet, blood was streaming from her side. I knelt down beside her to see that a large sliver of glass from the blast shattered window had dug itself deep into her side. "Cheri, I am hurting so much!" She whispered as I put my arms around her to comfort her pain. I yelled for someone to give her medical attention.

Moments later, medics arrived and Chantelle passed out as she was placed on a stretcher.

I traveled with her in the ambulance to the hospital. Chantelle was wheeled in for emergency surgery, still laying unconscious. I sat in the waiting room, worried and anxiously awaiting news as the doctors operated on her. It took over three hours to pull out the fragments of glass and suture her wounds. A doctor eventually emerged from the operating room. My anxieties lifted, when he told me that the injury had not been life threatening and that Chantelle would completely recover. I let out a sigh of relief. The doctor then informed me that he was going to keep her at the hospital for a few days under observation as a precaution. Also, that when she did return home she was to stay in bed to recover, for at least a week.

When Chantelle came home three days later I presented her with the largest bouquet of roses I could find. I also found it near to impossible to keep her in bed to recover, she wanted to get back to work. Finally, she gave in to my insistence and rested in bed. I fussed over her, making her dinners, seeing that she was comfortable and spent every moment I could by her side. Chantelle ran her fingers lovingly through my hair as I attended to her needs, "Careful Cheri, I could very easily get used to all your fussing and attention!" She teased. "…And, when I have recovered, I want to spend the whole night making love to you!" She added. "Well, if you are already thinking of that, it sounds like you are well on the road to recovery!" I answered with a twinkle in my eye.

A week later, Chantelle had recovered sufficiently to return to work. She meant what she had said about spending an entire night making love. Although I was concerned for her condition, Chantelle threw caution to the wind and beguiled lovemaking, turning nightfall into rapture, it was a wonderful sleepless night!.

The time for my final examinations were again approaching and I worried that I had not put enough time into my studies. With only a few weeks left, I put all my energies into absorbing the volume of cases, precedents and jurisprudence needing to be learnt to pass the exams. It was not sufficient, when the results were published, I had passed only three out of the four final subjects. As all four had to be passed in one sitting, I would have to take the examinations again the following year. I could understand the results, but was still very disappointed. I had a difficult time facing Chantelle, to tell her the news. "Oh Cheri, don't be so hard on yourself!" she said," With everything that is going on around you it is perfectly understandable, besides, I think it is wonderful that you passed three out of the four with the limited time you had to study! Next year Ivan, you will pass all four!" She consoled, putting her arms around my shoulders and gave me a loving hug.

As 1973 drew to a close, Chantelle fully recovered from her injury in the bomb blast. We settled in to enjoy the double festive time, for me it was Chanukah and Chantelle it was Christmas. My mother, Rae, was invited for dinners prepared on both occasions by Chantelle. Amongst her other graces she was a good cook, preparing lavish meals appropriate for each of the festivals. We were also treated to two phone calls over a period of a week from Chantelle's parents, Mr. and Mrs. Rouget, who diplomatically called and gave their best wishes for each of the occasions. I liked them a lot and the calls were typical of their thoughtfulness and caring.

Chantelle had often expressed her desire to see the Portuguese East African country of Mozambique. She had heard me frequently talk of its tourist and scenic splendor and also read that the cities of Beira and Lorenco Marques were modeled after the style of Portugal's towns. They indeed did have a distinct European flavor, with outdoor sidewalk restaurants and cafes. Beira had been a favorite beach resort for Rhodesians to vacation away from our landlocked borders. However, since the commencement of the guerrilla wars, driving the three hundred and eighty five miles to Beira was more than treacherous. With the FRELIMO rebels and Rhodesian guerrillas ambushing convoys of vehicles regularly on the road, as well laying land mines along the route.

The city of Beira itself, was still a reasonably safe place to visit within the confines of the town and beach areas. I surprised Chantelle with two air tickets and booked accommodations to spend the new year at Beira's Estoril beach hotel. She greeted the news of the trip with girlish happy excitement.

As we packed and prepared to fly out of Salisbury two days before new year, I cautioned her about the extreme heat we would experience in the port city. Although Beira was only a few hundred miles to the East, the hot and humid weather encountered there would be totally different to what we were used to. Salisbury was built on a plateau, five thousand feet above sea level, so even though it was within the tropics, the climate was a mild one. Winters were usually cool with temperatures in the mid forty to fifty degrees Fahrenheit and summers in the seventy to ninety's with low humidity. At sea level that all changed and the full impact of the heat and humidity of the African summers were felt.

True to my warning, as we stepped off the air conditioned commercial jet at Beira's airport, the heat and humidity hit us with a wallop! It was like walking into a hot humid sauna, from which there was no escape. It took a few hours to adjust to the change of climate and we laughed at the stickiness of our clothes which had become wet with perspiration and clung to our bodies. We checked into the hotel, changed into swim suits and made our way to the beach, a few hundred yards from the hotel.

Chantelle had taken to wearing one piece costumes rather than a bikini, to hide the scar received in the bomb blast. As she walked by my side, I gazed at her green blue eyes and sparkling blond hair which flamed with the wind. She looked like a goddess, even though I did not think it possible, each day that passed, I loved her that little bit more! As though she had read my mind, she stopped, put her arms around me and we kissed.

The searing heat of the sun allowed us to stay on the beach for only an hour. We returned to the hotel, showered, changed into light shorts and tee shirts and went into the city. Because of tradition and the heat, stores opened in the mornings at nine and closed at noon, when workers went home for a siesta, or, to the sidewalk cafes for a long lunch, returning to work at three in the afternoon, closing for the day at six in the evening. Life was very casual in this port city of a hundred thousand people. Walking along the streets we took in the sights, the buildings on each side were not fancy, more square and plain shaped, but what made them appealing was the artwork that adorned the outside facade of the structures. They had elaborate designs of painted ceramic tiles. It was just after the noon hour and the sidewalk cafes on the wide pavements were filled with people eating lunch. Chantelle and I stopped at one of the cafes to order lunch and take in the flavor of the passing life styles.

There were many uniformed Portuguese soldiers walking along the streets mingling with the civilians on the pavements and at the cafes. Some of the soldiers stopped to openly gawk at the beauty of Chantelle. Initially, I was sympathetic that they were a long way from home and ignored the blatantness of their behavior, though after a while, I started to become irritated, as the soldiers conversations in Portuguese turned to the fact that they would like to have sex with her. I turned to them and in fluent Portuguese told them to "Go and stuff themselves!" Embarrassed that their conversation had been understood the soldiers left the cafe.

After lunch, the two of us strolled towards the beach front near the city. We came to the multi-million dollar "Grand Hotel." Now abandoned, the hotel had been built with a view to making it the gem of the east coast. It had several hundred guest rooms, a larger than Olympic size swimming pool. The rebel war and politics had changed all those grand plans conceived for the hotel. The building was now empty and large cracks were beginning to appear in several places along its structure. Chantelle and I walked up the stepped entrance into the wide lobby which led into a huge ballroom, which had once been intended as the casino section of the building. Rats now chomped nonchalantly at scraps of remaining paint in the large room. On the floor we walked by an aging and soiled postcard, it showed a picture of the magnificence the building had exuded only a few years earlier. It was sad to see how much the place had deteriorated

The next evening, the Estoril hotel had a New Year's Eve dance. Chantelle dressed in a black knee length evening gown, with her silken hair swept back in a half bun. She looked strikingly beautiful. I started to have thoughts of taking her clothes off and making love to her without ever getting to the party. But I had something special planned for a little after midnight.

We danced the night away, at midnight we toasted in the New Year with champagne and joined the others celebrating, throwing streamers and blowing toy horns. When we returned to our table, I pulled out a black velvet box from my pocket and presented it to Chantelle. She took the box and opened it, inside there was a gold ring with a one and a half carat internally flawless round diamond. It was channel set with two square cut precious Sandawhana emeralds on either side of the sparkling center stone. "Will you marry me?" I asked. Chantelle had momentarily been surprised, then she looked at me, her face seemed to take on a glow and she said "Yes Cheri!…I was beginning to wonder if you were ever going to ask?" We leaned forward towards each other and our lips met over the middle of the table.

The band played the last tune at two in the morning. Chantelle and I were too filled with the excitement of our engagement to let the night come to an end. We took a stroll along the beach, walking with our arms around each other. It was a beautiful moonlight night, the reflection of the moon rippled over the ocean's waters. The sound of the waves breaking and lapping onto the sandy shore added to the romance of the night. The beach was deserted, except for the two of us. We walked near a cove and Chantelle stopped to embrace me in a kiss, then she took a step back, unzipped her dress and let it fall to the sand. We made love on the beach until the sun began to slowly rise bringing in a new day, and with it a new year.

Returning to our suite, we slept for a few hours, and were thoughtlessly awakened at midday by a maid wanting to clean the room. Still sleepy, we strolled to the beach to continue our relaxing and get in some sunbathing. Chantelle opened up a large blanket on the sand and we lay on it, I started to doze off. Suddenly, there was a screeching roar above us, we looked up to see three Rhodesian jet fighters screaming by overhead, no higher than fifty yards from the ground. The jets arched, following the curvature of the shoreline in a northerly direction towards the Tete province, a known guerrilla stronghold. The jets disappeared from sight, followed shortly afterwards by what sounded like distant claps of thunder. In the far horizon there were little puffs of smoke which could be seen rising skyward. The incident had caught the attention of the sunbathers on the beach. Almost mesmerized, we all stood on the beach with our hands shading our eyes, watching the strange event. It was obviously a military engagement.

Chantelle and I were puzzled by this occurrence as we returned to settle ourselves to rest on the sand again. Within half an hour, the three jets came roaring back over the beach still at very low altitude. As the planes passed over the bathers who were staring up at them, the lead jet fighter did a victory roll, the aircraft then sped away from the beach and out of view.

That night we heard the news broadcast, Rhodesian jets had successfully attacked a combined Frelimo and Rhodesian guerrilla base camp. "Deep in Mozambique territory!" The number of casualties inflicted on the guerrillas, was unknown. Chantelle turned to me "It is kind of scary, we thought that we had gotten away for a break from the fighting, yet, here we end up as spectators to the frightening events!" She said, almost fatalistic that we had been unable to escape the war, even for a brief time.

We returned home the next day and resumed our heavy work schedules. One month later, Chantelle was informed that one of her group of journalists covering the American withdrawal from Vietnam and the developing events in Cambodia, had been severely injured by sniper fire. She was to be re-assigned to replace him in Vietnam, while he recovered. I pleaded with her to resign her job and not to go.

"Cheri, I am needed to report the closing stages of the war to the world! Would you quit your job as a prosecutor, because I feared for your safety?" She asked. Understanding her point, I reluctantly replied, "No. I would not!" She held my face with her hands and kissed me. "Please, Ivan, we have so much that we both want to accomplish, be patient with me a little while longer. I am committed to you and we will be married soon, when the time is right for both of us!" she pleaded.

Within a week, I was driving her once again to catch a flight out of the country. We said our "Au revoirs," with a long kiss, as Chantelle prepared to go through the departure lounge. Once her flight had departed, I walked away, thinking of how much I was developing a dislike for these trips to the airport and saying farewell to Chantelle.

Chapter Thirteen

Developments were beginning to take place in other countries that would have a profound effect on the situation in Rhodesia. In Portugal, the *Estado Novo* governing regime had committed three quarters of its army of conscripts to fighting colonial wars in Africa. Despite their standard sophisticated N.A.T.O. military equipment and spending half of their national budget on these wars, they were not able to maintain control of the "Provinces". One of their retired military leaders had recently written a book critical of the regime and suggested radical changes. His revolutionary influence was spreading through Portugal like a wildfire. It was now a matter of time before the Portuguese government would be toppled, with it would come greater uncertainty regarding the situation of Rhodesia's Eastern neighbor, and present ally, Mozambique.

The United States gradual withdrawal from the theater of war in Vietnam, had resulted in a number of former Green Berets coming to Africa and signing up with the Rhodesian army, primarily joining the Selous Scouts. I met a few of those men at socials. The impression they gave me was that a majority had come to prefer a life of fighting, to them this was a form of continuation of the war in Vietnam against the communists. To a few, it meant fighting in a war, any war, period. One fact was certain, it was not for the pay, because the army pay was a pittance, in comparison to what these men could earn in civilian life, at home in the United States!

South Africa had been and would continue to be one of Rhodesia's staunchest supporters. Officially, That country had followed the United Nations resolutions and not recognized Rhodesia's declaration of independence. Quietly, it was very much in South Africa's interest to give whatever support to maintain this country which formed a buffer between them and the rest of Africa. The problem was Rhodesia was drawing too much international attention to the African situation. Politically, South African cabinet ministers started putting discreet pressure on the Smith government to come to some kind of terms with the rebel leaders. Even if it meant caving in to the majority rule issue and Rhodesia becoming a Marxist ruled country. Though these were two policies that their own "Apartheid" system was vehemently opposed to.

It seemed that it was in South Africa's interests to have Rhodesia go down as the "Sacrificial Lamb," and draw the line with the rest of Africa at their boundary of the Limpopo river, than have the present conflict grow on their doorstep.

Rhodesia had never adopted the South African "Apartheid" system. A substantial portion, between seventy to eighty percent of the Rhodesian army and police forces were made up of black members. They made a vast contribution to maintaining law and order. The Rhodesian government would certainly not have survived thus far without them. Almost without realizing it, the evolutionary process of a multiracial and integrated society had been speeded up. On reflection, it was the only logical progression from a situation where both blacks and whites were giving up their lives fighting together against the guerrillas. For those blacks not fighting with the guerrillas, this was a war neither about color or majority rule, but Rhodesians against a Marxist takeover. The changes taking place saw the appointment of black magistrates and the rapid promotion of peoples of the different races through the civil service, army, police and in civilian positions. Perhaps this was occurring too late to stop the war, but it was happening, setting the pace for the future, irrespective of the outcome of the war.

Chantelle and I kept in regular contact by phone, taking turns to phone each other once a week. Because of the different time zones, the calls were made early Friday evenings Rhodesian time, which coincided with midnight Vietnam time. Both of us were careful as to what was said, as the calls were very likely to be monitored in both countries. Chantelle did get across the message that the situation in Vietnam and Cambodia was not going well for the West and that she had her hands full with covering the breaking stories in that part of the world. She told me that she was likely to be in Southeast Asia longer than anticipated in view of the developments there. That was disappointing news, particularly as I had hoped to start making arrangements for our wedding date. Those plans would now have to be postponed to a more appropriate time for both of us.

A strong friendship was at this time developing between myself and the defense Attorney, Jay Patanak. Patanak was not particularly well liked amongst the legal fraternity. I believed that was because of envy, as Jay did an extremely good job for every case he was involved in, and sometimes in the process, left other attorneys with egg over their faces. Whether he was handling a matter "Pro Bona" or for the wealthiest of clients, the people he represented could trust that they were getting the best available legal advice from the man. I respected and admired that fact—wasn't that what legal representation was all about? I would say in response to critical comments made about Patanak by other lawyers, during casual conversations.

Patanak owned a large house with a swimming pool and a private tennis court, nearby to my residence. An invitation was often extended to me to play tennis on Sunday mornings with the Patanaks and their other guests. The days sports activities usually ended with a barbecue on the Patanak's lawn by the pool.

One of the regular tennis players was an elderly English gentleman in his early seventies, Bill Johnson. He was a good player who more than matched the younger tennis opponents he played against. Moving to Rhodesia in the late 1920's he had cultivated his own farm, growing tobacco in the Karoi region. Retiring from farming life ten years previously, he had moved with his family to live in the city to spend his retirement years. Now like many other senior citizens, who were too old to be called up for military service, he had volunteered to do protective duty on the isolated farms, protecting the younger farmers from Mondays through to Fridays, from terrorist attacks.

A few weeks after I had started playing regularly at the Patanaks, I noticed that Bill Johnson was absent. I asked Jay about him. Sadly, Jay turned to me and said, "Didn't you know Ivan, he was killed in an ambush on one of the farms he was protecting! Terrorists came in during the middle of the night last week and attacked the homestead, killing him, a young woman and her five year daughter." I shook my head, I had been so busy with court work, I told Jay, that I had not been aware Bill had been one of the week's casualties. Quietly, I thought about Bill Johnson's death, and the fact of my not knowing of the event—I knew that I could have taken a moment during my busy court schedule to read the names of the fatalities, but had avoided doing so. I wondered whether my behavior was as a result of my emotional defense mechanisms attempting to protect me from the pain of knowing. Or, had I simply dulled my senses to a cold acceptance that deaths of friends and acquaintances was now an everyday fact of life. At that moment, I did not have an answer.

Early in April, the senior prosecutor for the Regional courts suffered a heart attack. He was in his late sixties and had run the Regional Circuit Courts for over twenty years. Those courts handled the more serious cases for the Eastern Division of the country, which included Salisbury and covered the environs East, all the way to the borders with

Mozambique and South Africa. I was temporarily promoted to the post of a Regional prosecutor, during the senior man's absence.

Although, the case load was not as heavy in volume as the Harari courts, the cases being more serious took longer to complete. The work was substantially more dangerous as it involved traveling the circuit by car and usually alone, to the Regional Courts in Umtali and Fort Victoria. These were hazardous times to be traveling by car in view of the ambushes and land mines being laid along the roads by the terrorists.

I reviewed the cases to be tried for the days ahead; most were cases under the Terrorism Act, as well as Attempted Murders and Rapes. The case dockets involving terrorism were like reading grizzly horror stories, with the most heinous acts of barbarism and atrocities being committed. Most of the acts of brutality, surprisingly, committed by the guerrillas were against their fellow blacks—those that refused to join them or belonged to an opposing party. I thought to myself, "God help us if this is the freedom and democracy these people want to *impose* on the inhabitants of this country!" I saw no freedom, democracy or civility in what the terrorists were trying to achieve by means of force, only a subjugation of the people to the will of a particular party philosophy.

Jay Patanak appeared regularly as a defense attorney at the courts, usually in a civil action in another part of the building. Jay and I sometimes took a break from the stress of our work to have lunch together. On one of those occasions we discussed a recent trip that Jay had taken to London on behalf of one of his clients. Jay told of his perception of the way the Rhodesian story was being reported in the overseas press. "The media are painting us as the worst racists imaginable! Despite the atrocities committed by the terrorists not only against the whites but the blacks as well. The guerrillas are being portrayed as "Freedom Fighters" and come out smelling like a rose!" He said, and continued, "Yet, look at the double standard adopted; the press view the terrorist acts of bombings by the IRA at their own airports and buildings, completely differently, that is considered and rightly so, as barbaric acts of savagery. There is no difference between acts of terrorism, they are simply that; terrorists! Nothing can justify the indiscriminate taking of innocent lives. No matter under what guise or purpose!" Jay stated, starting to redden under his collar, at the improper treatment by the overseas media.

"Calm down Jay, you will give yourself a heart attack!" I told him. "Yes I know, but I can't help getting angry when I see the press feeding stories to armchair critics who have never been to this country, they use the misinformation from the snippets of news they hear to condemn us, without having any real idea what this part of the world is going through! Some of the business people I spoke to, thought Rhodesia was a part of Asia, others thought that we lived in primitive tree houses, the real insult was when I was asked why we were mercilessly killing the black people of the Country!" Jay stated, the redness of frustration had crept from around his collar to color his face. "I understand what you are saying Jay, I have seen the mis-reporting first hand with the way my cases have been recounted in the newspapers, sometimes I think I am reading about someone else's case, except my name appears right there as the prosecuting lawyer." I said, in agreeing with his frustration.

Jay calmed down a little and the subject changed, "Have you started traveling the circuit for Regional yet?" He asked. "I will be doing my first circuit starting this coming Monday. I have some interesting terrorist associated trials in Fort Victoria!" I replied, then I added, "I am also preparing for the final exams with London, which are only five weeks away, at the end of may. The two weeks study leave I am taking will actually be a refreshing break from court work!" He laughed "Is that the only break you ever get from work, to study?"

The following Monday, I traveled to Fort Victoria. One of the cases involved a policeman as the complainant and seven defendants on a charge of attempted murder, with an alternative charge, of conspiracy with terrorists to commit murder. The dossier showed that the policeman, a black, named Sergeant Clifford, had been decorated several times for

acts of valor and heroism. Part of his record showed that on one
occasion he had been out on patrol with his "Stick" a group of six
men, comprised of four black and two whites, near the Fort Victoria
area. They had been ambushed by a group of terrorists estimated to
number twenty-five to thirty men. In the firefight that had ensued, it
was apparent that they were hopelessly outnumbered. He instructed
the other five members of his stick to slip away while he remained
behind to provide them with covering fire. He held back the attackers, alone, for several hours, before being able to slip into the cover of
the veldt himself and make good his escape. He had been awarded the
Medal of honour for his bravery.

In this case, sergeant Clifford had returned to his village during his
leave, to visit his ailing mother. In order not to attract attention he had
worn his civilian clothes. The allegation was, that one of the accused, a
woman had recognized him and reported his presence to terrorists
camped nearby. Three terrorists had come into the village in the middle of the night, entered into the hut he was sleeping in and dragged
him out into the center of the village. The six other accused, one more
woman and five men, had joined the terrorists and helped them beat up
the policeman. The terrorists had struck him several times with their
rifles while the others hit him with sticks, breaking Clifford's arm and
beating him into unconsciousness. When he revived, his arms and legs
had been bound and they were dragging him to the top of a small hill.
There he was stripped naked by the villagers and tied to a wooden shaft.
He was then told that they were going to collect wood and burn him
alive in front of the villagers.

The terrorists had instructed the seven accused to stand guard over
Sergeant Clifford, while they went off to collect wood and awaken the
villagers to come and watch the execution. When the three terrorists
had left, he worked furiously at loosening the rope binding his arms and
was able to slip out of them. In the darkness he was able to untie the
rope around his legs. Waiting for the right opportunity, he made a dash

into the bushes, as he ran for safety he could hear the accused yelling an alarm that he had escaped, shortly afterwards the terrorists had given chase firing indiscriminately into the bushes. Sergeant Clifford had made his way walking twenty miles to the police station, where he reported the incident. The police had returned to the village and arrested all seven of the present accused.

In court all seven admitted their participation, but pleaded not guilty, saying they had aided the terrorists under duress and out of fear. In my mind there was no question of the accused acting under duress, they were willing participants! The case proceeded to trial and took a couple of days.

At the end of the trial, the Regional Magistrate acquitted all seven accused, saying that while he believed that they had been actively involved in the attempted murder of the policeman, there was a remote possibility that they had acted out of fear. In which case he preferred to err in their favour by acquitting them. Generally, I could usually gauge which way a case was going, the result in this matter was so unexpected, that it threw me completely. I had a difficult time looking the policeman in the eye, there was nothing I could say to change the fact of the acquittal. The policeman was obviously disappointed with the result, but he kept his composure. Shrugging his shoulder he left the courtroom.

After court that evening, I stopped in at the Reps theater bar, for a sundowner drink and saw the magistrate seated at a table. I walked over and the magistrate invited me to join him. "You looked very puzzled with my decision to acquit the seven accused today?" He asked. "Frankly, yes, I was very puzzled! Did you find something lacking in the evidence I produced in court?" I asked. "No, you actually did an excellent job with the facts you had at your disposal. However, my reasons for acquitting are what I stated in court. These are not normal times with the war going on, the accused are unsophisticated rural tribesfolk who may have felt a compelling fear with the presence of terrorists camped close by, to behave in the way they did. I had to give them the benefit of that doubt!" The magistrate said, looking directly at me. He could see that I was still not convinced, then he raised his glass and slowly took a sip from his drink. I took time to think about what the magistrate had said and responded, "I would be lying if I said that I agree with you, however all I can do, is present the facts in the best light that I can and then leave the decision to you, you're the one that has to live with the judgments you make!" I said, knowing that I was a little out of line with that comment. "Wait until you are on the bench Ivan, perhaps you too, will see things a little differently from the way you see them right now!" The magistrate wisely replied.

What the magistrate had said, created a major paradox in my mind. I thought about the words all night. Where did the law draw the fine line between the rights of an accused person by giving him every available benefit; as well as the balancing act of considering the rights of the victim who had suffered and looked to the courts to see justice being done? As I went to bed I continued to try to solve the conundrum. I looked at the argument from the accused's point of view, it was certainly beneficial in the case of doubt to err in their favour. But, the case I had tried that day had showed a willingness rather than duress on the part of the accused in the participation of the attempted murder. From the victim's point of view; had the policeman seen justice done by the system that he regularly risked his life for?

I fell asleep tossing the problem over in my mind. The sleep transformed into a nightmare, where I saw myself driving along a road with skeletons dressed in terrorist uniforms appear from hiding places along the sides of the bushes, attempting to ambush me with AK-47 rifles. As I drove I was being drawn closer to a skeleton of Death, dressed in dark cloak with his arms outstretched carrying a rifle in one hand. I awoke with a start, I was covered in perspiration from the nightmare. I realized that the case of the policeman was weighing much too heavily on my mind, causing the bad dreams. For my own sanity, I needed to come to some kind of terms with the situation. Even if an injustice had occurred, it was important to retain my objectivity. I sat up on the bed staring at the darkness in the room. Forcing myself to face the dilemma, I reasoned that the case was now over. I had to let go and move on to the other cases that lay ahead of me. That conclusion, gave me a little peace of mind and having made that resolve I was able to yield to a reasonable sleep for the rest of the night.

At the end of the week after putting in many extra hours of work, the circuit for Fort Victoria was completed. That Friday night I filed the last of the court dockets, and walked accross the road to the local police station. I wanted to ask if there was a convoy of cars I could join for the journey back to Salisbury. There were none. The member in charge explained that the last convoy for the weekend had left several hours earlier and the next organized escort was only due to depart the following Monday. I was going to have to do the return journey alone.

As I left the police station, I saw Sergeant Clifford parking his police vehicle. I walked over to him to offer an apology for the result in his court case. The bitterness I had anticipated was not there. The man actually showed a lot of understanding and strength of character over the acquittal. He thanked me for taking the time to discuss the matter with him, and that although he did not agree with the verdict, he told me, "I am just glad to still be alive!"

Returning to my hotel I packed my suitcase into the car and prepared to leave Fort Victoria. I started the drive back to Salisbury and began looking forward to a weekend's break away from the courts. Entering the highway, I noticed that mine was the only vehicle on the roadway. I put my foot down hard on the accelerator speeding up the car to make it a less easy target from a possible ambush. As I drove along the lonely highway my thoughts turned to the previous week's cases. I thought about sergeant Clifford, which in turn reminded me of the nightmare I had a few nights previously. I wondered whether that been caused solely by my troubled thoughts over the court case. Then, a cold chill passed over my body, as I speculated over the possibility that the nightmare could also have been some kind of premonition of a grizzly event that was to take place in the future. I decided to shake that apprehension from my mind. Some hours later, during the middle of the night I entered the outskirts of Salisbury and headed home. I let out a sigh of relief that the journey had been free of any incident.

The ensuing Monday I started a two week session of cases to be tried at the Salisbury Regional courts. Upon completion of those matters, I was due to travel in the third week to Umtali. The Umtali trip was to be my final weekly session before going on leave to study for the final exams. I perused through the dockets dropped off at the courts by the police. The Homicide section had delivered an inquest docket for my evaluation, that was being treated as an unsolved murder investigation. As I read through the documentation the facts it contained were fascinating and very puzzling. The case involved a white doctor who had a reputation of being a ladies man. He was in his early forties and had often bragged that he had slept with over four hundred woman, many of them being affairs with married ladies that had sometimes gotten him into trouble with their husbands. He was found dead in his bedroom, early one morning by his maid. At the time of his death, he had been having an affair with the wife of a wealthy real estate man. There was no evidence of any foul play or disturbance at the doctor's residence. The autopsy that was performed on him showed that he was in excellent health at the time of his death, His heart was in good condition, as was every other organ in his body. A check was made for any possible trace of any kind of substance or poison in his body or blood—none was found. Technically, the man should still be alive, yet nothing could be pinpointed as to the cause of death. Mystified, the police had searched every avenue and the conclusion they had reached was more than surprising, they believed that the murder had been committed by witchcraft!

Officially, the police had always taken the line of debunking witchcraft to the public. It was startling in view of that, to see the number of documents the docket contained marked, "TOP SECRET—FOR OFFICAL EYES ONLY!", dealing with the theory that this was a murder, which had been caused by witchcraft! One of the papers was from Professor Michael Gelfand, head of the faculty of medicine at the University of Rhodesia and one of the world's foremost authorities on the subject of African witchcraft. The documents detailed how different spells could be cast to obtain the death of a victim similar to the facts of this case! The police were suspicious that the spell had been cast by a powerful "Nganga" an African witch doctor, who was paid by the real estate husband to cause the doctor's death.

There was no possible tangible evidence to substantiate the suspicion of "Death by witchcraft" theory. I sent the docket back to homicide with the opinion that this would have to remain an unresolved mystery until they were able to come up with hard evidence—to link the suspect with the death, through the use of the occult! I knew that to do so, was almost a practical impossibility.

Without giving any details of the case, during a court break, I discussed the beliefs of witchcraft with my court interpreter—A sophisticated African man with a college education, by the name of Herbert, who was able to speak twelve African tribal dialects and languages fluently. The interpreter showed a respectful fear talking about the topic. He told me that not only did he believe in witchcraft but had seen an Nganga by the name of Solomon perform "magical" acts that were close to miraculous, near his home village in Umtali.

I was skeptical, telling Herbert that I believed the witch doctors fed off the fear of the unknown amongst the unsophisticated tribal villagers, as the main source for their influence and power. Perhaps, performing an occasional illusion, much the same way as a magician performed his magic act, to reinforce the fears and beliefs of the tribal followers. Herbert strongly disagreed. "The Nganga I have told you of, Solomon, has so much magical power with which he protects his village that both the terrorists and our own black security forces steer well clear of him and the village, because they are so afraid of what he would do to them!" I listened to what Herbert said, but continued to remain skeptical, "I think it is good thing that this witch doctor is influential enough to keep the fighting forces away from the village, but I still believe that his strength comes from prying on the fear of the unknown, rather than any real powers!" I told Herbert.

"Tell you what Ivan, we are due to do a circuit in Umtali in a couple of weeks. If you will agree to take me to my village to visit my family, I will arrange for you to meet with the Nganga, Solomon. It is a short distance from Umtali and as I have said the terrorists steer well clear of that area!" Herbert suggested. I could not resist the invitation, "I would be happy to do so!" I said, agreeing to the opportunity to meet with the Nganga.

A couple of weeks later Herbert and I were in Umtali. The last case that was due to be heard, was an involved white collar fraud, which had been set down for a two day hearing. The defense attorney, at the last minute, offered a plea bargain which was accepted by the court. That plea unexpectedly ended the circuit session on Thursday at midday, instead of the anticipated late Friday afternoon. Herbert approached me saying this was an ideal time to travel to his village to visit his family and to meet with the Nganga. With the time now being available, I agreed to take him to his home.

We left shortly after lunch and I drove the twenty miles through the countryside, to Herbert's family village. When we arrived, I noticed a distinct serenity about the tribespeople seated by their thatched huts and those casually ambling by the fields. This was something I had almost forgotten once existed in most villages, at a time before the start of the hostilities. It was wonderful to catch a glimpse of that life again. There was definitely something here, that had encapsulated the people away from the war going on in the rest of the country. Herbert took me to his family home and introduced me to his family. We sat down outside Herbert's thatched home and enjoyed the hospitality of his families home brewed beer.

After a couple of hours Herbert suggested that we should go and see the Nganga before it started to get dark. We drove a short distance to the adjoining village, parked the car and walked a few hundred yards to the top of a hill. There, at the top, was a large thatched house surrounded by a wooden homemade picket fence. Draped over the fence were an assortment of animal skins and a few large horned, antelope skulls. Herbert instructed me to wait outside, while he went in to speak with the Nganga.

As I waited, I began to feel the queasy feeling associated with venturing into the unknown. After a few long minutes Herbert emerged from the hut accompanied by an elderly, grey haired man wearing an animal skin loin cloth and headdress. He wore an animal bone necklace, several boned bangles adorned both his arms. Herbert introduced him to me as the Nganga, Solomon! I clasped my hands together to convey the traditional tribal greeting, which was also intended to mark my respect to the Nganga. "Welcome young man!" The Nganga said, in his native dialect. "My relative Herbert, has told me that you believe witchcraft is just an illusion and that you seek proof, is that true?" Solomon asked. "I mean no disrespect to you wise one, but that is true!" I replied, in the same dialect. The Nganga studied me for a few moments then he asked "Are you willing to part with a contribution of five dollars, to see a demonstration?" I put my hand into my pocket and pulled out a five dollar note, which I placed in front of the elderly man, then stepped back. "Yes, Solomon I am!" I replied.

"Come with me!" The Nganga said, leading the way towards an open field. Herbert and I followed. At the field, the elderly man stooped down and took a handful of sand in each hand. "Do you see that there is no strong wind?" The Nganga asked. There indeed, was only a very slight breeze, the two of us nodded in agreement. The Nganga threw the two handfuls of sand to the ground. The sand on touching the land surface began to swirl, like two tiny tornadoes called "Dust Devils." The swirling sand picked up momentum adding other debris to its motion and grew in size spinning faster and faster, continuing to grow until both dust devils reached a height of twelve feet. It was an incredible sight, to see these two miniature tornadoes a few feet apart from each other swirling about with such force. I felt a cold chill of fear as I watched the unexplainable happening. I witnessed the surge of force spinning in front of me with disbelieving intrigue. Suddenly, as if taking on a will of their own, the two swirling masses started to move from their stationary point. Almost in a parallel formation they moved away from us, towards the open field. Then in unison, they lifted off the ground to a height of a hundred feet, before slowly disintegrating into sand particles that drifted back to the ground. Watching the spectacle I found myself almost becoming a believer, "If this is a trick of magic, it is one that Harry Houdini would have been proud of!" I thought to myself. There was no rational explanation for what I had just observed! I turned to Herbert to see him snickering with laughter, at the look of astonishment I was wearing on my face.

Puzzled by what I had just seen, I thanked the Nganga for the demonstration. We left the old man and returned to the car. Herbert asked me to drop him off at the adjoining village, he wanted to spend the weekend with his family and would catch a bus back to Salisbury that Sunday night. As I dropped him at his village, Herbert asked, "Well Ivan, what do you think of witchcraft Now?" Still bewildered by the dust devils, I replied with a laugh, "Until someone can explain to me what I just saw, I don't think I will be as skeptical of witch doctors as I was before today! There really is, a lot about life, that we still need to understand!" I motored away still amazed by what I had just witnessed.

I went back to Umtali and returned to my office where I worked late into the night, updating and clearing my desk of all remaining dockets. I wanted to leave early the next morning for Salisbury, so that I could start my study leave for the final London exams.

At dawn the next morning, I packed my car and started the journey back to Salisbury. Sitting with the government issued Uzi machine gun on my lap for protection while I drove. I looked at my watch as I passed by the town of Marandellas, forty-eight miles from Salisbury, it was six thirty in the morning. I was making good time and would be home well before breakfast.

As I rounded a bend thirty miles from home, I caught sight of a group of men gathered by the side of the road in front of me. There were eight of them, and they were standing over the motionless body of a black man. Thinking they were part of the security forces I slowed down momentarily, before realizing that the body was of a dead postal worker and the uniforms of the men were those of terrorists. I slammed my foot down on the accelerator pedal as I saw the men turn and raise their rifles at me. Steering with one hand I lent out of the car window with my rifle, opening fire with the Uzi. Simultaneously, the terrorists opened fire with their AK-47 rifles at my oncoming vehicle. Bullets ripped into the car and the front window shattered from a slew of bullets. I aimed at two men crouched by the roadside firing at me, and set off a burst of rapid fire at them, they both went down. The other men dove for cover by the roadside as my car closed in and then continued to pepper the car with bullets. I began to fire wildly as I was having difficulty controlling the car as well as firing at the attackers. My car passed the terrorists and a hail of bullets ripped into the drivers side of the vehicle. One of the bullets tore through the door and into my stomach. I concentrated on accelerating away from the ambush with my head lowered to the point where I could just barely see over the shattered windscreen. Eventually, steering the car out of rifle range.

I felt my stomach, blood was streaming out. My hand become covered with the sanguine fluid, as I explored the open wound I focused on keeping conscious until I reached the safety of Salisbury. I could feel no pain, just darkness creeping in, trying to overcome my body. Reaching the city I continued to struggle to stay awake and headed in the direction of the Salisbury General Hospital. Barely with enough strength left to control the vehicle I drove into the entrance of the hospital. I slammed on the brakes as the car headed towards a tree in the parking lot. Stopping mere inches from the tree, I slumped forward onto the car horn and lost consciousness. The sound of the horn blaring in my ears, was the last thing I remembered.

The next time I opened my eyes, my vision was a blur. I could make out that I was in a hospital room, a drip hung by the side of the bed with a tube leading into my arm. I could see the figures of two people who were standing over me. One looked like my mother, the other, Chantelle. I thought that I was hallucinating, and blinked my eyes. I looked again, the outlines became sharper—it was Chantelle!

"Am I dreaming ?" I asked. "No Cheri! How do you feel?" Chantelle asked, softly stroking my forehead. "Chantelle, what are you doing here?" I mumbled. "Hush Cheri, don't get excited, you have been unconscious for five days!" She gently replied. As happy as I was at seeing her, I was still confused by her presence. Chantelle smiled knowingly in anticipation, "It was my turn to phone you on Friday night, I tried to get through several times. When there was no reply, I phoned your mother to leave a message. She told me what had happened and that you were in Hospital. So, I caught the first available flight out of Vietnam and have been here for two days now!" She said. "Maybe I should get shot more often, if that will result in getting you to come back and see me!" I Quipped. My mother and Chantelle laughed at my response. "Well we know that you are getting better, if you still have your sense of humor!" My mother, Rae said, bending over to give me a kiss.

I remained in the hospital recovering for another ten days. Chantelle never left my side, she ate with me, looked after my needs and slept in the uncomfortable looking wooden chair by my bed. She would fall asleep snugly holding my hand. The touch of her soft fingers was the greatest feeling of comfort I could sense as I would doze off to sleep.

Sometimes I would awaken in the middle of the night and look at the beautiful form of Chantelle, asleep in the chair holding my hand. I loved her so much, and knew that there could never be a woman so perfect for me, as she was.

I attempted in vain to get out of the hospital to go and write my examinations. Chantelle with the assistance of the doctor talked me out of the idea. "Ivan there is always next year, you are in no condition to try and write any kind of exams at the moment!" Chantelle chided me, making sure I remained in the bed. "This final examination is beginning to frustrate me, it always seems that I am fated to prolong the wait to get that damn degree and go into private practice!" I complained. Chantelle knew exactly the right buttons to press when I got angry, "Has anyone ever told you how funny you look when you get Angry?" She teased. "No, but I think you just did!" I replied, we burst out laughing at the comment.

The day I was to be discharged from the hospital, Black from Special Branch, now a chief superintendent in the police, came to visit me. The visit was a surprise and cordial. As Black was about to leave, he said to me, "By the way, we were able to suppress the news that you were shot by the Ters from the media. We do not want the other side to get any morale boosters, by knowing that they got a prosecutor. As far as everyone is concerned you have been away on study leave and have been writing your exams!" He said, then turning to Chantelle, he asked, "We would appreciate your co-operation with this, Miss Roget!" Chantelle nodded her head in compliance.

I returned home with Chantelle to receive a royal welcome from our little dog, Tiny. I had not seen him for a few weeks. I had dropped him off with my mother to look after, before setting off on the ill fated Umtali circuit. Tiny did somersaults at seeing the two of us together at the house.

Chantelle remained in Salisbury a further week to watch my recuperation. Satisfied that I was well on the road to recovery and would soon be returning to work, she sat by my bed and told me that she would be returning to her job covering the story as it unfolded in Vietnam, the next day. Sadly, I accepted the fact. Chantelle tried to lighten up the circumstances that she was leaving, by promising that she would return to spend the New Year together. We also, made plans to become married the following year after I had written my final exams, in August of 1975.

The following weekend, I received a visit from Amos accompanied by Motorcar's widow, Sheila, who was visiting from Inyanga. They had heard that I had been "ill" and came to see how I was recovering and whether there was anything they could do for me. We sat in the garden with my little dog Tiny scampering about, playfully sidling up to my visitors for attention. We talked for a while and I asked about the situation at Sheila's village. "Things are very bad! We are caught in the middle of the endless fighting between the terrorists and government forces!" She replied. "What do you intend to do?" I asked. Amos interceded at this point, " Ivan, she is too shy to ask you, but we have always looked on you as a father caring for his children! Sheila is thinking of abandoning her plot of land and moving to Umtali for safety and to be near her children at school there—she would like you to help her find a job in that city!" He explained. "Do you need money, Sheila?" I asked. " No, there is still plenty of money left from what you gave Motorcar, also we have the comfort of the rubies which are hidden away in a safe place!" She said, "But, if you could help me with finding a job with a place to stay in Umtali, I would like to get away from being captive between the fighting and killing around my village!" she stated. "What kind of work are you looking for? I enquired. "I did work before as a maid and would be happy to do that again." she replied. "I will contact some friends in the area and see what I can for you" I told her. I proceeded to contact a prosecutor in Umtali by telephone and arranged for an interview for her, the following week. My sympathies was with her and the other villagers, those good and simple folk in the remote areas that were carrying the brunt of the hardships from the conflict.

I took Amos aside and talked to him confidentially, telling him of what had happened during my return from Umtali. I spoke of the firefight that had ensued with my receiving the bullet wound to the stomach. Amos nodded his head, saying that he was already aware of the circumstances of the event. He proceeded to relate to me, that a security force patrol had come on to the scene where the attack took place, shortly after it had occurred. They had found and recovered the bodies of the dead postal worker and the two terrorists laying by the side of the road.

Chapter Fourteen

The Estado Novo government of Portugal fell in May of 1974, over-thrown by a junta of young military officers dissatisfied with their leaders. Marcello Caetano who had ruled Portugal was replaced by General Antonio de Spinola, the man who had authored the book, *"Portugal and the Future"* which had been so influential in bringing about the fall of the regime. The new leader had advocated in his writings a political solution instead of the present military tactics implemented. The translation of that theme was to hand the "Provinces" in Africa over to the rebel leaders, although they had no political or economic preparation in the running of their countries, and grant independence.

The coup in Lisbon threw that country's entire administration of the territories into disarray. Amid the political shambles, the transfer of power and granting of independence of the African countries was quickly negotiated. In the wings, as far as Mozambique and Angola were concerned, the Soviets waited to step in as the new force of influence.

Rhodesians watched the developments with anxiety as the former friend and ally Mozambique, was about to be transformed into hostile territory. The white settlers there, numbering close to half a million were about to be repatriated or thrown out. In time the loss of those white businessmen and their expertise would prove to be an economic disaster, turning Mozambique into one of the poorest, most war ravaged countries on earth.

While the rest of the world stood back applauding the birth of the soon to be new "Democratic" nation, the Soviets waited to step into the new country. The Soviet Union had backed and supplied the FRELIMO rebels led by Samora Machel. Once that group took power, it was an easy next step for the Marxists to move in. The newly formed opposition RENAMO party backed by the West, particularly the American C.I.A. and South Africa, was running a distant second place.

To the North in Uganda, Idi Amin was beginning to practice discrimination against the Asians in the country. Some fifty thousand Ugandans, purely by reason that they were of Asian descent, were given an ultimatum to get out of the country by a fixed date or face the consequences. From Amin's past behavior of the genocide of opposing tribal groups in Uganda, and his irrational behavior, the Asians took his threats seriously. Abandoning their homes, businesses and property, they left the country in droves emigrating mostly to Britain, one of the few countries offering sanctuary to them.

Rhodesians watching the events taking place around them, saw the developments as a justification for the stand they were taking. The question that perplexed many Rhodesians about the events taking place to the north in Uganda, was that Idi Amin was a tyrannical dictator; having seized power in a military coup in January 1971. He had ordered the deaths of tens of thousands of Ugandan tribespeople from opposing tribes. Headed a blatantly corrupt government. Openly gave safe haven to terrorists, as exhibited by the hijacking of the El Al airline jet and the subsequent famous rescue by the Israelis in freeing the hostages. Yet, other than a hue and cry about his outrageous behavior by the press and world leaders, nothing was done. No steps were taken at the United Nations to declare Uganda a threat to world peace. No threat of sanctions were made, or contemplated. No focus of attention was placed on helping that country's civilian plight other than the regular media reports of interest, regarding Amin's bizarre behavior.

Rhodesians were coming to strongly believe that the world was adopting a double standard. A frequent comment bandied about at many Salisbury gatherings was; "It is all right if you are a dictator, murdering and suppressing the civilian population, affording no democratic privileges of the citizenry to vote; provided you are a black leader! But, on the other hand, should you be white and defending your place of birth and home, you are branded, irrespective of your true beliefs, as a racist and a bigot!"

I returned to work at the Regional courts. As agreed With chief superintendent Black, I maintained the pretense that my absence had been due to study leave and the writing of the London exams.

A few days after my return to work, there was the sound of an enormous blast nearby the court building, the reverberation from the sound of the explosion caused the court tables to clatter and windows to rattle. It was almost the lunch hour, I requested a court adjournment. I left the courts and walked a few blocks towards the city, reaching Manica road. The street was teaming with fire engines and police cars. All the attention was focused on an alley behind some shop buildings.

Speaking to the police, I was able to get the sketchy facts; it appeared a terrorist had been carrying a bomb in a large suitcase and was walking along the alley, when it had accidentally detonated. The bomb had ripped the man apart so badly that there were very few fragments of him left, making identification impossible. The blast fortunately, occurred in an isolated alley with no other injuries resulting, there was however, major physical damage to the rear of the stores on either side of the explosion.

Amongst the rubble, the police were now left with the dilemma of having to guess where the ultimate destination of the bomb was intended, and, how many more innocent lives would have been lost, should the terrorist have completed his mission.

The authorities introduced drastic new measures in an attempt to prevent potential bombers from having easy access to the city. Instead of shoppers having to succumb to body searches only as they entered the stores, they now had to submit to being randomly rounded up as they walked in the streets, herded into two straight lines, one line for women the other for men. Where full body and bag searches were conducted. I submitted to these searches on several occasions and each time, couldn't help thinking, how close the country was to becoming a police state.

During one of the random searches I found myself standing in line next to Stan Garrick, the would be politician from Highlands who had enunciated the idea of U.D.I. and lost so badly years previously on that platform. I asked him about his daughter Shana. Stan proudly told me that Shana was now married with three children. "How time flies!" Stan said, "Do you remember when I was standing for the Highlands constituency, advocating U.D.I., and everybody thought it was such a wild idea! Look at us now, that is exactly the policy the present government has implemented!" Garrick added, to emphasize how right he had been all along. I responded whimsically, "Your idea certainly is the one that has been accomplished. How right that course is for the country, with all the lives that are being lost, only time and the events of history will be the judge its wisdom!"

Garrick was slightly taken aback by my comment and remained uncomfortably silent for the remainder of the search.

As the end of 1974 approached, the war gradually escalated. The guerrillas were beginning to take heart from the upcoming independence to be granted to Mozambique and expanded their attacks.

Zambia and the other African leaders meeting at the Organization of African Unity were encouraged to increase their support for the rebels.

Rhodesia was beginning to find herself increasingly isolated from the rest of the world. Much needed foreign currency was increasingly diverted to the military and the war effort.

Royal Cycles, as well as many other corporations that depended on foreign imports, saw their allocation of quotas to buy imported parts being diminished. Royal's quota was now reduced to twenty per cent of the level it had been at, prior to U.D.I.

I visited my mother and the business frequently. It was apparent to me that the corporate pressures and strains were weighing heavily with her. She openly talked about selling out her interests. Benny, on the other hand, from his self-seeking interest of not wanting to lose control of the corporation, was opposed to the sale of Royal cycles.

The relationship between Benny and me had evolved to the stage of greeting each other politely, there was never any conversation between the two of us. When our paths did cross, I noticed that Benny would keep to a cautious and dignified distance away from me. Perhaps, it was the mellowing of time, that was replacing his unfriendly disposition. Whatever the reason for Benny's change in behavior, it was of little concern, my main interest was in my mother's well-being. To that extent, as long as she was safeguarded, I had no quarrel with Benny.

The guerrilla leaders outside the country had begun a propaganda blitz of feeding the overseas media with stories that the black tribespeople in Rhodesia's outlying villages were being badly treated by the security forces. That news filtered back to Salisbury. It caused concern with the local courts, which had prided itself in the English tradition of the separation of powers and being a watchdog of the individual rights of all the peoples in the country to fair play. In order to allay those concerns the authorities arranged for forty magistrates and prosecutors to be flown to the trouble spots of the North-Eastern districts to see and evaluate the conditions for themselves.

I was one of the prosecutors assigned to travel to the "Hot Spots!"

The team of legal observers assembled at Salisbury airport early on a Saturday morning and were ferried by an air force Dakota twin engine aircraft, to the points we were to see. The flight to our first stop, Mount Darwin, took two hours. I sat by a window, looking down. The countryside underneath displayed the most beautiful array of lush green growth and colors. It was almost difficult to perceive that below all that lavish greenery, men on both sides stalked each other with deadly intentions.

At the Mount Darwin air strip, a convoy of armored trucks met our group of lawyers. We were then transported to the police base for a combined breakfast and briefing of the operations in progress within the area. At the base introductions were made with the commanding officer, though for me, no introduction was necessary, it was chief superintendent Black! "We are going to have to stop meeting like this!" I wryly commented, drawing a laugh from Black and a raised eyebrow from a Regional magistrate standing nearby, who overheard the remark.

Black led the group towards what looked like a very large mound of earth in the center of the camp. At one side of the mound there were steps leading downhill. We took the few steps down and almost at ground level, we came to the entrance of the operations center. A quick tour by the senior policeman showed it was fully self contained with sleeping quarters, mess room, a small bar complete with a man serving drinks behind the counter. The bartender was actually an off-duty policeman taking his turn serving drinks.

After a detailed briefing and a less than gourmet breakfast, Black approached me and pulled me aside. "How are you coping with your stomach wound?" He asked. "Everything has healed up just fine. Thank you!" I reassured him. "Good!" Black stated and went off to gather the rest of the observers for a tour of the base. Surprisingly, the compound was an open field, there were no barbed wire enclosures or fortifications, as I had expected to see. The perimeters merely had several fairly deeply dug foxholes for defense.

There was a large concrete slab to the side of the base. On closer inspection, the concrete had several places on and around it where blood had dried layering its surface. Black explained solemnly, "This, gentlemen, is where we bring the casualties from both sides. Sometimes, they are the bodies of farmers who have been murdered on their farms, other times the security force members that have been killed in action, as well as those terrorists that have been killed in the firefights! Here they are placed in body bags before their final journey to Salisbury." I stared at the blood stained slab, a cold chill swept up my spine, as I thought of the number of dead that must have been placed on that spot before being moved to a final place of rest! I stood for several moments blankly staring, lost in thought at the ultimate sacrifice of the people losing their lives in war.

My thoughts were disturbed by chief superintendent Black making an announcement that we would shortly be leaving for our next destination; a large village, situated on the Northernmost tip of Rhodesia, bordering with Mozambique. I said farewell to the chief superintendent and we made a vague arrangement to get together at Reps Bar the next time Black returned to the city.

The flight was a short hop of forty-five minutes to our next stop, a hastily built dirt landing strip by the Mozambique border. The strip had been constructed adjacent to a thatched village of several hundred inhabitants. At this remote place conditions were primitive. There was more than good reason to surmise that had it not been for the war, the villagers would have rarely been in contact with civilization. Now, they had a landing strip with aircraft and armed soldiers guarding the village.

As the magistrates and prosecutors left the aircraft we were informed that we had a free reign to move about the village and interview whomever we wished. The military officer present added a warning not to approach the border fences too closely, for fear of being shot by terrorist snipers on the other side. In an act of what could only be described as stupid inquisitive bravado, I walked to the furthermost point of the fence bordering Mozambique and peered through the barbed wire to the other side. A soldier came running up behind me and not wanting to infringe on my freedom of movement, he crouched down alertly beside me. His weapon raised pointed across the border to afford protection. I realized my action was endangering both our lives, I apologized to the soldier and walked to a safer spot closer to the middle of the village. I then began to mingle among the villagers, observing their living conditions.

I saw an elderly couple near their hut, the woman was grinding corn in a large cauldron, turning the corn into the staple African diet of mealie-meal. The man was passing the time seated on the ground outside his hut, smoking tobacco. I approached them, speaking in Shona, I asked if I could interview them and they agreed. I asked whether they had any complaints about the treatment from the security forces. They replied, that apart from the inconvenience of having soldiers on their doorstep, they had none. They did however have complaints which were focused on the fighting going on between the opposing forces around them, which they said was making life with their mobility outside the village very difficult.

During the conversation it also emerged that the couple had been put in a terrible dilemma regarding their family. They had five children, all sons, the eldest had become a policeman; while their middle son had gone off and joined the Z.A.N.U guerrillas. The situation had been further complicated when the middle son returned to the village and convinced their youngest child to come away with him and join the rebel forces. The remaining two children wanted to have nothing to do with the conflict and moved to the city to find jobs. "Tell me sir, what is an old man to do, when he knows that his children will be involved fighting each other on different sides?" The elderly man asked, his hands outstretched despondently, as if reaching for an answer. I wished I could give the old man an answer, but did not have one. The only thing I could do, was to encourage his hope for the safe return of all his children.

I moved on to several more interviews, before being called to join with the other prosecutors and magistrates in an "Indaba", a meeting with the village chief and his tribal elders. We sat as customary, in a circle around the chief's hut. The chief began answering questions from the visitors. Surprisingly, the chief leveled accusations at the terrorist groups, complaining that their activities were breaking down the traditional values of the tribal system. His main complaint was that the tribal way of life, which was based around the tribal chieftain working in council with the elders, administering the villagers, was severally being undermined by the black political parties. He cited as an example Z.A.N.U. the predominant political party in the area, which had been demanding the villagers allegiance to their party and no longer to the chiefs. "We had in the past, no quarrel with the whites or the black neighboring tribes, we are simple people. All we ask is to be left alone to carry on our traditional way of life!" He stated as the meeting ended.

The prosecutors and magistrates started to head back to the aircraft to be ferried to another village and more interviews, when the air force pilot came running towards us. "Gentlemen, I am sorry, but there has been a change in plans!' He stated, and explained, "We have just received a request to assist with a "casavac"—a casualty evacuation! A farmer's vehicle has just hit a land mine on the road by Mount Darwin. We will be flying back there, to pick up the two injured civilians, we will be taking them aboard so that they can receive treatment at the hospital in Salisbury!"

Arriving at the Mount Darwin airstrip the plane's doors were quickly opened and army medics lifted up two stretchers aboard the aircraft. In the one bed was the farmer, a man of Indian descent, his right arm had been shattered and he had wounds to his forehead. The second bed had his farm foreman, a black man, with injuries to his chest and a broken left leg. They were both conscious. Barely had they been placed aboard when the plan took off again, heading for Salisbury.

Two of the female prosecutors aboard, had some nursing training and assisted the army medics comfort the wounded men during the journey back. Arriving in Salisbury, a helicopter was waiting to airlift the men for treatment at the general hospital.

It was early evening, I said goodbye to my fellow workers and drove back home. I had a dinner party to attend with friends that night. The day had been an emotionally draining one for me and I was really in no mood to go anywhere. But, I realized that the change of ambiance would be good for me, so I forced myself to shower and change to attend the gathering. Dressing in a dinner suit, I drove to an old colonial style home near the city. The party was being given by friends that I had grown up with, a Rhodesian born couple named Paterson. They had dated during their school years and married shortly after completing college. The pair were now celebrating their tenth wedding anniversary. To mark the occasion, they had invited over fifty guests to their house for a night of dinner and dancing. On arrival at the house I was warmly greeted by my hosts and began to mix with the other guests. Gradually, the friendly atmosphere eased some of the tension on my emotions.

I sat down at the dinner table to enjoy the good meal being offered to the guests, while watching the warm and friendly interactions of the people around me. "You're very quiet tonight, Ivan, are you all right?" The woman seated next to me enquired. I smiled back and replied, "Yes I am fine, thank you. I am just a little tired from a busy day!" I went back to observing the guests. It struck me, as I watched the laughing and talk-ing, how much my friends still clung to their old way of life. Looking around, no one would ever have suspected that there was a war going on. Yet behind each of those smiling laughing faces sharing the happy occasion, everyone had been touched by the war. All of the men in the room had been called up and done military service of some kind. Most of the woman were involved with volunteer work, helping at hospitals or charity work. Many knew someone who had either been injured or was a casualty of the fighting. Three of the women present had lost their husbands in action, and were widowed by the war. Yet, life went on as usual, for the moment! It took courage to maintain that positive attitude these people had seemed to achieve, with the hardships going on around them. They had been able to adapt to the difficult circumstances, and were getting on with life the best they could.

Alice Paterson, the hostess, walked up to me and gave me a friendly kiss on the cheek, "Come on Ivan, you are so deep in thought, that you are beginning to resemble the statue of 'The Thinker!'" She said teasingly. "There is always a time to enjoy life! Come and dance with me?" She invited. I danced with her, had a few too many drinks of brandy and put aside momentarily, the events of the day.

Chantelle returned to Salisbury from Vietnam on the last day of December, 1974. Gratefully, she had arrived in time to spend New Year's eve to share our little haven at the house. We settled in to spend the precious hours we had together to ring in 1975 with just the two of us. Working as a team, we cooked a festive dinner of roast beef complete with Rhodesian champagne, as we laughed and talked. It was wonderful to be with her again! Time seemed to fly as we chattered away the night, listening with interest and being enraptured with the other's experiences during the time we were apart. I had bought streamers and party hats for use at the midnight hour. We made it until eleven-thirty, before succumbing to making love by the dinner table and leaving a string of clothes behind us, as we made our way gradually to the bedroom.

Tiny, our little dog cocked his head in confused amazement, as we closed the door behind us, locking him out of our intimate moments.

The love making continued unabated through to the morning of New Year's day. It seemed that Chantelle and I couldn't have enough of each other and by midday we both lay exhausted in the bed, just holding one another.

Before her arrival, Chantelle had told me that she would only be returning for a brief period of two weeks to Rhodesia. She was due to fly back to her post in Vietnam via a short stopover in Ethiopia to report on events that were taking place there. Ethiopia's Emperor, Haile Selaise who had ruled that country for over thirty years and was known as "The Lion Of Africa!" had been dethroned the previous September, in a

Marxist backed coup. Civil war and anarchy had developed, adding one more country to the list of Africa's communist instigated upheavals.

Chantelle and I talked about the emerging conflicts on the African continent. Chantelle made the comment which I had already begun to believe, "I think World War Three, has already been started by the communists, except they have been clever enough to get locals to do the fighting for them. Look at how country after country has fallen to their way of life without them having to send in their armies or their own soldiers being required to fire a single shot!" She stated.

She went on to tell me of the situation in Vietnam, Cambodia and Laos. "That is turning into a disaster for the West, the nail in the coffin has been the withdrawal of American troops. The South Vietnamese, as bravely as they are fighting, have not been able to hold their own against the Vietcong guerrillas. I think we are looking at only a few months before Saigon will fall, and with that, the whole region will become communist!" She predicted.

Then she said, "This will be the last time that I will return to cover the stories in South East Asia! Ivan, I have missed you so terribly! Each time I cover the stories of fighting and see the bloodshed, I think of us and what might be happening over here to you!" There was an air of quiet determination in her words. "When will you be coming back?" I asked. "I will return by July, after you have completed your exams!" She replied. "Permanently?" I asked hopefully. "Yes, my love, permanently! Would you like to set the wedding date?" Chantelle asked, snuggling into me.

I hugged her, "How about the middle of October?" I suggested. "Perfect, cheri!" She said.

We wasted little time in telling our families of our plans, and phoned Chantelle's parents in Brussels. Her parents told us that they would fly to Salisbury for the wedding. Her parents sounded ecstatic that Chantelle was to settle down from the dangers of her career to a married life. They ended their conversation to us with the wish; "Make us grandparents of many children soon!"

The remaining time Chantelle had in Salisbury, seemed to pass by in a blur. She kept busy with making preparations for the wedding and I juggled my time between work and helping her with the arrangements.

On our last day together, Chantelle's departure somehow seemed different from all the other occasions when we had bid each other 'Au revoir'. This time, we clung to each other, relishing each second before her flight departed. Finally, she had to go to board her flight. When she reached the steps to the aircraft on the tarmac below, she turned to blow a kiss at me in the terminal building. She smiled, but there were tears in her eyes as she gazed up at my direction. She looked so incredibly beautiful! She turned, walked up the steps and disappeared inside the plane.

It was with reluctance that I returned to work after Chantelle's flight had departed. There were a number of cases awaiting trial and it was with forced deliberation, that I threw myself back into my job. My mind kept wondering and my thoughts were traveling with Chantelle. The same day, I was informed that the senior prosecutor for the Regional courts had recovered from his heart condition and was due to return to his position in a couple of weeks. His eventual return would mean that I would be scheduled to return to Harari, to resume my duties at those courts.

Shortly afterwards, during one of my morning tea breaks at the Regional common room, I was seated talking to a police inspector. We were in the midst of discussing a case I was involved in prosecuting, in which he was the investigating officer. Unexpectedly, one of our newer prosecutor's attached to the lower courts by the name of Lillian, interrupted us with a knock at the door. She informed me that her magistrate had suddenly been taken ill and as a result her case load for the day had folded. Lillian wanted to know if she could sit in to listen to the day's regional cases I was trying, to assist her accrue more trial experience. I invited her to join us. She sat at the tea table and casually made the comment "The workers are not doing a particularly good job of repairing the roof!" I looked at her and asked, "What are you talking about?" She looked at me and replied, "The repair work that was started a couple of days ago, has been left unfinished. The workers have left one of their pipes, sticking out precariously from the elevator shaft at the back of the building! It is a strange looking thing, it has fins at on end which are projecting over the building!" She said, complacently. I looked at the inspector and replied "I was not aware that any work was being done on the building, would you show us where you saw this pipe sticking out from the building?"

The three of us walked to the back section of the building, and Lillian casually pointed out the "Pipe"......Both The inspector and I stared in horror, as we looked at the projectile sticking out of the elevator casing at the top of the building. It was an unexploded rocket that had dug itself into the shaft! The missile had obviously been fired from the nearby Kopje, a high hill that overlooked both the courts and Salisbury, from a point of half a mile away.

"CHRIST! Get the building evacuated, Ivan! I will call the bomb squad!" The inspector yelled, as he ran for the police radio in his car. I ran into the entrance hallway of the court building, bumping into the senior public prosecutor Sarij Ahmed, nearly knocking him over. I grabbed Ahmed by the arm, pulling him to one side, I explained about the missile on top of the building.

"We do not want to create a panic amongst the members of the public in the building! Ivan, you take the bottom two floors, I will take the top two. Tell the prosecutors involved in trials, to remand their cases until tomorrow and adjourn their courts, as we are having an 'emergency bomb drill!' Get them to pass the word and to make sure that everyone leaves the building." Ahmed ordered. I took off to tell the people on my assigned levels to evacuate, getting the other co-workers to pass on the message. Twenty long minutes later, the last of the people streamed out of the courthouse to a safe distance five hundred yards from the building.

"Bloody inconvenient, I was in the middle of my cross examination!" One of the defense attorneys complained, as we watched the bomb squad arrive in their trucks and enter the courthouse. "It seems they are turning this into a full scale drill with the 'bomb boys' doing their bit of practice on the building." A magistrate observed. I and the senior prosecutor, said nothing to break the illusion that this was merely a drill. Taking the initiative, Ahmed addressed the gathering. "Gentlemen, sorry for the inconvenience, but as you can see the Bomb squad have turned this into a full scale drill. Which is obviously for our future safety in the event that there should ever be a real bomb threat! It is likely that they will be here for a couple of hours, so I suggest we go home and start afresh in the morning!" I was not sure how many had been fooled by Ahmed's glib explanation of why the courts were being closed for the day, but in the circumstances, it was the best that could be done to cover what was really happening.

I walked across to the parking lot to my car and saw the police inspector. I approached the policeman and asked about the dismantling of the rocket. "Thank goodness, the missile had a dud explosive head!" The inspector told me, "It will be another few hours before the squad will have it completely taken apart!" He added, as he walked away towards his patrol vehicle.

I returned to my post at the Harari courts the following week. The one good element of being at these courts was that I received visits from Sergeant Amos more frequently. Amos's career was doing well and he informed me that he was about to write the police Sub-Inspectors exams for promotion to that post and with it, to have command of his own police station. He also informed me that Sheila was happily working in Umtali and was pleased to be near her children.

The pressure of the workload at the courts continued to be heavy over the next couple of months, with very little relief of the number of cases flowing in, being anywhere in sight.

As The Easter weekend approached, I found that I was scheduled to spend much of the time on patrol doing police reserve duties. Although, despite that task, I looked forward to the four day break from the courts.

By late night Easter Monday, I had almost completed an uneventful weekend of foot patrol duties. I was walking alongside the University Buildings, in Mount Pleasant. It was a crystal clear night, with no clouds in the sky. I stared upwards, and admired the stars above of the Southern Hemisphere, shimmering like multi faceted diamonds sending out sparkles of light to the heavens. My police radio suddenly crackled into life disturbing the tranquillity. "Attention all police reservists! We need volunteers for an emergency search party to fly to the Victoria Falls region to assist the army and police there, looking for survivors of a commercial aircraft crash. The plane with approximately a hundred passengers, is believed to have been shot down by terrorists. Those able to volunteer, please make your way to your local police post for transport to helicopters at the New Sarum Airfield!" I ran to the Mount Pleasant police station, arriving just in time to jump aboard a truck about to leave for the airfield.

"What has happened?" I asked of the regular police officer and member-in-charge of the truckload of men. "I am not too sure, but it seems that those sons of bitches used a Russian Sam-6 missile to down an Air Rhodesia plane filled with Easter holiday makers, returning to Salisbury from the Victoria Falls!" He said.

Our truck load of men arrived at New Sarum at three a.m., to see a flurry of activity taking place at the airfield. The military hangar was ablaze with lights as helicopters were pushed out, their motors ignited and started, warming up the engines ready to ferry passengers. Amid the blur of activity, someone called out "Ivan, over here!" I looked to see Amos with a group of fourteen Selous Scouts boarding to take off in one of the choppers. I ran over to their position. "We are about to depart do you want to travel with us?" Amos asked.

I signaled with a nod of the head that I did, and joined in behind the file of men entering the helicopter.

In a matter of minutes we lifted off the ground and were airborne, heading towards the Victoria Falls to begin the search for survivors.

On board with the Scouts was a Hottentot soldier, one of the few pygmies who had been recruited by the Rhodesian army from the Kalahari desert, in South Africa. These tiny men, no more than four feet tall, with perfectly proportioned little bodies, were undoubtedly the world's best natural trackers. Stories of their hunting skills, tracking abilities and sense of smell to find water in the desert were legendary. It was very comforting to know that he was aboard, if anyone could track down survivors he would be the one to find them. For me, it was fascinating also listening to the Hottentot talking with the other soldiers, most of the words that he uttered were articulated with a loud clicking sound to express himself.

One of the other Selous Scouts on board, known only as "Gray" was an American and a former Green Beret. He was a well built, tall, fair haired, good looking man, who had a flamboyant character. He spoke so loudly, that everyone on board couldn't help but be aware of his presence. Even he silenced, as the lieutenant leading the group signaled for quiet as he took a lengthy radio call through headphones he was wearing.

"Okay, loosen up men!" The lieutenant said after the call, "Here is the situation as far we know. An Air Rhodesia Viscount turbo jet aircraft, with ninety-seven civilian passengers on board was hit with a Sam-6 rocket launched by 'ters' shortly after take off, at eight p.m. last night. The plane crashed forty miles from the Victoria Falls airport. The crash site has been located, army and police personnel have begun arriving, to help at the scene. We have also established from one of the injured at the site, that there are fourteen survivors who took off several hours ago, trekking through the bushveld to try and seek help. It seems that they did not know whether we were aware of the attack on their plane and that it had crashed! Our task, is to find them and get them back to safety, before they are found by the terrorists. We will offload by the crash site, the tracker will follow the spoor leading out from that point! Move fast men, heaven knows what will happen if the 'ters' get to them first!"

Flying low, barely over the tree tops. The helicopter came within sight of the crashed plane and landed nearby, the time was just after seven in the morning. The Hottentot was the first to jump to the ground. He spent a few moments surveying the bushes around the crash location and then took off running into the undergrowth. The men from the chopper took off at a fast pace, following behind him into the bushes.

As the group ran through the tall grass, Amos turned to me, "Make sure you keep up Ivan, the Hottentot is capable of running for hours, without stopping!" Conserving my breath, I nodded in acknowledgment and maintained my pace with the other men. The Hottentot displayed the most incredible stamina, glancing at a broken leaf or twig to calculate direction while still on the run. He zigzagged through the undergrowth, sidestepping the overgrown tree roots and thorn bushes. He slowed down from his run only momentarily, allowing the rest of the group to catch up with him before speeding off again on his search for the survivors.

After nearly two hours of keeping up with this tireless tracker, I felt totally winded and on the verge of passing out. Forcing myself to pump up whatever adrenaline was left in my body, I kept running. Gratefully, the tracker stopped for a few seconds to examine some displaced leaves. I took in some heavy gulps of air, my heart raced with exhaustion. "This way!" The Hottentot said in a clicking voice, pointing to his right and taking off again. We ran for another fifteen minutes. Abruptly, the tracker came to a halt and stared at the heavy grass ahead of the group. "There!" He said, crouching down and pointing in front of him.

The Scouts approached the location cautiously, clearing out the grass in front as we moved forward. The American, Gray, led the way. There was a low moaning sound coming from behind the bushes. Gray advanced forward and stopped "Sweet Jesus, NO! This can't be!" he yelled out, at the scene in front of him. I moved forward, my stomach tightened into a knot and my body stiffened at the sight of total carnage, that came into view in front. All fourteen survivors of the plane crash, lay scattered in blood stained tall grass. The men, women and children had each been shot, their bodies lay motionless at the site of the slaughter, on the ground. Several gaping bullet wounds on each of the bodies attested to the merciless way that they had been gunned down.

We searched to find the victim that had let out the earlier low moan that we had heard. Hoping that at least one of them was still alive. The Hottentot found him, a young man in his early twenties, laying against a tree stump bleeding from several bullet wounds. Gray tried to comfort and administer first aid, but it was hopeless, the young man was drawing in his last breaths of life. I could not stand to watch the man dying. I walked away towards a tree which I leant on, covering my face with my hands, I wept unashamedly.

The young man died in the soldiers arms. Gray, the Selous scout who had been holding him lowered the lifeless head to the ground. He walked over to a nearby tree and smashed his fist into its side. "Bastards!" He yelled, "It wasn't enough that these civilians had to survive a plane crash, the 'ters' had to shoot them down in cold blood, while they were looking for help!" He cried out.

The lieutenant, who had kept stone faced throughout, took command of the situation. He ordered the soldier manning the radio, to call in our position and the circumstances at the site. Turning to the Hottentot, he asked "How many and how long ago?" The Hottentot walked around the perimeter of the carnage, looking at imprints in the grass and examining broken twigs and leaves. "Sixteen terrorists, three hours have passed!" He responded with a click. "Shit! We are less than two hours from the border with Zambia!" The lieutenant exclaimed. "Gray, take your stick of six men, see if you can engage them before they can cross the border!" Without another word, Gray and five other soldiers disappeared into the bushes.

The lieutenant turned to the Hottentot, "Retrace the journey the survivors took before being murdered here! I want you to recreate and tell me the circumstances, of how they were captured and killed!" Pointing to Amos and me, the lieutenant ordered, "You two, go with him to provide support and fire cover!"

The three of us took off into the bushes, lead by the Hottentot, carefully retracing the steps taken by the victims. For the first time in my life, I hoped that we would run into the terrorists and engage in a fire fight; I was eager to avenge the deaths of those innocent civilians.

After an hour and a half of searching through the bushes, the Hottentot stopped. "Here is where the terrorists camped last night!" He said. Further down, He pointed out; "This is where the survivors accidentally walked into the camp. They then walked together in this direction!" The small soldier said examining the path, as if the broken grass, leaves and twigs were speaking to him, recounting the events of the previous night! We came to a flattened bed of grass at one site, the Hottentot carefully examined the spot. "Two of the women were raped here!" he said sadly.

Continuing to ascertain the events from the evidence on the ground, we eventually returned to the place where the bodies of the victims were discovered by the Scouts. "They were walking slowly, perhaps too slowly for the terrorists. The survivors were grouped together at this spot, the terrorists moved back several feet and opened fire on them!" The Hottentot said, ending the recreation of events. He took off to speak to the lieutenant, to tell him of the evidence he had uncovered leading to the killing of the civilians.

Hours had now passed since our arrival and the military began the last stages of clearing up the scene. The bodies of the victims were picked up by helicopters and flown to Salisbury. Gray and his men, emerged back through the bushes to the scene of the tragedy. His stick reporting that their pursuit had not resulted in any contacts with the terrorists, who had made good their escape into Zambia.

A military helicopter arrived and picked up the remaining men and myself in the late afternoon, we flew back to Salisbury.

The news of the missile attack and subsequent murder of the crash survivors had already been broadcast over the media airwaves to an outraged Rhodesian public. Condolences and messages of sympathy swarmed in from all parts of the country, to the bereaved families.

From outside the country, leaders of Z.A.P.U. took pride and credit for the downing of the aircraft and bragged to the world at how effective they had been in shooting down the plane.

Some leaders of the black African countries, lauded the behavior of the downing the commercial aircraft, by the "Valiant freedom fighters" of Zimbabwe.

The international community remained silent, not a word of official condemnation was spoken, for the acts of downing a civilian aircraft, of the rape of innocent women or the subsequent brutal murders of the surviving crash victims. Eight children had died in that brutal act of savagery, and on their behalf, only silence.

A few days afterwards, an inter-denominational service for the fallen victims was given at Salisbury's largest church, the Anglican Cathedral. The service was broadcast to a nation that mourned its loss. The host Anglican priest delivered the sermon.

I was seated in the church and listened to the priest. He gave the most powerful speech I had ever heard a man make. The priest talked about the victims and the "deafening silence," heard from around the world at the atrocities committed on helpless innocents. "Listen carefully, my friends for the words of condemnation from the world community— the silence is deafening!" He said, ending the sermon.

Chapter Fifteen

In the political sphere, Portugal made the announcement that Mozambique was to be granted independence on the 25th of June, that year, under the leadership of Samora Machel. With that, the future destiny of that country was sealed. Whites were being repatriated out of the country in droves, fortunately they had a country to go to, which was Portugal. However, it still meant leaving their homes, businesses and in many cases a lifetimes worth of work building up the country behind. Some not wanting to leave Africa, came to Rhodesia and South Africa.

Chantelle and I continued contact with our regular weekly telephone calls to each other. In early April, during one of those weekly phone conversations, Chantelle told me how the situation she was covering in Vietnam had deteriorated dramatically. The Vietcong were advancing on all fronts and the general consensus was that Saigon would shortly fall, perhaps in a few weeks! There were mass evacuations taking place. She told me that she was going to try and cover the events in Saigon for as long as possible, but in the event that the city fell, she would be moving her base to Cambodia to cover the story from there. Chantelle mentioned that should she move, I may not hear from her for a little while, but as soon as she was re-settled she would phone and give me her new address and phone number.

Amos had written his Sub-Inspectors exams and passed. He was excited to tell me the news during one of his visits to the Harari courts.

His promotion was scheduled to take effect at the end of the year, with it he would be assigned the command of his own district police post. He told me that he hoped it would be in the vicinity of Salisbury.

Royal Cycles had attracted a group of businessman who were interested in buying out the corporation. The group was headed by a young man still in his late twenties. He had emigrated from Denmark to Rhodesia six years earlier landing in the country with three hundred dollars to his name. He had found a job, and began buying property cheaply from people leaving the country. In a few years he had succeeded in becoming a multi-millionaire, heading several groups of companies. The satisfactory purchase Of Royal Cycles was to be his biggest financial coup. Rae discussed the pending sale of the company with me, I offered to review the legal documents and to help in any way that I could.

An article appeared in the business section of the Salisbury newspaper about the pending sale; which Rae read with interest concerning the sale being subject to a "Satisfactory offer being made to purchase the company." and commented to me, "It will be even more satisfactory for me to walk away from the business and the headaches of coping with the import quotas!"

Benny had been given an incentive to go along with the sale. He had been offered a percentage of the purchase price received, when the company was sold. The real intention of that offer was intended not to alienate the greedy man into doing something that would jeopardize the negotiations, as well as keeping his interest in the deal to realize the maximum sale price.

"How is Benny taking the proposed sale of the business?" I asked my mother. "Actually, considering the circumstances, very well! He is pushing to get the highest price from the buyers, to increase the amount he will get as his percentage of the sale. He has told me that with the money, he is going to buy property which he will lease out and retire, to live on that income." She replied.

The senior prosecutor for the Regional Courts had given his best efforts to returning to work. However, the continuing pressures were proving to be too much for his heart condition, and he submitted his resignation. I was promoted to the permanent post of Regional prosecutor, effective from the date that I returned from writing the elusive final London examinations.

As the end of April approached, the news reports of events taking place in Vietnam gradually began to overshadow for a time, our own local news. Dramatic footage was carried on T.V of the hasty evacuation of the American Embassy in Saigon. The footage showed the numbers of people struggling to get aboard the last flights of helicopters taking personnel out before the city fell to the communists. I did not hear from Chantelle, whose turn it was to make the weekly phone call. I tried not to worry about her, she had amply prepared me for this possibility. But despite that, I was still very concerned knowing that the situation must have been chaotic with the events taking place where she was stationed.

I keenly followed the events as they developed in Southeast Asia, all the time thinking of Chantelle and what she must be going through. I could not help thinking how glad I was that she was due to come home for good. Even though there was a continuing war situation in Rhodesia, we would be together sharing our lives. Chantelle could settle down with the knowledge that she had achieved her ambition, and the experiences from covering the stories in Vietnam, to fill her memories for a lifetime.

The following week, I again, did not hear from Chantelle. I tried phoning her number, it was no longer in service, as were most numbers in Saigon.

I began my study leave the following week, always nearby the telephone, running to pick it up every time it rang, just in case it was a call from Chantelle.

The third day of my leave I did receive a call, though it was from Mister Roget, Chantelle's father. His voice was raspy and somber, as he greeted me. I sensed immediately, before any further words were said, that something was seriously wrong. His voice hauntingly betrayed the bad news he was about to relate to me. "Ivan, I regret to have to tell you, we have just been informed by the news agency, that Chantelle has been killed in a helicopter crash!" Mister Roget said, as his voice choked up tearfully. "Dear God! No!" I exclaimed, I could not believe what I was hearing. My world felt completely shattered by the news!

Chantelle's father haltingly tried to overcome the grief showing in his speech to explain the circumstances, "She was covering the evacuation of the city of Saigon, from a news agency helicopter. We do not know whether the craft developed engine trouble, or was shot down. But, the helicopter crashed in flames, killing everyone on board!" I paused for a moment. " Is there any possibility she could have survived the crash?" I questioned, grasping at the vague hope Chantelle may have escaped from the helicopter. "None!" Roget somberly replied. "The rescue party recovered personal articles from the charred remains that identified her positively Among those articles were the remnants of jewelry you have given her. There was a diamond and emerald engagement ring as well as part of a pendant with the emerald and gold cross. I know that Chantelle never went anywhere without wearing them!"

I spoke briefly with Chantelle's mother, expressed my sympathies to the Roget family and put down the phone.

At that moment, I experienced my world become engulfed in a feeling of sorrowful darkness. I turned to our dog, Tiny, picked him up and hugged the little animal. I closed my eyes imagining for a second that Chantelle was there with us. Tears began to flow incessantly and without any control down my cheeks.

Rae, my mother, did her best to give me support and comfort on hearing the news, but my preference was to be left alone. I did not see or speak to anyone for several days, refusing to answer the telephone each time it rang. I tried to throw myself into the studies, but that was to no avail. My mind was not on the work and my eyes blankly stared at the words in the content of the books, nothing seemed to penetrate. Unable to sleep or concentrate, I could think of nothing else but Chantelle.

Just prior to the exams, I took a trip to the library in a vain attempt to do some research. I came across a book that detailed the derivation of names. I looked up "Chantelle." The literal translation was French, meaning "Her Song!" I thought about her name. She had truly been my song. Even more than that, Chantelle had been my "Song of Africa!"

A few days later, I started to write the London examinations. The lack of sleep, stress and exhaustion finally caught up with me. I passed out halfway through writing the paper, and landed in the hospital for two days.

After my discharge from the hospital, I went to visit a stone mason. I asked the owner to engrave a granite memorial plaque, with the following inscription:

CHANTELLE ROGET

"MY SONG OF AFRICA"

1945–1975

When the plaque was completed, I paid for it and drove towards Lake MacIllwaine. I steered off the main road, to the remote wild life spot that I had taken Chantelle to view a few years back, while I was the Youth Mayor. I stopped by the watering hole we had visited and enjoyed so much. I looked at the scenery from the same position where we had once stood and watched the animals casually drinking. Now, because of the terrorist threat the locality was uncared for and had become overgrown with shrubbery.

I knelt down and dug a small hole in the ground. I was going to leave the small memorial to Chantelle at this site. As I completed digging, I sensed that I was being watched. I knew that my being at this place was flirting with death, but I no longer cared.

From a distance of a hundred yards away, hidden in the bushes, a group of eight terrorists watched my solitary work digging at the earth. A seventeen year old member of the squad, raised his rifle and had me squarely in his sights. The leader of the group moved forward and pushed away the barrel of the rifle aimed at my back. "It is bad magic to shoot a madman or a fool!" He whispered to the members of his group. "Let us see what this man does! I believe that he is grieving the loss of someone close and does not care whether he lives or dies, why else would anyone come to this place alone and unarmed?"

They watched as I completed my ritual of placing the memorial stone to hopefully, forever face the watering hole. It would always have a view of the animals lazily basking and drinking from the water.

I stepped back to inspect the position of the memorial, then I heard the rustle of bushes nearby. I knew what had caused the sound but continued to stare at the plaque. The rustle grew closer, I ignored the sound.

The moving rustling sound stopped directly behind me. I thought, "If I am going to die, I could not think of a better place to be!" I braced myself for what I expected to happen next.

A few seconds passed then I felt a hand being placed on my shoulder. I impassively turned, coming face to face with the guerrilla leader. "Do you speak Shona?" The leader asked. "Yes, I do!" I responded in the native dialect. "You are grieving the loss of a loved one?" the man asked. "Yes, the woman I was to marry." I replied. "You lost her in this war?" The leader asked. "No, she was a newspaper reporter and died in a helicopter crash covering the story in Vietnam!" I told him. " I am sorry for you!" The man said. I nodded my head in acknowledgment.

We both stood there for a few moments, observing the memorial. The guerrilla leader spoke again, "Go home and finish your grieving. Hamba gashi—go in peace! For today, I have no quarrel with you!" With that the guerrilla leader turned, walked away and disappeared back into the bushes.

I stayed at the spot a few minutes longer, taking a look at the scenery before returning to my car and driving back to Salisbury. During the drive back, I reflected on my close brush with death and the encounter with the guerrilla leader. It became clear to me that even in times of armed conflict, there was still always a moment for compassion and humanity, as displayed by the man who should have been my mortal enemy.

The event at the wilderness site, somehow, rekindled in my grieving heart, a light of hope. A hope of the inner kindness that could exist amongst all men simply by taking the time to understand and show empathy to fellow human beings.

Still burdened from the emotional strain of coping with the loss of Chantelle, I resumed my court duties at the Regional Courts.

I noticed that in addition to the regular overload of cases waiting for trial, some of the more recent cases submitted for prosecution involved elements from the international criminal circle.

Perhaps Rhodesia's "Outlaw" status was becoming a lure for individuals attracted by the possibility of finding refuge away from their own countries legal systems. Such as men who were wanted for serious crimes, or those who had their own illusions of creating a new world order, started to trickle in to the country.

Most were in for a rude awakening. Rhodesia may have been a political outcast, but it still maintained very close connections with the international police organizations, such as Interpol, as well as the police fraternities in other countries.

I become involved in a deportation case, involving an American based "Hit man". Shortly after his arrival in Rhodesia, the New York police department had forwarded a rap sheet showing the man's prior arrest record, it showed that he had been arrested eight times on charges of murder. He had been acquitted on each of those charges. He however, had been convicted on three other charges, two of culpable homicide and one of manslaughter, for which he had served a total of seven years in prison.

The man, who was in his mid forties, arrived in court wearing an expensive business suit. I noticed that the man had the coldest looking eyes I had ever seen. I spoke to him before the case. He was very relaxed about the deportation order, saying that he would not be fighting it. He was also, very casual about his past history. Knowing that he could not be re-tried in the United States on the cases for which he had already been acquitted, he openly bragged that he had actually committed the murders that showed on his rap sheet.

He went on to say that he had been sent to Rhodesia "on a hit" against a man that had swindled his "Employer" out of several million dollars. He did refuse to divulge who the intended target was, but merely added the comment that now that he was being deported, his "employer" would likely send out someone else, to do the job.

Another case involved a "con artist", from America. He had arrived in Salisbury. Staying at the most expensive hotel, where he proceeded to rack up a bill of several thousand dollars over a period of six weeks with the promise to pay as soon as his funds were "wired In!" He also proceeded to buy a house which he promptly re-sold and bought six businesses without laying out a single penny. When he was eventually arrested, he continued to insist that money was being wired in to him. Unable to raise bail he was placed in the remand cells.

Several times prior to the trial date he requested a meeting with me, as I was to prosecute the fraud case. Each time we met, the man would protest his innocence and then try to sell me a piece of property in Florida.

I resisted the overtures to buy the property at the "bargain" price offered.

When the trial date came up, I was amazed on my entry into the courtroom, to see the con man sitting at the back of the court in a huddle with the investigating officer, a police inspector. He was still negotiating the sale of the Florida property! The con artist then went into the trial with the weirdest defense; that he was still waiting for money to be wired in. The facts of the wiring, and his reasons for the non payment of the large debts accrued, changed each time the circumstances suited him during the trial. He was convicted and sentenced to five years in prison.

Without serving a single day of his sentence he was promptly deported; apparently trying to sell each person he came in contact with on the way to the airport, a piece of the property in Florida.

L. Ron Hubbard, the founder of the American Scientology movement, immigrated to Rhodesia. On his arrival he bought a large sized farm estate, at which he was allegedly going to "retire".

I had remembered seeing a large neon sign of the Scientology movement on Hollywood Boulevard, in Los Angeles and was vaguely familiar with its concepts. Articles in the local newspaper and television, gave credibility to the man's background and stature. Hubbard had impressed Rhodesians by referring to the country as a "Paradise" and a "Garden of Eden."

The police took a different view of his reasons for settling in the country and watched his activities. On the surface it appeared that Hubbard was living a low profile, quiet life on his farm. However, in secret documents, that came through my office, undercover agents disclosed that Hubbard had a definite agenda for the future of Rhodesia. According to the intelligence, Hubbard intended to turn his farm into a commune for members of his group, which would eventually expand to take over the country. Rhodesia was to become the world headquarters of his movement, as well as turning it into a nation based on the concepts of Scientology. It was highly unlikely that Hubbard would succeed in his goal, but the police had their hands full with the war and decided the best way to deal with the situation was to nip his plans in the bud. He was brought up on a deportation hearing and I was assigned to the case.

Hubbard was a pleasant and charming man, though, he fought the case tooth and nail, alleging that his aims were purely benign and really no threat to the country.

He lost the case and was deported back to the United States.

Mozambique achieved its independent status, the new leadership now strongly under Soviet influence turned hostile towards the former friend, Rhodesia. That territory now became a safe haven for the Z.A.N.U. party, providing their group with a solid base from which to expand the war and launch their guerrilla activities against Rhodesia.

With the increased guerrilla incursions, the list of casualties on both sides increased dramatically.

The guerrillas began a radio broadcast from Mozambique, preaching subversion and a "Death List," announcing the names of people who were to be targeted for execution in Rhodesia. That list included all politicians, leaders of the community, judges and prosecutors, as well as anyone else that opposed their activities. It was no surprise to me to hear via the intelligence sources, that mine, was one of the names on the list, by the fact of my being a prosecutor.

As the months rolled by towards the end of the year, I found myself totally immersed with my work. My social life had become non-existent, more by desire than lack of opportunity. In the past, I had comfortably socialized with the knowledge of Chantelle being an integral part of my life. Whether we were together or thousands of miles apart, I had always felt her closeness to me. Now there was a huge void, an emptiness which I did not know could ever be filled! Although grateful for the wonderful memories of her that I would always carry with me as part of my life, I also tried hard to remind myself that there was still a future for me to look forward to. The problem I constantly faced was the difficulty to imagine living it alone, without Chantelle.

New Years eve, my friends were able to convince me to join them to bring in 1976, at a dinner dance. There were many single people celebrating the occasion and I forced myself to join in the dancing, drinking and even flirt a little.

As the new year rang in, I took a glass of champagne, walked outside the party, into the clear summer moonlit night. Alone, I gazed up at the heavens in a moment of reflection. My thoughts filled with cherished memories of Chantelle.

Chapter Sixteen

The political face of Africa was rapidly changing. Many of the new leaders who had come to power had turned their countries into one party states. Other leaders had been quickly deposed of, by their military, allegedly, because of rampant corruption, the swift deterioration of living standards and genocide.

Those who did the deposing usually found themselves too, soon being overthrown, while other leaders, just became outright dictators. Political philosophies changed with leaderships and depended on who was in power for that moment. Control of African countries had become a surrealistic game of political musical chairs.

The guerrilla war, combined with the sanctions imposed against the country, were beginning to have a biting effect on Rhodesia's economy. Before U.D.I, Rhodesia had been a bread basket of Africa, openly exporting goods and supplying food to neighboring states. Now what little that was exported, was done covertly, for fear by the leaders of those black African States who were buying, of being discovered and accused of supporting Rhodesia.

The rhetoric and the reality became two different things; Kenneth Kaunda, President of Zambia was one of the loudest vocal opponents of the Rhodesian government. Yet, although he allowed terrorists to launch attacks into Rhodesia from bases inside his country, he continued to do business with this country. So did Mozambique, which depended heavily on trade with its neighbor for its foreign currency existence. Trade continued and in some cases increased slightly with the countries of Botswana, Malawi and Zaire.

Political gamesmanship was a fact of life that Rhodesians were becoming all too familiar with, in regard to their neighbors.

Royal Cycles was finally sold. With the proceeds of the sale my mother Rae, decided to retire from business life. She invested the principal received from the sale with a bank, with plans to live off the interest dividends. She also made arrangements to buy a round the world air ticket, with travel to America to see brothers and sisters that she had not seen for over fifty years. Rae also planned a visit to my sister, Babette and her husband, who had now retired from active ballet dancing in England and had opened a school for ballet in Melbourne, Australia. The last leg of Rae's journey was a stop in London to see her eldest son Leon, and family.

Rae and I sat at dinner one evening at her apartment, shortly after the sale of the business. I listened to my mother talk with enthusiasm of her travel plans to visit our families in the different countries. The length of her travel was scheduled to take ten months, she would leave in April and return to Rhodesia at the end of January the following year. As we talked, I felt a surge of eagerness to travel as well. I found myself wishing the pressures of my work were not as heavy, as I longed to be able to take a real holiday once again. In the past, most of my breaks from work had been to take study leave for the London Exams.

Rae and I talked about the London examinations due to take place in the middle of May. I had a copy of my mother's travel itinerary and promised to phone her, once the results came out. I still held onto my plans to resign from the prosecutor's office and to go into private practice as an Advocate, when I had completed this last and almost elusive hurdle of obtaining the London LL.B. degree.

Amos had now been promoted to his new rank of sub-inspector. With this promotion, had came the command of his own police post. He was named officer-in-charge of the West Harari police station.

The months seemed to fly by, late April arrived and I took my mother to the airport to begin her around the world adventure.

Little had changed in my routine of working by day on the heavy load of court cases, studying at night for my exams, plus the regular call up for nightly and weekend police reserve duties. Occasionally, when time permitted I would stop in at reps bar for some brief socializing.

When he was in the Salisbury vicinity, Chief superintendent Black, also, was an occasional visitor to the bar. He and I sometimes ran into each other there, we would pull up a couple of chairs, sit and talk over a few beers. There had been strong rumors, that Black was now head of the Rhodesian Special Branch unit. This was the Rhodesian equivalent of the British Secret Service, although Black would not openly admit to that fact.

I stopped in one evening at reps, just before I was due to start my leave to study for the forthcoming examinations. Black was at the bar and walked over to speak to me. "Glad to find you here Ivan, I was hoping to run into you!" Black said, pulling up a chair. He continued, "There has been an important development, with regard to Mozambique, that I would like to discuss with you. Can you come down to police head-quarters tomorrow evening to see me?" Black asked. I agreed, and the policeman got up to leave, as he did, he inquired "By the way, I believe that you can speak Portuguese fluently, is that correct?" I smiled in reply "Yes I can, but with a British accent!" Black nodded and walked away.

The next evening I arrived at police headquarters and was escorted through to the Special Branch section. I was led into an office, where Black was seated behind a desk. On top of his desk was a large Manila folder, with the words "Top Secret" thickly printed across the cover. Standing by an open window, pensively looking out of the office, was Major Swartz. We greeted each other and I sat down on the seat in front of Black. "Thank you for coming to meet with us, Ivan!" Black acknowledged.

The policeman then proceeded to come right to the point of the meeting. "Ivan, I believe you are aware, despite the Rhodesian political deadlock, that we still work closely with intelligence sources of other countries, especially in matters of mutual concern, such as the communist infiltration into this part of the world?" I nodded that I was aware of that fact. Black continued; "We work particularly closely, swapping information with the American undercover and the British MI-6, intelligence services!"

Black opened the manila folder in front of him, "The American Intelligence has provided us with information about a Cuban troop ship that recently offloaded a few hundred Cuban soldiers at the port of Beira. They were heavily equipped with weapons and sophisticated Soviet armaments. The troops were quickly loaded onto several trucks, which set off in a Westerly direction. Presumably, headed somewhere close towards the Rhodesian border, that is where our sources lost track of the Cubans!"

Major Swartz entered the conversation; "We believe that the Cubans are basing themselves somewhere near Villa de Manica, inside Mozambique. They are the advance party for future sorties of Cuban troops, who intend to attack Rhodesia!" Swartz paused a few seconds, then he continued, "What we need to do, is find out exactly where this advance party is located. Once we have the location pinpointed, we can send in air power to knock them out, before they can complete setting up a base of operations! If we can accomplish that, it will send a strong message to the Cubans and the Soviets, that we are capable of hitting them, should they attempt to set up future bases!" Swartz concluded.

Black and Swartz both momentarily stared at me, and I was now starting to feel very uncomfortable. "Why are you telling me this?" I asked. Black nervously shuffled the papers in the Manila folder, "We want you to go undercover into Mozambique with two other men, and get that information on the location of the Cuban base, back to us!" He said.

"You're crazy! Why me?" I blurted out. Black looked at me with a firm gaze, "If I remember correctly, that is exactly what we said to you, when you came to us with your wild idea of going after "One Eye." Both you and Amos, proved us wrong! No, we are not crazy! We have given a lot of thought to a plan that we think will work! Why you? We picked you, for several reasons. One of which is that you proved to us how effective you can be, when you went in after "One Eye". Also, You speak Portuguese and Spanish fluently, which will allow you to pass off as one of the Cubans soldiers. finally, you have started your study leave, which provides a good cover for your absence from work!" Black stated.

"When is this "undercover" work supposed to take place?" I asked. "In four days time!" Swartz replied. "Jesus! Do you realize what you are asking of me?" I asked in astonishment. Black nodded his head, "We know precisely what we are asking of you. We know that it means giving up the opportunity of completing your final London examinations and being able to go into private practice—for the moment. We know it means seriously risking your life, if you are caught, there will be no mercy, you will be shot as a spy! We know that should you succeed, no one must ever know what we asked you to do. So, there will be no payment of any kind, or even a thank you, particularly from other Rhodesians, whose lives you may help save! But, make no mistake, getting that information will save a lot of Rhodesian Lives!" Black said flatly. "Does that about cover, what we are asking of you?" The policeman asked, his voice taking on a latent compassionate tone.

I nodded my head in resigned acceptance. "Explain the plan to me!" I uttered.

Swartz began to outline the strategy. "In four days, we will be making an air and ground strike against a terrorist base just inside Mozambique. The attack will provide us with a diversion and the cover to get you across the border. While the ters are pre-occupied with the air strike, one of the helicopters carrying your group, will fly you deep into the Gorongosa game reserve and drop you off there."

Swartz continued, "Your group will consist of three men. You personally, will be dressed and pose as a Cuban corporal. We know that you and Sub-Inspector Amos work well together, so he will be the second member of the team. Amos has been briefed and will be posing as a Z.A.P.U. guerrilla. The third member of the team will be sergeant Patrick of the Selous Scouts. Patrick, for your information, is formerly from Mozambique and an ex-terrorist, that has come over to join our side! He will pose as a FRELIMO soldier from Mozambique."

I interrupted Swartz, "Isn't that risky, having an ex-terrorist on the team—what if he decides to change sides again, once we are in Mozambique?" Black shook his head "That is highly unlikely, Patrick has proved himself to be highly effective for us, since he came over! The chances of him turning on you, are less than minimal." He said. I raised my eyebrow, "Thanks for that bit of reassurance!" I stated caustically.

Ignoring my remark, Swartz continued, "We picked Gorongosa as the drop off point, for the simple reason that since the Mozambique war, the area has become neglected and allowed to go totally wild. Conditions are so primitive with malaria and Tsetse fly infestations, plus the abundance of wild animals, that even the terrorists give the place a wide berth. You should be able to penetrate deeply towards your objective without being detected. We estimate that it will take you a three day march to come out of the game reserve, in the vicinity behind Villa de Manica. From there you will have to play the situation by ear, as you see fit! You have three objectives; one is to map the precise location of the Cuban base. The second is to establish their numbers and types of armaments. The third is to get that information to us and yourselves out of there as quickly as possible!" Swartz concluded.

Black entered the briefing, "As you hold the post of Captain, you will be the ranking officer on this mission! Do to have any questions, Ivan?"

He asked. I sank back into my seat, and answered; "Yes, do you have any brandy? I think I need a good stiff drink!"

Black smiled, "Good, as you have no questions, we will have your Cuban outfit ready for you in three days, at which time you will meet Patrick!"

Three days later, Amos and I traveled to Nkomo barracks thirty miles from Salisbury, the headquarters camp of the Selous Scouts. There, we were introduced to Patrick, a tall, thin, muscular man, with several scars visible across his face. We were taken into an operations room, for a final briefing by major Swartz, on our mission.

The three of us changed into the covert disguises, in preparation for the drop off, scheduled to take place early the next morning. Going in under the cover of darkness and the diversionary planned attack on the terrorist base, we hoped would give us a good start of our mission into Mozambique, undetected.

As nightfall approached, Swartz stopped by to see how we were doing. "Try and get some rest men. We leave for New Sarum airport at three a.m.! You will have a tough few days ahead of you. Good luck with the mission!" He wished, as he left us in a barracks room to make our final preparations.

Early the next morning we received our wake-up reveille from a soldier beating on the barracks door. His effort wasn't necessary. None of the three of us had been able to sleep. We had each spent the hours prior to this moment wide awake and deep in thought about the mission. We loaded our equipment on to the trucks with the Scouts traveling to participate in the attack on the terrorist base. Arriving at new Sarum the three of us climbed aboard one of the ten helicopters waiting to transport the troops. Our chopper was the last to take off traveling at the rear of the convoy.

As we approached the target base near the Mozambique border, low flying Rhodesian jets screamed by our helicopters, taking the lead assault to hit the targets. Their job was to strategically soften up the enemy, before our ground forces offloaded from their transports to continue the attack from the ground. As we closed in on the terrorist encampment, our helicopter pitched right of the convoy and veered off to the South, flying low over the dark shadowed outlines of the tree tops.

The helicopter proceeded to fly us towards our planned destination, away from the ensuing combat that was beginning to rage in the distance behind us. I watched with awe, the backdrop of distant bursts of incandescence from the firepower being exchanged. Explosions from mortar shelling illuminated into the night and spewed into the air, as the battle between the opposing forces raged. Ahead, in the direction we were now traveling, all that could be seen was the blackness of a moon less night. After nearly an hour of low flying through darkness the helicopter circled a clearing and landed. Amos, Patrick and I scurried off the chopper. The pilot gave us a thumbs up gesture for good luck and lifted the helicopter back up into the air.

The three of us looked around cautiously as the first rays of light began to streak across the wilderness, bringing in the dawn of a new day. Here, in the middle of one of Africa's largest game reserves, the area teamed with an abundance of wild life of every kind. The tropical bushes, trees and grassland had not missed man's incursions into its domain and grew unfettered in all directions. The ongoing conflicts had caused an abandonment of the region. It was now no longer being restricted by man cutting pathways and roads to inhibit its growth.

The malarial mosquitoes and tsetse fly, also flourished in this region. In order to protect ourselves from those deadly bites, we had worn heavy protective underclothing; despite the searing African heat.

After checking our equipment, the three of us set off on our trek. We had over eighty miles to cross, through dense jungle territory, which needed to be covered in three days or less.

Walking through the rough terrain, I could not help but marvel at the sights of raw Africa. In each direction I looked there were herds of zebra, antelope, elephant and African buffalo, roaming the range.

Occasionally, the peaceful tranquillity of the animals grazing would be disturbed by a lurking predator, causing them to stampede in all directions sending up clouds of dust in a protective screen.

All day we trekked through the heavy bushland. We were careful in rationing our water, not wanting to risk drinking from the rivers and lakes we passed. The fear was of contracting the dreaded Bilharzia or sleeping sickness from the infested waters.

Marking good time by early evening, we calculated that we had traveled a distance of thirty miles that day. Night approached and we sat in an open clearing to rest. Patrick made a request to build a small fire so that he could cook us a meal. I had seen no signs of any other human activity in the vicinity, to which the fire would be a tell-tale sign of our presence, so, I agreed to the request.

The three of us sat around the small campfire eating the rations cooked by Patrick. This was the first opportunity we had to relax since the start of the mission. I observed Patrick in the glow of the small fire, the man spoke very little. My impression of the ex-terrorist was that he was more a man of action than words, which I felt was good. I wondered what hidden stories Patrick had in his past that brought him into service with the Selous Scouts, which in turn had led him to this point in life with Amos and myself, in this wilderness.

We settled to rest for the night, each of us, was to have a four hour shift in guarding our camp.

In the early hours of the morning while Patrick was on point duty, he quietly communicated an alarm to Amos and myself. Reaching for our weapons we went on the alert. "What do you hear, Patrick?" I asked. Before he could answer, there was a large crunching sound of something very large, breaking through the bushes in front of us. "A herd of elephants, perhaps ten or twelve of them, they are coming this way!" Patrick whispered. "Do not run, lie flat on the ground. The elephant are sensitive creatures. They will smell that you are there! As long as they know that we do not threaten them they will be gentle and merely step

over us. Do not panic! Lay absolutely still and they will not harm us!"
Patrick stated. Amos nodded in agreement.

Flattening myself on the ground I muttered to myself, "Shit! What a
great way to find out if elephants will not harm anyone who is not a
threat! I hope these guys have sensitive noses and gentle feet!"

The heavy crunching sound of several large feet walking through the
undergrowth, drew closer and closer, and entered the clearing where we
lay. I shut my eyes tightly, as I felt an elephant's trunk over my body,
smelling the human presence. Gently, the elephant lifted his feet, carefully stepping over me. A second and third elephant did the same.

As the last Animal passed over us, Patrick let out an ear piercing
scream, causing the herd to stampede off into the night. I released the
safety catch off the Russian rifle I had been issued and shone my torch
in Patrick's direction. The light showed Patrick gagging and flailing
wildly at his head with his hands. "The bloody elephant shitted on my
head!" He screamed.

The top half of Patrick's body was covered in elephant dung! This
was without doubt, the funniest sight I had ever seen. Coupled with the
relief that the man was unhurt, I doubled over with laughter. Amos,
who was standing close by, had tried to keep a straight face, but the sight
of Patrick with dung all over his head was too much for him, and he too,
cracked up with laughter, tears rolled down from his eyes. " I thought
you were a shithead!" Amos blurted out in-between gasps of air from
laughing. Patrick's outrage eventually gave way to seeing the funny side
of what had happened, he also joined in the laughter.

The three of us settled down in an attempt to get some more sleep,
before starting out again on the following day's lengthy journey, that
lay ahead.

The incident with the elephants, seemed to break the ice with the
new member of our team. Patrick's attitude relaxed and he showed a
new-sprung friendliness towards Amos and myself. He joined in our
casual conversations as we trekked under the hot African sun. Stopping

by a watering hole, we took a break to eat lunch and watched the animals also arriving to take a drink from the muddy waters. Flies buzzed around us in their hundreds, for each spoonful of food we ate, we had to take several more swats at keeping the pests away from us.

At nightfall we stopped our trek, exhausted, we searched for a place to spend the night. Having learned from the previous night's experience with the elephants we decided to set camp by some tall trees. Each picking our own tree, which we climbed up, to sleep in for the night.

Sleep was uncomfortable in the trees, but, the night passed without further incident. At dawn the following morning we prepared for the last and most dangerous leg of our trek. By nightfall, we hoped to come out on the Eastern side of Villa de Manica, entering the town through the roadway as though we had just come in from the direction of Beira.

Setting off on our march, we made our way through the tall tropical grass. The grass was sometimes taller than the top of our heads, making visibility difficult and frequently we were unable to see what lay ahead of us. As we marched I sensed a presence and signaled the other two to halt.

We stooped, motionless in the grass, listening for any kind of sound. Behind, there was the slight sound of rustle in the tall grass. With silent signals, the three of us separated into defensive positions in the bushes. The subdued rustling sound drew closer. Each of the men released the safety catches from our rifles.

Through the bushes, a large lioness crouching in a hunting stalk broke apart the tall grass. It stopped motionless, smelling the air, looking for directions to find its prey. It seemed, that the lioness was stalking after the three of us!

Suddenly from a hiding place in the bushes behind our position, a gazelle, leapt through the shrubbery into the open and ran off. The lioness pounced into action chasing after the buck. Both huntress and prey soon disappeared into the undergrowth. Leaving behind them only the sounds of heavy rustling as they broke through the grassland, continuing the saga of the struggle for survival, and of life and death in the jungle.

Relieved that we were not the target of the lioness's stalk. The three of us resumed our trek.

By late afternoon, we reached the main road, leading into Villa de Manica. Nearby was a farm store. We scouted the shop for a few minutes. I then spoke to Patrick, "You are native to this area, go into the store and speak to the owner under the pretext of buying some goods. See what information you can get out of him about the Cuban camp!" I instructed. Patrick ambled into the store, he emerged half an hour later, with a bottle of Anise liquor and some canned meat. " Did you find out anything?" I asked. "Yes, the camp is about ten miles from here. The store owner is not sure exactly where, but he says soldiers from there come regularly to the store to pick up ground corn and assorted vegetables." Patrick replied. "Good, we will wait in the bushes until one of the soldiers comes by!" I told Amos and Patrick.

The three of us slipped under the cover of the bushes on the side of the road. A little while later a Soviet type Jeep skidded to a halt outside the store. A Cuban private, accompanied by a Frelimo soldier stepped out of the vehicle and went into the shop. My Group came out of the bushes and began walking to the store as the Cuban and Frelimo, came out carrying goods. The Frelimo Soldier, tripped and dropped some sacks of ground corn. The Cuban began yelling at him, calling him "Stupid and incompetent!"

This gave me an idea; I turned to Patrick and began to yell loudly at him in Portuguese. "Idiot, I told you to check if there was any oil in the vehicle! Look at us now, because of your imbecility we are stuck with having to walk back to the camp!" I cursed, putting on a stance of anger. The Cuban approached, "What is the matter corporal?" He asked. "This imbecile, did not check if there was any oil in our vehicle and it seized up, four kilometers back!" I said, pointing in the direction behind us.

"I can give you a lift back." The Cuban offered. He approached closer to Patrick, "Phew! This man smells like shit!" He commented, as he smelt the residue of the Elephant dung. "You know how it is, these men never take a bath!" I stated casually.

Looking at Amos, The Cuban asked "Who is this Man?" I explained "He is one of the Rhodesian guerrillas, I was taking him to help us, back at the camp." The Cuban gave me a curious look. Fearing I had given the wrong answer, I tightened my finger grip on the trigger of my rifle. The Cuban shrugged his shoulders and walked to his vehicle. Amos, Patrick and I followed and climbed into the back of the car.

The vehicle set off and after a few kilometers the Cuban turned the vehicle onto a dirt side road. Driving down a bumpy, recently constructed roadway. We drove for another ten kilometers into the countryside, before abruptly coming upon a very well camouflaged encampment. I made a mental note of the directions we had taken to get to this place. Looking around, I saw the camp had been surrounded with camouflage netting that hung from the trees.

I observed how well these people had been able to hide themselves and their equipment from the possible scrutiny of air reconnaissance. Alighting from the vehicle, I thanked the Cuban for the ride and we proceeded to lose ourselves amongst the soldiers and flurry of activity taking place at the camp. Finding a quite corner, I gave the other two their instructions; "Amos get a count of the number of personnel on the base. Patrick, check the defense perimeters and weaponry. I will check the armaments the Cubans have stored in their armory. We will meet back here in two hours! Hopefully by then we will have all the information we need—and can get the hell out of here, using one of their vehicles. Understood?" I asked. Amos and Patrick nodded their heads in acknowledgment. "Let's do it!" I ordered.

Mixing with the other soldiers, I made my way to where the armaments were stored. There was a wide array of weapons. They ranged from SAM-6 anti-aircraft missiles, anti-tank rockets, rocket launchers, additionally, there were other weapons that I had never seen or heard of before this night. Casually, I walked into a tent next to the weaponry. I asked the private on duty there, for a rooster of equipment, as I "Had been ordered to do an impromptu armaments check!" The private handed me a clipboard which detailed the list of weaponry. I thanked the soldier and walked away. Quietly, I let out a heavy sigh of relief. My heart had been pounding from the risk I had just taken.

Two hours later, Amos and Patrick and I met at the pre-arranged spot. We each signaled a thumbs up, to indicate the success of our assigned objectives. "Okay, let's get out of here!" I whispered.

We made our way to the car pool. I walked up to one of the open vehicles. A private was seated nearby. I turned to the Cuban, "Is this vehicle fueled? We need to transport this Rhodesian comrade back to his group near Villa de Manica." I said, pointing to Amos. "Yes sir! The vehicles are all fueled up." The private replied. "Good, we will return later, perhaps in the morning." I said to the Cuban, the three of us got into the vehicle, I started it up and drove out of the camp. "Shit! talk about living on the seat your pants!" I exclaimed, as we distanced ourselves from the Cuban encampment. "What was the personnel count, Amos?" I asked. "Three hundred Cuban soldiers and a mixture of forty Frelimo and Rhodesian guerrillas!" Amos replied. "How good are their defense and fortifications around the camp. Patrick?" I enquired. "Very good! They are surrounded with machine gun bunkers, SAM-6 anti aircraft missiles, plus other weapons that I have never seen before!" Patrick replied. I remembered the unusual weapons I too had seen. "Perhaps the Soviets intend to test some new weaponry against Rhodesia?" I commented, as we came out of the dirt roadway and traveled on to the main road towards Villa de Manica. The main road beyond that town, led to the Rhodesian border.

Driving slowly through the town of Villa de Manica, we passed by groups of Frelimo soldiers and Rhodesian guerrillas walking along the side of the roadway. Receiving and returning the occasional comrade hand wave as we passed by the soldiers and the town, onto the stretch of road leading back to Rhodesia.

After driving for several miles, we came across a dilapidated signpost laying to the side of the road. The sign had the words "Rhodesia, 2 kilometers" printed across its face. I looked at my watch, it was three in the morning. "Let's dump this vehicle off the side of the road in the bushes. It will be safer to cross the border on foot, through the grass cover!" I ordered.

The three of us pushed the vehicle into the bushes and covered it up with foliage, before setting off through the semi mountainous terrain towards the Rhodesian border.

Dawn started to break as we crossed back into Rhodesia. We stopped our trek to rest for a few minutes in a gully. "What a relief to be back!" Amos stated.

"Halt! Drop your weapons!" A voice from behind the gully, threatened. The three of us taken by surprise, dropped our rifles to the ground and stood up, with our hands raised.

A group of thirty guerrillas, emerged from behind the cover of the bushes, their AK-47 rifles pointed directly at our small team. We had walked straight into a terrorist ambush point! "Who are you?' the lead terrorist asked. Amos, who was wearing the same guerrilla uniform as the terrorists, answered. "Comrade, we are friends! I have with me, a Frelimo and Cuban soldier!" He explained. "What are you doing here?" The leader demanded. "We are doing a reconnaissance of the Rhodesian border, in preparation for the Cubans to help us attack this country!" Amos replied. One of the other terrorists spoke out, "He lies! They are Selous Scout spies! Let us shoot them now!" He said, taking up a threatening stance.

"Comrade, why would we be here wearing our true uniforms if we not checking out the countryside. If the Rhodesians saw us with these uniforms they would surely shoot us. Come, let us get on with our purpose, we are wasting time. We have much work to do before we return to make our report! The cadres will be angry with you for delaying our work!" Amos replied, with a touch of indignity.

The leader walked up to me and poked me in the chest with his rifle "Who are you?" He questioned. I replied in Portuguese. "Answer me, in English!" The leader demanded. "He does not speak any English!' Patrick interceded, "That is why I came along, to interpret between the two comrades!" he stated. The leader turned his attention on Patrick, and proceeded to question him. I listened, grateful for the man's background as a former terrorist, Patrick was able to answer most of the interrogation questions, with ease.

"Very well, you may proceed with your work!" The leader commanded. Both Patrick and Amos thanked the terrorists and we set off walking in the direction of Umtali.

After a few miles, I turned to Amos and Patrick, "Keep walking, I am going to backtrack to see if the Ters have been following us. I will catch up with you a little later." I took off under the camouflage of the foliage surrounding the bushes. Scouting back I saw no sign of the guerrillas and returned to catch up with Amos and Patrick. Meeting up with them, I said "Okay men, there is no sign of them. We are fairly close to the main road, lets lose these uniforms and weapons, before we run into trouble with our own security forces!" "What are we going to wear for clothing?" Amos asked quizzically. "We should be fairly close to a village, perhaps we can buy some clothes from the tribesmen. We have been lucky getting this far. Let's not push it by wearing these clothes with our security boys around!" I instructed.

Stopping by a village, I paid one of the tribesmen handsomely, for three sets of raggedly looking shorts and tee shirts, which we changed into. Patrick looked at me and started laughing. "What's so funny?" I asked. "Heh, heh, heh! You look so funny, dressed in a torn tee shirt and dirty shorts!" Patrick guffawed. I chose to ignore him.

We walked to the main road that led into Umtali and waited. After a short while an army truck approached, and I flagged it down. Giving the driver urgent instructions to get us into the city. The three of us were then flown from Umtali by helicopter, back to Nkomo barracks near Salisbury.

Changing out of our raggedy clothes, showering and dressing back into our normal clothing, I drove the three of us to Police headquarters in Salisbury.

Swartz and Black were waiting for us at the Special Branch offices. "Congratulations on successfully completing your mission men!" Black said as we sat down for the debriefing. "What information do you have for us?" He asked. Amos, Patrick and I each took our turn in disclosing what we had seen and learnt. The real coup was the clipboard I handed over, containing the list of armaments contained at the Cuban camp. At the end of the meeting, Swartz leaned back on his seat. "Excellent! With this information we know their precise location and the firepower we can expect. We should be ready to move against them with an air and ground attack in two days!" He informed us.

As we stood up to end the meeting, I addressed the two senior officers. "Before we leave, I would like to place on record the bravery and valor of both, Sub-Inspector Amos and Sergeant Patrick in obtaining the information. As their commanding officer on this mission, I am commending them for a medal of valor!" I stated. Black nodded his head in agreement, "Very well! They will both deservedly receive that citation." He said.

Outside the police station the three of us shook hands before parting to return to our respective homes. "Good night Amos." I said. Then turning with a friendly wink to Patrick, I said, "Good night my friend, keep out of the way of elephants in the future!"

A couple of days later, late on a Sunday afternoon, I was working in my garden with "Tiny" the little dog, by my side. Overhead, Rhodesian jets suddenly roared by, the jet at the rear, broke formation. Flying low over the Salisbury suburbs, the jet proceeded to do a slow precision victory roll over the city.

I knew the mission they had just accomplished!

Chapter Seventeen

My Mother was now at the point in her journey where she was visiting her family at Seattle, in America. I phoned Rae, dreading the thought of having to tell her that I had not written the final London examinations. "Why Not?" she asked. "Mother, I can not tell you over the phone, the reason why. Something important came up with my work. I will explain the situation when you return, but I will definitely write the examinations next year!" I stated firmly. "I hope so, Ivan. It would be good to see you put the examinations behind you and go into your own practice!" She said. I put down the phone, wondering how I could explain the situation, without revealing details of the mission I had been sent to accomplish in Mozambique.

I returned to work, knowing that when the list of candidates passing the London examinations would be published, my name was going to be missing from the pass list. I hoped that I would not deemed academically inept, by my associates at work, when that happened.

The attack on the Cuban base inside Mozambique seemed to have its desired effect. Other than sending in "advisors" to that country, the Cubans refrained from sending any further large scale contingents of troops into Mozambique. The Cubans instead, concentrated on sending their forces into Angola, where conditions were more receptive with the local movement.

I reviewed the work load to find the number of cases still continually increasing, most of them being terrorist associated trials. Cases which in normal times would have been regarded as "heinous, savage atrocities," were now commonplace. I looked at one particularly grizzly case and after reading the facts, I was surprised to find that I had insulated my emotions substantially. I was no longer being shocked or upset from the wretchedness inflicted on the victims. I had adjusted to this format of life and now simply looked to the facts of each case, in preparing the matter for presentation to the courts. I wondered if a certain amount of callousness had of necessity become a part of me, because of the brutality of war?

As the end of the year approached, Z.A.N.U. began to establish strong bases in Samora Machel's Mozambique. The guerrilla incursions intensified into Rhodesia, from along the seven hundred mile border between the two countries. Rhodesia's military was being stretched to the limit as they also had to cope with the Z.A.P.U. guerrillas coming in from the several hundred mile border with Zambia.

The Z.A.N.U. and Z.A.P.U. factions too, were at odds with each other, primarily, because of their competing backers from the East. Not only were they fighting the Rhodesian troops, but they were fighting each others forces. Their clashes left many of their troops dead in the field.

South Africa, covertly, began sending contingents of their army to help the stretched Rhodesian military protect the borders. Despite this assistance, the South African Prime Minister, John Vorster had already come to the conclusion that the Rhodesian situation was frail and that the Smith regime was doomed. Vorster began to apply pressure on Ian Smith to come to terms with moderate black leaders and pass the reins of government on to them, in majority rule elections. What Vorster did not take into account was that The Z.A.N.U. and Z.A.P.U groups had their own agenda's for taking over the country, there was no room for passing of the reins to moderates.

The final nail in Rhodesia's future course, came with the election of Jimmy Carter, as President of the United States. The man's meddlesome activities in Rhodesia's affairs, made him particularly disliked amongst Rhodesian whites, who believed he had no real comprehension of the situation. From the pressures he applied to the government, it appeared that he was ready to hand over the country to the guerrillas and their communist backers. Fortunately, though as a weaker counterbalance, there were also United States leaders that were more sympathetic, who seemed to understand the situation a little more clearly. They were prepared to help work towards a more equitable resolution of the fighting. Amongst them was Ronald Reagan.

The feeling amongst many Rhodesians, who had now endured nearly twelve years of the hardships of sanctions and war, was to stand fast and keep up the fight for their country. Aware that the rest of the world was at the point of writing us off, we became even more determined to survive the odds and the increasing pressures to abandon our pro-Western culture.

The Military stretched to the limit, continued to hold their ground against the guerrilla incursions. In the process tales of extreme heroism performed by men of all races emerged. Tales of sticks—groups of six men, patrolling the bush coming into firefight contact with terrorist groups of twenty to thirty men, and able to come out on top.

Tales of boldness, where the country's tiny air force, consisting of six outdated Vampire jets, bought before U.D.I. in the early 1960's, went on the offensive into Zambia to strike at terrorist bases. In one of those strikes, one Vampire jet flew low over Lusaka international airport, where that country's newer and faster military jets were stationed. The pilot of the Vampire jet, who identified himself to the air control at Lusaka, as "Green Leader," courteously requested the control tower to keep Zambia's jets grounded. "We mean you no harm!" The Green leader told the tower, as he circled the airfield. He explained that Rhodesian air and ground forces were conducting a strike against

Rhodesian terrorist bases inside Zambia. He added the Rhodesians would prefer no interference from Zambia's military, any planes attempting to take off would be shot down. "Green Leader" apologized for the inconvenience, but added that the mission would shortly be over. The Zambian control tower complied by closing the airfield.

A Jumbo jet carrying international passengers, at that time approached Lusaka airport and was instructed by traffic control to circle at high altitude and await further instructions. After twenty minutes of circling, the irate pilot of the Jumbo jet unaware of what was going on below, asked for the reasons for the delay. The tower responded that there was a "situation" going on, which would shortly be over and the jet would be allowed to land. The Pilot of the Jumbo jet caustically commented, "Who the hell is in Charge down There?" The air traffic controller calmly responded; "Well, for the moment, it appears that the Rhodesians Are!"

While these stories helped boost Rhodesians morale and encouraged them to keep up the fight, they were not being told the full story. It had became impossible for the Rhodesian military to patrol the borders of several hundred miles with its neighbors. Some portions of the boundaries were land mined in an attempt to curtail cross border incursions. In other areas, tribespeople were moved and placed in "protected villages", with military guards. The protected village concept proved to be very unpopular, displacing many villagers from their homes into these new and unfamiliar, communes. Worldwide press condemned the protected villages as being "Concentration Camps!" Which gave more credibility to the guerrillas.

Certain areas of Rhodesia, were simply left unsecured and the guerrillas were allowed to take over those border portions of the country. The guerrillas infiltrated the tribal villages in the South-east border region that were left without military patrols. They mingling with the tribespeople, to the point where they took over the villages, setting up their own administration of the region. Most of the Rhodesians in the cities were oblivious that these developments were taking place.

Rae arrived back in Salisbury from her around the world trip. She told me of her experiences during her travels. America had truly been wonderful she told me, recounting how fulfilling an experience it had been to finally see the brothers and sisters she had not been with for over fifty years. She told me of the hours they had spent together reminiscing about their childhood days. How she had enjoyed Los Angeles, gambled a little in Las Vegas and spent time with her eldest brother and three sisters in Seattle. The long flight to Australia, where she had joyfully spent time with Babette, her husband Michael and their two teenage children Peter and Fay. From Australia, Rae had flown to London to see Leon, his wife and their teenage daughter Colette. I listened fascinated with her news of our families living in other parts of the world.

Rae, also broke the news to me that she had decided to emigrate to Cape Town, to spend her retirement years. I received the news with mixed emotions. Sadly, because it meant my mother would be leaving Rhodesia and it would be more difficult for us to see each other. But also, with a sense of relief that with her living in Cape Town, my mother would be living out of harms way of the increasing war situation and dangers that now existed in Rhodesia. Rae told me, that she would leave the country once the immigration formalities for permanent residency had been approved by the South African authorities, a process which normally took about six months.

I began to concentrate on writing and passing my London Exams, determined now, not to let anything get in my way. I wanted to make sure that I had that internationally recognized degree, should the situation in the country deteriorate to the extent that I was forced to emigrate. The degree would serve as a cushion, knowing that the strict exchange control regulations would force me to leave all my savings and money behind.

I approached my study leave in May 1977 with apprehension, afraid that something would happen again, as in the past, to prevent me from writing the examinations. Nothing did, I was able to complete sitting the papers, this time without interruption. Now, it was a matter of waiting for the results.

I returned to work and felt as though a weight had been taken off my shoulders. Five weeks later, the results were published. I had passed the examinations and was to be awarded the LL.B. degree at last.

The results, when they arrived came as an anticlimax. The many years of trying to complete writing the examinations. The delays which for one reason or another had made the completion of the degree so elusive to accomplish, had built up an expectation in me. The expectation had been that my life would change drastically, that was not the case, everything around me remained the same. The only fact about my life that changed, was that I now started to make preparations to go into private practice.

The Provincial Magistrate for the Harare courts stopped in to congratulate me on completing my degree. He told me that he was at the Salisbury courts for a meeting with the chief magistrate. The purpose of the meeting was to review candidates for appointment to the bench of a new magistrate. He wanted to Know if I would agree to my name being submitted!

I was very reluctant, explaining that I did not want to make a career of working as a civil servant. The provincial magistrate was very persistent, saying that he considered me to be of judicial caliber. He also emphasized the honor of being elevated to the magisterial position. After much persuasion, I agreed to a tentative submission of my name, on the understanding that there was a strong possibility of my withdrawing from the running in favor of going into private practice.

I discussed the nomination with my old friend Jay Patanak. Jay was excited about the offer and very much in favor that I accept the position, if it were offered to me. "Ivan, it is an honor that most people would jump at the opportunity of having. Besides, should you decide that the bench is not for you, you can always resign and come into private practice! Should you do that, you would enter private practice with judicial experience, prestige and honor!" Jay said, encouragingly.

Rae was delighted at my nomination and she too encouraged me to accept the appointment to the bench. I decided to go along with the invitation, submitting to the ritual scrutiny that accompanied the candidacy of such appointment. I submitted to Interviews with the Provincial and Chief Magistrates, who gave their endorsements. The heads of the Ministry of Law and Order, and Justice also endorsed my nomination, as did the Attorney General's office.

After two months of government paperwork and bureaucracy, a hearing was set before the Public Services board. The board consisted of nine members, all senior officers in Justice, Law and order, the Attorney General, Director of Public Prosecutions and the ranking Public Services Officer. Although the hearings were reputed to be grueling and rigorous, it was generally accepted that anyone who made it as far as that hearing, was virtually assured of the appointment, it was the final rubber stamp of approval.

On the appointed day, I appeared before the board. The meeting was in a large room, with a long conference table along the side of one wall and a solitary chair set in the center of the room. I was to sit in the chair. The positioning of the chair was intended to make the person being interviewed feel uncomfortable, it succeeded in its purpose.

The interview began and continued for an hour. The hearing took on a friendly tone from eight of the nine members of the panel. The Ninth member, was the representative from the Public Services board, he neither smiled or asked many questions and appeared to distance himself from the other panel members. At the end of the hearing I thanked the panelists for their cordiality and returned to work. The findings of the hearing would be announced in three weeks.

At this time an Anglo-American proposal was submitted to the Rhodesian government. The plan proposed the introduction of black majority rule, in which the interests of the whites in the country would be protected. It proposed the merger of the Rhodesian security forces with the guerrilla forces of Z.A.N.U. and Z.A.P.U., into an army of national unity. The problem with this proposal was that Sithole's Z.A.N.U. and Nkomo's Z.A.P.U. armies were equally at conflict with each other, as they were with the Rhodesian government. The only factor that those two nationalist factions could agree on was despising Ian Smith's pro-western white government.

Bishop Muzerewa's umbrella group, The United African National Congress was more amenable to the proposals. They entered into negotiations with the Rhodesian government, and brought with them, although reluctantly, the Z.A.N.U and Z.A.P.U. parties to the negotiating table. The negotiations floundered and dragged on, in an attempt to come to an agreeable settlement between the different groups. Terrorist activity was increased substantially by the guerrillas in order to maneuver into a better bargaining position.

I was called into the Director of Public Prosecutions Office to review pending cases awaiting trial. At the end of the meeting the Director said to me. "Ivan I have the decision of the hearing on your appointment as magistrate in this letter!' He said, handing over an envelope. "Before you read it, I wanted to give it to you personally, as I believe the contents merit an explanation! What that letter says, is that you will have to wait two years for the appointment. Frankly, and off the record, eight members of the board voted in favor of your elevation to the bench immediately. The ninth member, from the Public Services Board was against you. He said that it would set an "unusual precedent" to appoint you as magistrate as you had only just obtained your London degree. That was the only ground he could find to argue on and bluntly, it is horse shit; as you undoubtedly have the experience! I believe that his real objection is that you are Jewish, although we could never prove that bigoted attitude. We argued with him, but the decision of the board has to be unanimous. So we reached a comprise, to appoint you to the judicial position in two years…. I am sorry Ivan, but it was the best we could do in the circumstances!" I thanked the Director for his efforts and candor, and left the meeting with a feeling of disappointment.

With the benefit of hindsight, I found myself regretting that I had agreed to become involved in the candidacy for magistrate. My thoughts became focused on leaving the civil service and starting my own practice. The one thing I was not going to do, was to let myself feel down and become upset over the decision that had swayed against my appointment. I was determined not to allow that public service bigot, the added satisfaction!

I went back to the courts and prepared to submit my resignation at the month's end. As though reading my intention, Chief Superintendent Black arrived at my office a few days later. "Ivan I have heard what transpired with your appointment to the bench…and am quite frankly, disgusted at the outcome!" He stated. "I appreciate your thoughts!" I replied, "But, that event has merely confirmed my decision to go into private practice!" I told Black.

"Well, that is why I have come to see you. With the way things are going, we are losing a lot of valuable people, either through the war, those leaving the country, or being lured into the commercial world. I have come to ask you to delay your decision to go into private practice!" I stared at the policeman for a few seconds. "For the last several years, my life really has not been my own. Now that I have the opportunity to do something for myself, you want me delay that decision again?" I asked. "Yes Ivan, I am! With the negotiations going on between the different political parties. There is a possibility of us achieving a settlement. Should we get to that point, we need every available person to maintain stability through Law and Order. You have the respect of both blacks and whites as being judicially sound and fair in your prosecutions! It is essential that people like you stay on a little while longer, to help the country get through what may prove to be one of its more difficult periods!"

"I really do want to go out on my own! I have always thought of this position as a stepping stone to get the experience, before going into private practice!" I replied. Black looked at me with a firm gaze, "Yes and it can continue to be! To be honest, one of the options we had considered was to actually let you resign, then, once you were in private practice we were going to call you up, and second you back into the prosecutors office—on military pay! However, that is an underhanded way of doing things. We would prefer for you to stay on voluntarily!" Black said, offering me the veiled threat as a means of playing his trump card. "Is this what you consider to be the art of friendly persuasion?" I snapped at Black. "Sorry Ivan but we do need you to stay on a little longer." Black said, apologetically. I knew he was leaving me with no choice. "Only…a short while longer!" I stated, angrily, pointing my finger at Black. "Agreed!" Black said, with a smile, as he picked up his police hat and left the office.

My mother Rae's documents came through granting her permanent residency in South Africa. She prepared to leave at the end of the year. She had tears in eyes as she began to package her belongings for shipping and storage, I quietly helped her. "It is strange Ivan." She said, "When I arrived here over fifty-five years ago to marry your father, this was a country in the middle of the wilderness. It was full of wild animals, the dreaded Malarial diseases and a barely developed society. I was afraid of traveling into what was then the interior of a dark continent I had the tears of a newly arrived bride. Now that I am leaving after being a part of a nation, both black and white who have toiled together to turn this country into the jewel of Africa. I again have those tears. Tears of a widow leaving the country I love!" She said.

I turned away from her, I did not want her to see the tears that were rolling down the side of my face. I knew and understood how she felt about leaving Rhodesia. So much of her life was entwined with this country, it was very hard on her to be leaving it.

On the day of her departure many friends came to the airport to say goodbye to Rae. Among the crowd were Benny and Amos. I hugged my mother as she parted and watched her walk to the aircraft. Amos stood next to me and put his hand on my shoulder. "She will be all right, be happy that she will be safe away from the war here, and you will be able to see her again soon!" Amos said, consolingly. I nodded my head in agreement as we watched the plane taxi to the runway. Shaking hands with Amos to say goodbye, I started to make my way out of the airport building. Benny walked up to me. "Do you have a few moments to stop and have a drink with me at the bar?" He asked. "Why?" I queried suspiciously. "I think that it is time we had a talk!" Benny said, there was a pleading look in his eyes.

We sat at a table in the bar lounge and ordered tea and sandwiches. Benny started the dialogue, "Ivan, since Royal Cycles was sold, I have had a lot of time to myself. I have used that time to invest…. and also to do a lot of thinking! Frankly, I wanted to tell you that I am ashamed of the way I treated you and for creating the obstacles that stopped you from coming into the business. I have not been sleeping well lately, so for my own peace of mind, I wanted to speak to you, to offer my apologies for what I did!" I watched Benny as he spoke, there was for the first time an air of humility about the man. I thought a few moments about what Benny said and replied, "You know Benny, I often think how different my life would have been without your malevolence in stopping me from coming into Royal Cycles. In a way, I suppose I should thank you! Because of you what you did, I became more determined to succeed! I probably would never have started my own business or gone on to complete my law degrees. Perhaps, had the situation gone more smoothly between us, we would still be working together today in the cycle business, and I would be looking forward to spending the rest of my life selling bicycles! In the light of the experiences

I have had over these last years, and the fact that I now look forward to a life as a lawyer, I am content that the situation has turned out in this way!"

Benny extended his hand to me, "I am glad that you were able to achieve what you did, it still does not excuse my behavior…I am Sorry!" I took Benny's hand and shook it. In that moment, we put the past behind us.

Chapter Eighteen

As 1978 rolled in, the negotiations between the Rhodesian government and the Nationalist parties reached a stalemate. It seemed that some of the nationalist factions, particularly the Z.A.N.U. wing operating from Mozambique, wanted more than they were prepared to give. Although many points had been agreed on by all the parties, there were a few issues where it become impossible to satisfy the demands without one of the parties losing ground. The Anglo-American proposal lost its backing from the British and American politicians.

Ian Smith decided to go for an "Internal settlement" with Bishop Muzerewa's U.A.N.C. and Sithole's Z.A.N.U. parties, which were leaning towards an equitable agreement to end the fighting. A public referendum was held in which the Rhodesian public were given the choice of voting to accept or reject the internal settlement for majority rule. The vote was overwhelming in favor of the settlement. With a clear mandate from the Rhodesians, the first majority rule election in which every person over the age of eighteen could vote, was scheduled for June of 1979.

The effect of the internal settlement was to split the Z.A.N.U. party. Sithole who had been the unquestioned leader since the inception of the party, found himself at odds with his lieutenant Robert Mugabe, who was leading the guerrillas fighting from Mozambique. The party now had an internal Rhodesian leadership with Sithole agreeing with the settlement, and an external leadership under Mugabe in Mozambique, determined to fight on.

Joshua Nkomo and his Z.A.P.U. party seemed to be sitting on the fence vacillating between going for the internal settlement or staying out of it and continuing the war. Finally, he opted to join the previous adversary Robert Mugabe in a loose alliance, linking the external Z.A.N.U and his Z.A.P.U. parties into a new group, which they now called the Patriotic Front or PF. The real effect of that alliance was that they would refrain from fighting each others armies.

I was convinced that irrespective of what the outcome of the majority rule elections were. Once majority rule had been achieved the whites would be quickly forgotten about and thrown into the background as an insignificant issue. The real issue would then emerge...the power play would begin between the Marxist giants from the East, the Soviets and Chinese manipulating for a foothold on this small but resources rich country.

Even though an internal settlement had been reached, the external factions continued the guerrilla warfare and increased their activities in urban terrorism through 1978. A massive bomb blew up a church situated in the suburb of Borrowdale during the middle of the night. The sound of the explosion resonated throughout the rest of Salisbury, waking the sleeping city. The bomb destroyed the church and killed its black caretaker.

A rocket was launched by terrorists from the Kopje, Salisbury's highest point, to the nearby main fuel storage depot. The rocket hit the largest gasoline storage tank which exploded into flames, a chain reaction followed with the other nearby tanks going up in flames, millions of gallons of gasoline burst into white flames. The entire night sky around the depot was lit up by the blaze from flames leaping two and three hundred feet into the air.

I like most other people in the city had been awakened by the sound of the explosions from the fuel tanks erupting. I looked at my watch. It was close to midnight. I walked outside my house and looked in the direction of the city. Although I was more than five miles from the site of the explosion, I could clearly see the huge ball of flames lighting up the entire area in front of me. The T.V. station had tuned off for the night, so I turned on the radio, which began broadcasting reports of the missile attack at the gas depot.

I decided to drive to the site of the attack, to see what was happening. When I arrived the place was a hive of activity, every available fire engine in the city was there. Fire fighters, the police and military were desperately trying to bring the flames under control and were losing the battle.

I walked up to the leaping flames. For a moment there was a sense of surrealism in the inferno which blazed into the night around the buzz of human motion. People were scurrying around trying so desperately to control the fire. I stood watching the activity taking place, there was little else I could do.

A short distance away, Chief Superintendent Black was leading the security forces, combing the nearby kopje for any sign of the terrorists responsible for the missile attack. He was probably more than aware that the search was an exercise in futility, that the perpetrators had quickly made good their escape from the scene and were long gone by now.

It was close to two in the morning when I left the scene to return home. The fire blazed for several days and the Rhodesian authorities eventually decided to call in the help of the famed American fire fighter, Red Adair, to bring the inferno under control.

Under constant pressure from the attacks by external Nationalists, the Rhodesian government and internal factions pressed forward to implement the internal settlement. One of the terms of the agreement was a change of name to the country, which after the general elections would become known as "Zimbabwe-Rhodesia." An open invitation was also extended to Mugabe and Nkomo's groups to join in the general elections. They declined and persued the guerrilla war to the maximum.

By early 1979, everything was in place to proceed with the elections. International observers were invited to see that the elections were conducted in a free and fair manner. A few countries sent their observers as referees to the free choice of the people.

The elections took place in June 1979. In which Bishop Muzerewa's party won the vote count by a substantial majority, he become the new prime Minister in the new shared parliament. Ian Smith was appointed to the position of Minister without portfolio, under the terms of the settlement agreement.

White Rhodesians waited with baited breath to see the changes that would overtake the country with the new black Prime Minister in power. Smith moved out of the Prime Minister's residence to make way for the new leader. Muzerewa took occupancy by side stepping the available Mercedes vehicle and traveled to his new residence by means of an Ox-cart filled with his furniture. The significance of the Oxen driven cart was to show his "humility and association" with the tribal way of life.

Rhodesians continued to await significant changes to their way of life. Nothing changed, life continued exactly as it had been before the transformation of power. There was also, no international recognition of the new government, because the Patriotic Front had chosen to stay outside the settlement.

What was almost surprising was the intensification of the fighting. The Patriotic Front launched all out offensives across the borders from Mozambique and Zambia against the new multi-racial government. In retaliation the Zimbabwe-Rhodesian forces carried out cross border attacks on the guerrilla movements. Two hundred of the Selous scouts were ferried into Mozambique where they attacked a large Z.A.N.U. military base. They went in singing the company battle hymn, with weapons firing, leaving nine hundred guerrillas dead when they left Mozambique.

Similar attacks were carried out into Zambia, even to the extent that the Selous Scouts hit Nkomo's home and headquarters in the city of Lusaka. Nkomo was barely able to escape the attack with his life.

The internal settlement had not achieved the desired peace for the country. In the pursuit of putting an end to the fighting, Smith and Muzerewa were invited to meet with President Carter in Washington. Meetings took place at Camp David, in Maryland over a long weekend. From Maryland, Smith flew to California for meetings with leaders that appeared to be more sympathetic to the Zimbabwe-Rhodesian situation. Ex-President Gerald Ford and the Presidential candidate, Governor Ronald Reagan.

For Zimbabwe-Rhodesians following the news at home, it was clear that Reagan wanted to help achieve an equitable resolution to the fighting and would have liked to send American troops into the country to put an end to the war. But, he was still a candidate for the Presidency and there was nothing he could effectively do at this time, other than give morale support.

Returning to Zimbabwe-Rhodesia, The British through their Foreign Secretary Lord Carrington, applied pressure on Muzerewa and Smith to re-negotiate a new settlement that would include the Patriotic Front. Despite warnings from Ian Smith, Muzerewa was confident that he could win any future election which included the opposing Patriotic Front, he agreed to a new conference to be held in London.

The conference was held at Lancaster House in December of 1979. Under the chairmanship of Lord Carrington. During the meetings one of the legal advisors to the Zimbabwe-Rhodesian team mysteriously, committed suicide.

An agreement was finally reached by all sides. Under the agreement Rhodesia would renounce its declaration of independence. There was to be a short transitional period where the country would come under British supervision and rule. During this time there was to be a cease-fire, the guerrillas were to be disarmed and immobilized. A new constitution would be drafted which incorporated the principal of one man one vote. Also, for the first ten years the rights of the whites would be protected by having twenty seats in the one hundred seat legislature. The date for the new elections was set for February, 1980.

The agreement sounded good—on paper.

Muzerewa remained confident that he would win the fresh elections. All the leaders of the different groups began to posture their parties in early January to campaign for the elections. There were the UANC, led by Muzerwa. Z.A.N.U. (internal), led by Sithole. Z,A,N.U. (Patriotic Front), led by Mugabe. Z.A.P.U. (Patriotic Front), led by Nkomo and The Rhodesian Front, led by Ian Smith, as the leading contenders.

Problems arose with some of the guerrillas from both sides of the Patriotic front. They refused to be disarmed and took off into the bushes to take up new careers as armed robbers. Others cached their weapons in secret hiding places for possible use at a later time. A couple of bombing attempts were made to assassinate Robert Mugabe, the attempts were unsuccessful, but caused finger pointing between Ian Smith, Nkomo's group and the UANC. Who all denied any involvement in the attempts.

The general election was duly held in February 1980. After the voting, It took a few days to count the results which were sent in from across the country. When the votes were tallied, the final results sent shock waves throughout the military and police.

The day the results were to be officially declared on the radio, Major-general Walls, head of the security forces made a brief statement before they were announced. He appealed for calm and an acceptance by the public of the results. The listening public braced themselves for an upset result of the elections. Robert Mugabe's Z.A.N.U.(PF) party had won fifty-seven seats. Joshua Nkomo's Z.A.P.U {PF) party nineteen seats, Bishop Muzerewa, three seats and Sithole's Z.A.N.U.(Internal) party a single seat. Ian Smiths party won all twenty of the seats reserved for the whites.

Robert Mugabe's party had won the elections, and he was to become the future Prime Minister. The shock was how poorly Muzerewa's party, which had been so successful only a few months earlier, had done. Sithole the founder and leader of the Z.A.N.U. party was now brushed aside by his former underling. In conformity with the way history has always treated the winners, Mugabe found himself being credited with the "Liberation of Zimbabwe!"

Independence was to be formally granted by Britain on April 18th, 1980. The name "Rhodesia" would cease to exist and the country would in the future, be referred to solely as Zimbabwe.

The prosecutors office had an influx of new employees. Former terrorists were now appointed as prosecutors. I and the other Senior prosecutors were instructed to take these men under our wing and train them to be ready for their appointment as Magistrates within three months. I shook my head in disbelief! Here were men who a few short weeks ago were guerrillas in the bush, now they were to be elevated to the bench, with minimal training. The situation was clearly lopsided. While people like myself, who had worked for ten years to gain the experience, had only now reached the point to be considered for the appointment to the position of magistrate. I did not like what was happening. I feared for the quality of the standard of justice that would be meted out by these totally inexperienced people.

One of the new prosecutors assigned to work with me was a close relative of a future Z.A.N.U cabinet minister. He was flamboyant and threw his weight around—the typical characteristic of an individual who did not know what he was doing but, wanted to impress everyone with his knowledge, which he clearly lacked. At the end of this particular new prosecutors first work week, he joined me and a group of our other colleagues for a weekend social at the Meikles hotel. The group had been multi-racial for several years, but somehow the new man just did not fit. He was boisterous, loud above everyone else and as the evening wore on he became very, very drunk.

I watched the man attempting to spurt words of wisdom through a slurring mouth that had taken on its own vitality and will with the intake of alcohol. At the end of the evening, I said good night to the remaining colleagues at the hotel and glanced over to see the new man, slouched over his armchair in a state of semi-consciousness. I left the hotel with misgivings about the men coming into power and hoped the example I had witnessed that night was more an exception, rather than the rule of what was to come.

Part of the settlement agreement reached at Lancaster house between the parties was a political amnesty. All cases pending before the courts of a criminal nature which involved political activity prior to the cease-fire, were granted immunity and to be dropped.

I returned to work the following Monday and began reviewing the pending cases to ascertain which of them fell under the amnesty category. Those that did, I would forward to the Attorney General for a "decline to Prosecute" endorsement on the docket.

One particular case I considered carefully; the circumstances of the case were that a band of guerrillas had gone to a tribal village. At the village they had called out the black tribal Headman, under the pretext of accusing him of being a "sellout" to the Zimbabwe-Rhodesia security forces, had robbed him of his money. The guerrillas then raped his daughter. They took the headman into the center of the village, where in front of the villagers they had slit his throat. The Headman did not die. The guerrillas in order to complete killing the man, threw his body onto a pile of grass and wood setting fire to the brushwood, leaving the Headman to burn to death. The guerrillas then left the village.

Incredibly, the Headman survived his throat being slit and the fire. He crawled out of the blaze with severe burns. Walking and crawling, he made it to the nearest police station fifteen miles away. He collapsed at the police post and was rushed to hospital. Although maimed and disfigured for life, with intensive treatment at the hospital, was able to survive. When he regained consciousness, He identified his attackers to

the police. The police were able to capture and arrest the men responsible, who were now awaiting trial.

I looked at the aspects of the case; The robbery was for financial gain
and not political. The Rape on the young woman certainly had nothing
to do, by any stretch of the imagination, with politics. The heinous
attempts at murdering the Headman were perpetrated as a continuous
act in furtherance of the Rape and robbery. I decided the case did not
fall into the political amnesty category and set it down for prosecution.

The guerrillas in this case, or "Freedom Fighters," as they were now
officially termed, awaited trial in prison. They were well connected with
officers of the incoming political regime.

A "Comrade" official from Z.A.N.U. came in to see me. His purpose
was to persuade me to recommend to the Attorney General's office that
the matter be dropped from prosecution. I refused, explaining my views
that this case was outside the realm of politics. I also made it clear that
with the new government coming into power, it was important to continue a confidence in the public's trust that law and order would be
maintained. The official expressed his anger with me for continuing the
case and stomped out the office, threatening that this was not the end
of the matter.

A few days later a senior member of Z.A.N.U., who had been desig-
nated for a top cabinet post in Mugabe's new government, took a band
of freedom fighters to the home of a white farmer. There, he proceeded
to murder the unarmed man by emptying a full carbine cartridge from
his AK-47 rifle into the farmer. There was no excuse for what the official
did—it was blatant murder! The official was arrested by the police but
soon released on instructions from the new government. Not only had
the official committed murder, but he continued his ranking and was
appointed to the cabinet post. There was a major outcry by the white
population. For once the media joined in the hue and cry which gave
the case international attention.

The cabinet member was re-arrested, charged with murder, granted bail which was previously unheard of in a murder trial and returned to his cabinet post.

I during this time, continued to receive pressure to drop the case where the Headman and his daughter were the victims. I maintained my position, I received a call from a new senior official in the Attorney-Generals office. The official requested that the docket be sent to his office for closure.

I protested the political interference, "What about the separation between the judicial and executive bodies?" I argued. "We are supposed to work independently without interference, irrespective of who is in power!" I stated. "Ivan I agree with you on that aspect, but these are not normal times. We are all walking on thin ice." The official replied and continued saying, "You are due for the judicial appointment in a couple of months, do you want to ruin that opportunity by standing firm on this matter?" I thought for a few seconds, "Yes, I do! If this is the way the judicial system is going to be in the future, I do not want to be a part of it!" I paused and added, "I will be forwarding my resignation with the case docket in the morning!" The official's voice at the other end of the telephone showed surprise and sounded as though he had been taken aback at my statement. He cautioned me to handle the situation with diplomacy, otherwise he warned, I would find myself at odds with the new government.

Heeding the official's warning, I submitted a simple letter of resignation with no explanation. I would have to complete a one month period of notice.

During this period, I watched the changes that took place in the country.

Samora Machel had advised Robert Mugabe not too make the same mistake in Zimbabwe, that Mozambique had made in throwing out its whites. The loss of the white expertise from that country, had left Mozambique in the disastrous position of having its businesses, goods and services virtually in a state of collapse. Consequently, nothing was being done to encourage the white population to leave Zimbabwe.

Exchange control regulations were maintained, making it very difficult to emigrate out of the country. A family wishing to leave the country would be permitted to take out the maximum amount of One thousand dollars, with which to start a new life. A couple with two children, would find it impossible to start a new life elsewhere on that meager amount. Those that did leave the country, had to do so by leaving all their other assets behind.

The statues of Cecil John Rhodes, Jameson, and Alfred Beit were torn down. The street names were changed to "Stalin", "Tito" and "Lenin", all Marxist figureheads. The new regime was removing anything to do with the British "Colonial Era".

Perhaps that was appropriate for the new government, but, they were forgetting that it was due to the philanthropy of men like Rhodes and Beit bequeathing much of their vast fortunes to the country, that Roads and bridges had been constructed. Hospitals that had saved many lives were built. Schools providing for their education were erected. Scholarships provided for the advancement of the people, as well as many other services. That now, was all relegated to the "Colonial Era!"

The new regime ordered a fleet of brand new gleaming white Mercedes motor vehicles for its cabinet ministers. As far as the ordinary people, peasants and tribal villagers, nothing changed. Despite the years of promises, there were no fancy cars or houses for everybody.

The new government raised the minimum wage to a hundred dollars month for the poorer workers. A tax of thirty per cent on the sale of all houses, was also introduced.

There was an influx of diplomats and "Advisors" from communist countries. Mugabe's bodyguard was an imported Vietnamese man.

Although, blacks were moving into government positions, the commercial and agricultural worlds remained exactly as before. Despite the talk of nationalizing many industries.

There were already rumblings of dispute emerging between Mugabe's Z.A.N.U. and Nkomo's Z.A.P.U. parties. The whites were already being forgotten about, in this developing power play. Bishop Muzerewa was dragged protesting into court and detained in prison without charges being filed, under the Emergency powers act.

The Selous Scouts who had been so effective at counter insurgency against the freedom fighters, were to pay the price of having been too good at what they did during the war. For the first time in the country's history a command was disbanded without formal ceremony. They were quietly and unceremoniously disbanded, leaving Nkomo barracks deserted, having earned the hatred of Mugabe.

I watched all these events taking place, and felt a shiver run up my spine, as though I could feel the cold chill of the wind blowing in from the communist East! I loved the country of my birth, but the changes taking place and the Marxist philosophies that were gradually being implemented, was a way of life I did not wish to succumb to.

I thought hard about the decision I was about to make—that it was time to leave "Rhodesia"—the name Zimbabwe, had not quite yet, penetrated my vocabulary.

I hoped that in time the country would mature and once again be a wonderful home for people to live in. A place where the inhabitants could freely roam the open spaces, enjoying the spectacle of the wildlife and picturesque African plains. But, for now, there was too much upheaval and too many recent and raw memories for me, of the country that once was, to accept the new Marxist philosophies that would soon be replacing it.

I called my mother in Cape Town to tell her of my decision to leave the country. Rae urged me to emigrate to South Africa. "Mother, we have just been through a difficult war in this country. I am young enough to start a fresh life somewhere else, but if I were to come to South Africa, it would be like going from the frying pan into the fire!" I told her. "Why do you say that?" She asked. "Because, South Africa is the next place targeted to go through what just happened in Rhodesia! It may take five or ten years, but it will take place. I would like to go to a country where I will have the chance to settle for good, without having to worry about having to pull up roots and starting over once again in the future!" I said. "Where will you go?" She asked. "Either Europe or America, depending on which place will allow me to immigrate to their country!" I answered.

I saw Amos a couple of days later and told him of my resignation and plans to leave the country. Amos surprised me by informing me that he too, was going to leave Zimbabwe. "Where will you go ?" I asked. "Botswana!" Amos replied, "I have spoken with Sheila, Motorcar's wife, she is going to go there as well with her children. We are going to take the rubies and sell them to a dealer there. We will use the money to buy our own homes and start a bicycle and hardware business in the capital city, Gaberone!" I was delighted for Amos, "That's wonderful news! I am glad to hear that Sheila is going with you!…If you ever need a cycle salesman, just let me know!" I teased. "In the meantime, let's go and have some lunch together? My treat!" I offered.

Chapter Nineteen

Chief superintendent Black visited me in my office at the courts, "I heard that you have resigned your position as a prosecutor?" He asked. I nodded my head in acknowledgment. "I have also heard that you intend to leave the country?" He said, more as a statement, than a question. "As usual your intelligence sources are accurate!" I replied.

"Where do you intend to go?" Black enquired. "That's been a bit of a problem. Most countries that I would like to settle in, need me to have a bit more than the eight hundred dollars the government is allowing me to emigrate with, but my first choice is to live in America." I replied. "Well I may have some good news for you, Ivan. It seems that you have some friends in the American intelligence service, they are grateful for the work you did in Mozambique, uncovering the location of The Cubans and their equipment. I have been asked to pass a message to you; should you decide to go to the United States and apply for permanent residency, you may find that your request will be processed favorably! But, after that bit of help you are on your own." Black told me. "Thank you. getting permanent residency, will be the only help I need!" I replied gratefully.

Black stood up to leave, he extended his hand. "Well, I suppose this is Goodbye! Thanks for what you did for us and good luck in America!" He said. I shook the policeman's hand, "It certainly was an experience working undercover, and one that I wont forget for a long time!" I answered with a smile, "By the way, how is Patrick the ex-terrorist handling the changes?" I asked. "Patrick and several other former Selous Scouts have left the country and joined the Botswana army. It seems that the government there is only too pleased to have soldiers of that caliber join their military." Black responded and with a wave to me, he left the office.

The last day of my tenure as a prosecutor, I stood alone in my office. I looked around me, the wall shelves and the desk that had once been filled with law books and case dockets were now empty, cleared, ready for my departure. I looked at my watch, the end of the day was a mere hour away. A farewell party had been organized for that evening, a party that would officially end my prosecuting career.

I had spent much of the day reminiscing, thinking about the events over the last several years. I thought about those close to me who had lost their lives, my father who had worked so hard to build a family and the bicycle business. Chantelle, the woman I had loved so much, was now gone. Motorcar, the warrior and best friend I had ever known. Enock, the friend who had became a terrorist. It was difficult to digest those events that had taken place over the last ten years and yet keep in perspective that I had to look to the future.

The country's economy was a mess. There were a glut of houses being sold on the market, primarily because so many people were leaving the country. Some people in their anxiety to leave had merely abandoned their mortgages, and gone. I had sold my house for a mere pittance of what it was worth, just to clear the remaining mortgage. The money I received from the sale of the house was really irrelevant, as everything in excess of the eight hundred dollars that I was allowed to take out the country had to go into a frozen bank account. There was no access to that account from outside the country. The sum of Fifteen thousand dollars, payment from my pension fund paid out from ten years of service to the country, also went in the frozen account. The hardest part of the sale of the house was having to give away my little dog, Tiny.

Fortunately, I had found a good home with friends of mine who were remaining in Zimbabwe.

I looked out the office window, I thought back to the book I had read as a teenager, "Gulliver's Travels." The unnecessary war, over which way to cut the egg was finished, for the moment. The once enemies were now becoming friends. Paving the way for existing friends to become the enemies of the future- I was thinking specifically of Mugabe and Nkomo! There was no doubt that the two factions would soon be fighting with each other—this time without the whites in the middle to intervene in their dispute.

I thought about my pending departure from the country, I had booked my flight for the middle of May, that was fifteen days away. Although the authorities were stringent in allowing people to take money out of the country, there was some flexibility in the purchase of airline tickets, provided they were paid for within the country. I had bought a ticket that took me to Cape Town, where I would visit my mother for a few days. Then I would fly to Brussels for a couple of days to see Chantelle's parents, before flying to my final destination of Los Angeles. The relatives I had stayed with as a student in Hermosa Beach, my uncle Jack and aunt Emily, had both passed away years earlier. I had written to my cousin Elaine, the former beauty queen, living in Beverly Hills. In my letter I explained that I was leaving Zimbabwe and had asked for her help, with a place to stay briefly, while I sorted out my residency status and found a job. Elaine had not replied to my letter, which made me nervous—without a place to stay I would run out of money in a matter of days in America!

My thoughts were interrupted by a soft knocking on the office door. Khamila, one of the office legal secretary's for the past five years entered. She was a short attractive dark skinned lady of Indian descent. In her hand she carried the metal nameplate from my office door. There was a hint of moisture and a look of sadness in her eyes. "I thought you might like to keep this as a souvenir." She said handing the plate to me,

"We are really going to miss you around the office!" she said, with a tear trickling down her cheek. Watching her thoughtful gesture, brought a lump to my throat. It was difficult enough having to leave, but seeing this tender show of emotion made the situation even harder. "Come on Khamila, we have a farewell party to go to, there is no time for sadness, only time to look to the future!" I said, and gave her a thank you kiss on the cheek.

Close to a hundred and fifty friends I had made in the legal world over the past ten years were at the party, which was being held in the large prosecutor's common room. I was particularly glad to see Jay Patanak as one of the guests. There was a presentation of an engraved sterling silver box to me from the Attorney-General and court staff. I made a farewell speech, had a couple of drinks too many and went home to sleep off the forthcoming hangover.

With the sale of my house, I moved into a residential hotel for the remaining two weeks left in the country. The last few days before my departure seemed to fly by.

The day before my departure, I still had not heard from my cousin, Elaine in America. Concerned, I sat down and drafted another letter again asking her for her assistance. I ended the letter by writing, " In case you did not receive my first letter. I pray that this letter reaches you before my arrival and that you understand my predicament. The funds that I have been allowed to take out the country are minimal. I hope that you will be able to put me up for a brief while, so that I will have the opportunity to look for work and find my own place. Your assistance and help, will be much appreciated."

I sent the letter off, in the naive belief that if the circumstances were reversed, I would have done everything possible to help any of my relatives.

The next day, I prepared to leave the country. My worldly possessions had been reduced to two suitcases and Eight hundred dollars in travelers cheques. This was what I hoped to start my new life in America with.

Amos had offered to drive me to the airport and I was glad for his companionship. When Amos arrived at the hotel, I asked him to drive in the M.G.B.

At the airport, we bade each other goodbye with a hug. "Where do you want me to take your car, Ivan?" Amos asked. "Take it with you wherever you go, Amos!" I replied handing over the car's registration, "Its your car now! Good luck and fare well my friend—Hamba Gashi, Amos!" I said, as I turned to leave for my flight.

The few days that I spent with my mother in Cape Town, was like enjoying pure nectar from the heavens! My mother had a tiny apartment in the suburb of Seapoint, it was all that she could afford on the small allowance that she was allowed to receive from her funds in Zimbabwe. But the pure pleasure of seeing and being with her again, made her home feel like a palace.

The serene beauty of Cape Town and the added bonus of not being involved in a war situation with the pressures of court work, was the tonic that I needed. I played and frolicked in the Atlantic waters near Rae's apartment like a teenager.

I flew to Europe and was met in Brussels by Chantelle's parents. They were full of kindness and treated me as if I had become the son-in—law they never had. Their home was full of pictures of Chantelle. I ran my fingertips over the walled photographs as though I could touch Chantelle one more time. I stayed in Brussels for two days with them, before catching a flight to New York.

I Had finally arrived in America! I checked into a cheap hotel near Times Square and phoned my cousin, Elaine, in Los Angeles. The maid answered the phone. "I am sorry but they are asleep, and can not be disturbed until eleven a.m., that is the time they wake up!" She said. I looked at my watch, it was eleven-thirty a.m. New York time. "Please, this is important, tell Elaine her cousin Ivan, is in New York. Ask her to phone me." I said, leaving the phone number of the hotel where I was staying. "Very well." The maid replied and hung up the phone.

With the three hour time difference between New York and Los Angeles, I decided to take a walk and return to the hotel to wait for Elaine's call at eleven in the morning her time. I returned to the hotel a couple of hours later and waited for the return call, I waited until the evening, nothing happened. I phoned Elaine again, this time an answering machine clicked on. I left another message for Elaine, and waited. Eventually falling asleep by the bed. The next day, I phoned at eleven in the morning Los Angeles time. The maid answered, Elaine was still asleep, the maid said she would give her the message. I sat by the telephone and waited. Early evening arrived, again there was no call. I was starting to feel desperate and felt certain that there was a lack interest from my cousin to help me. I phoned one more time and the maid answered, Elaine and her family had gone to a party. I left a message that I would be flying into Los Angeles the next evening, I gave the maid my flight and arrival time. I thought that If Elaine did not show, I would have to try and sort out something in quick fashion while the money I had, lasted. A feeling of apprehension started to overcome me, I was flying into a city which I had last visited nineteen years previously. I did not know anyone, where to go, or what to do, once I was there. It would be a matter of trying to find my way around and to make some place in Los Angeles, my destination.

The next night I flew into Los Angeles airport, my stomach was in a knot, wondering where I was going to go once the plane landed? As I emerged from the plane I caught sight of Jody, my cousin and Elaine's younger sister. She waved at me. "Sorry we did not get back to you, but we have all been pretty busy lately!" She said, with a coy smile. I heaved a sigh of relief—prematurely, the American dream I had come to seek, was about to turn into a personal nightmare!

We drove to Elaine's house in Beverly Hills. It was a magnificent large two storied home on Rodeo Drive. Elaine and her husband Dave, were not there to greet me, they had gone out for dinner. So I was left alone to unpack in the room provided to me. The family arrived back late that night and although I had waited up for their return, Elaine barely greeted me, and her husband was so drunk that he scarcely made it up the stairs before passing out.

As I had already guessed, Elaine had very little intention of extending me a helping hand. She had, in the nineteen years since my last visit to Los Angeles, become a women of notable wealth and success. She had come to own several apartment blocks and a couple of thriving businesses in the Beverly hills area. She indeed had more than the capacity to assist, but, she had also become a selfish, self centered, bad tempered woman. She was more concerned with what others could do for her, and had very little regard for what she could do in return. I was now a refugee with nothing to offer—she had no incentive to help me.

So, my adventures in America had begun.

Elaine was an event all by herself. During the next couple of days I tried desperately to get advice and information from her about sorting out my situation, none was forthcoming. I needed to get started somewhere, so I walked the streets of Los Angeles stopping in at different legal offices to get the information. Elaine was kind enough to invite me to join her and some guests for a dinner out at a posh Italian restaurant the first week. During the dinner her husband Dave became very drunk. To show her displeasure, Elaine picked up a large bowl of spaghetti from the center of the long table where the guests were seated and proceeded to dump the contents over his head. I cringed with embarrassment.

When we arrived back at the house, Elaine still in a violent mood, berated her husband. Then she turned to me and asked if I was happy with the accommodation. I replied that I was and appreciated their hospitality. She then proceeded to tell me that similar accommodation at a hotel would be costing me Five hundred dollars a night! If it had been her intention to make me feel even more uncomfortable—Elaine had succeeded!

The next morning she advised me that the strain of the last few days had been too much for her and that she would be spending a week at her beach house to relax. I would have to find somewhere else to stay while she and her family were away. But, the good news was that she had one of her apartments in Beverly hills being vacated by a tenant—she would let me stay in it rent free for a period of three months, when she returned from her vacation. I gratefully thanked her, I packed my worldly belongings and Elaine dropped me off at a cheap motel on Santa Monica Boulevard.

During the week Elaine was away, I did my best to find my way around by bus and managed to file my application for residency at the Immigration service in downtown Los Angeles.

Elaine arrived back from her vacation and I was able to move into the apartment building as promised. One week later, she phoned to inform me that she had found a paying tenant, I would have to move out at the end of the week. I was starting to feel devastated. My cousin arrived at the apartment building to inspect it, before I moved out, handed me two hundred dollars—I did not see her again!

I moved back into the cheap motel. I estimated I had a week left before my money ran out. To save money, I walked to where I had appointments and existed on one Macdonalds hamburger per day.

That became quiet a learning experience for me. I also did a lot of thinking, mostly as to how I was going to survive! Looking around at all the wealth in Beverly hills and Santa Monica, I realized that this was a place where the "American Dream" could be lived. Though, it was very conditional on having two essential ingredients! One was having money, the second was to have friends to help get into a position to get there. I had neither!

Desperate, I telephoned my relatives in Seattle. My one cousin Alvin, was an Attorney who gratefully, understood the situation and sent me money and an air ticket to Seattle. The other was my aunt Mathilda, my mother's widowed elder sister, she was eighty-six years old and never fortunate enough to have children of her own. She was a person of very little means and lived in a tiny home, yet, she offered me a place to stay for as long as I needed. I gratefully, flew to The North-West of the country.

The relatives in Seattle were far more down to earth and more helpful than those in Los Angeles. My aunt Mathilda was the dearest, sweetest woman, I had ever met, who showed me nothing but kindness. She opened her tiny two bedroom home to me and literally cared for me until I sorted out my immigration status and was allowed to find a job six months later.

The adventures and experiences over a period of nearly twenty years in America, since that time, almost paled my experiences in Africa. I thought that one day perhaps, I would write a book about my experiences and the risks I had taken in this new land. Maybe, I would title the story "The loneliness of the company!" To express the sentiment that although, one can be in the company of many people and yet at the same time feel totally alone in the struggle for survival. I had struggled for many years, been on the verge of poverty and fought my way through the business world to where I now owned my own corporation, wholesaling diamonds.

During the passing years I had remained in contact with Amos and Sheila. They had done very well with their bicycle and hardware business in Botswana and expanded into a handfull of new business ventures. It had always been a joy to receive their letters and hear their news. Tragically, they were both killed in 1990 when they were involved in a motor vehicle accident while traveling on business from Botswana to South Africa.

My mother at the age of ninety emigrated to Australia in 1991 to live with my sister Babbete. Babbette also a widow had now moved to Perth, Western Australia. My mother continued to live an active life in Perth until she passed away at the age of ninety-four. Her last wish was to be buried in the country she loved so much, Zimbabwe. In accordance with those wishes, her body was flown for burial in that land.

The blur of the memories through the ripples in the waters of Lake Washington, began to diminish. The rain had begun to intensify and I found myself returning to the present time, it was approaching night-fall and the New Year's eve.

The chauffeur who had been standing so firmly and patiently at attention next to the Rolls-Royce vehicle parked by the side of the road, approached me. He was carrying a cellular telephone in his hand. "Sir, there is a call for you from your Seattle manager!" He said, handing me the phone. It was Peter Gordon, the manager running operations for the West coast of the "Bender Diamond Group."

"Hello Ivan, just wanted to let you know that there has been a slight change in plans for the celebrations tonight. The governor of Washington State has canceled the millennium fireworks and street party we were going to attend at midnight. The secret service have arrested a man who is believed to be a terrorist carrying explosives crossing into Washington from Canada. So as a precaution all public parties have been called off because of the bomb threat. Though, every-thing is still in place for our company dinner party tonight! If you approve we will all be meeting at the Space Needle, at eight and stay there instead, to ring in the New Year. There is a magnificent view from the revolving restaurant, which is several hundred feet high, towering over the city and the waters of the Puget Sound. We have a reservation for fifty people, is that all right with you?" Peter asked. "That's just fine, Peter, I will see you there tonight." I replied, putting down the phone and returning to the Rolls-Royce for the journey back to the city.

At the party that night, I mingled with the guests. One of the newer employees, a young lady in her late twenties who was attending the company party for the first time approached me, "Mr. Bender, are you really from Africa?" She asked. I nodded, "South Africa?" She asked. "No, The country next to South Africa, a place once called "Rhodesia" now it is known as Zimbabwe!" I replied. "Do you ever go back there?" She asked. "No, although I travel to South Africa often to buy diamonds, I have never returned to Zimbabwe, I have too many fond memories of the country, as it once was, and that is how I would like to remember it!" I replied. "Do you miss that country?" She enquired. "Yes, a lot, its a place that is engraved within my heart and I think of it often!" I answered, with a tone of nostalgia. "Are you married?" She probed. "I once had someone I was very much in love with, but no, I am not married." I told her and moved on, to mingle with the other guests.

The party entered into full swing, Peter Gordon always the good manager, came over to see how I was doing. I assured him that I was having a good time. Peter apologized, "Sorry we did not do something a little more exciting, but this is a quiet city!" He said. I looked at Peter and smiled, "Don't be concerned, I have had enough excitement to last me a lifetime. I am perfectly happy now to settle for peace and quiet!" I answered with an appreciative twinkle in my eye.

The party progressed and as midnight approached, I watched the guests crowd together in one section of the revolving restaurant to bring in the New Year. I quietly slipped away to an empty section where I could be alone.

There, I looked out across the spectacular view of the Pacific Ocean. It was a clear night and the stars were out sparkling in the sky. In front of me, reflections of the stars sparkled with shimmering bursts across the waters of the Puget Sound.

I raised the glass of champagne I held in my hand. I remembered my family and friends and drank a toast to the memory of Chantelle and of Africa.

THE END.

Printed in the United States
58793LVS00005B/1-51